LANDSCAPE, WELL-BEING AND ENVIRONMENT

Well-being is now firmly established as an overarching theme of key concern to all professionals that work, manage or design the environment. However, well-being is a complex multidimensional issue rooted in the ways that we encounter, perceive and interpret the environment. No one discipline alone can claim to have sufficient knowledge to fully explain the types of interactions that occur, therefore there is a need to draw together a wide range of professions who are exploring the consequences of their actions upon the well-being of individuals and communities.

This edited work addresses the above, consisting of a collection of studies which embrace different aspects of environment, landscape and well-being to consider current approaches to well-being research and practice that fall outside the traditional concepts of well-being as part of medical research, making links with architecture, landscape design, environmental perception, social interaction and environmental sustainability.

The contributors originally presented at the international conference, 'Well-Being 2011' jointly hosted by Birmingham City University and the Royal Institute of British Architects (RIBA); the chapters have been developed to present a coherent series of themes reviewing a wide range of literature, presenting case studies appropriate to diverse audiences.

Richard Coles is Professor of Urban Landscape and Environmental Interaction, with a background in forestry and issues relating to urban greening. He has a particular interest in examining how individuals perceive the landscape and has developed a range of theoretical perspectives which model user/environment interaction and from which the current emphasis on well-being stems. His initial training in biological sciences and current work within a design school of architecture allows him to adopt a unique stance to investigation and where he has received grant funding from the UK research councils and the EU. With Zoë Millman he has developed a range of well-being initiatives which target the landscape, walking, memory and cultural engagement.

Zoë Millman is a post-doctoral researcher at Birmingham Institute of Art & Design, with a background in museums and the history of art and architecture. She was awarded her PhD, 'Landscape narratives and the construction of meaning in the contemporary urban canal-scape' in 2012 (Birmingham City University / British Waterways). Her current research relates to how we perceive, remember, give meaning to and ex~~   ~~'scape. Zoë's recent work has used creative rese~~   ~~e perceptions, identities and well-being in part~~   ~~l national organisations.

LANDSCAPE, WELL-BEING AND ENVIRONMENT

Edited by Richard Coles and Zoë Millman

LONDON AND NEW YORK

First published 2013
by Routledge
2 Park Square, Milton Park, Abingdon, Oxon OX14 4RN

and by Routledge
711 Third Avenue, New York, NY 10017

Routledge is an imprint of the Taylor & Francis Group, an informa business

© 2013 selection and editorial material, Richard Coles and Zoë Millman; individual chapters, the contributors.

The right of the editors to be identified as the authors of the editorial material, and of the authors for their individual chapters, has been asserted in accordance with sections 77 and 78 of the Copyright, Designs and Patents Act 1988.

Every effort has been made to contact and acknowledge copyright owners. If any material has been included without permission, the publishers offer their apologies. The publishers would be pleased to have any errors or omissions brought to their attention so that corrections may be published at a later printing.

All rights reserved. No part of this book may be reprinted or reproduced or utilised in any form or by any electronic, mechanical, or other means, now known or hereafter invented, including photocopying and recording, or in any information storage or retrieval system, without permission in writing from the publishers.

Trademark notice: Product or corporate names may be trademarks or registered trademarks, and are used only for identification and explanation without intent to infringe.

British Library Cataloguing in Publication Data
A catalogue record for this book is available from the British Library

Library of Congress Cataloging in Publication Data
Landscape, well-being and environment / edited by Richard Coles and Zoë Millman.
   pages cm
   Includes bibliographical references and index.
   1. Human ecology – Psychological aspects. 2. Human ecology – Health aspects. 3. Environmentalism – Psychological aspects. 4. Well-being – Environmental aspects. 5. Landscapes – Psychological aspects. I. Coles, Richard, 1949– II. Millman, Zoë.
   BF353.5.N37L36 2014
   155.9′1–dc23

ISBN: 978-0-415-82998-4 (hbk)
ISBN: 978-0-415-83151-2 (pbk)
ISBN: 978-1-315-88306-9 (ebk)

Typeset in Bembo
by HWA Text and Data Management, London

Printed and bound in Great Britain by
TJ International Ltd, Padstow, Cornwall

CONTENTS

List of figures vii
List of tables viii
List of contributors ix

Introduction 1
Richard Coles and Zoë Millman

1 Exploring the potential for a 'double dividend': living well and living greener 7
Louise Reid and Colin Hunter

2 Modelling well-being and the relationship between individuals and their environments 20
Sara Warber, Katherine Irvine, Patrick Devine-Wright and Kevin Gaston

3 Synchronising self and city: an everyday aesthetic for walking 38
Fiona Bannon

4 Towards a landscape of well-being: the role of landscape and perceptions of place in human well-being 53
Lindsay Sowman

5 Interactive urban landscapes for well-being and sustainability 72
Janice Astbury

6 The contribution of greenery in multi-family houses as a factor of well-being 87
Irene Yerro Vela

7 Third places for the third age: the contribution of playable space to the well-being of older people 109
Benedict Spencer, Katie Williams, Lamine Mahdjoubi and Rachel Sara

8 Kids in the City: differing perceptions of one neighbourhood in Aotearoa/New Zealand 129
Penelope Carroll, Lanuola Asiasiga, Nicola Tava'e and Karen Witten

9 Culture's place in well-being: measuring museum well-being interventions 147
Erica Ander, Linda Thomson and Helen Chatterjee

10 Using woodlands to improve individual and community well-being 167
Liz O'Brien and Jake Morris

11 Children as explorers: revealing children's views on well-being in intensifying urban environments 184
Christina Ergler and Robin Kearns

12 Landscape, well-being and environment 200
Richard Coles and Zoë Millman

Index 218

FIGURES

1.1	A unifying framework for the double dividend	15
2.1	Post-park state following use of urban green space	25
2.2	Interconnected Model of Well-being	31
6.1	Pflegi Areal, green spaces, Patientenhof	94
6.2	Pflegi Areal, green spaces, Innenhof	94
6.3	Pflegi Areal, green spaces, Samaritenhof	94
6.4	Hegianwandweg, semi-private outdoor space	97
6.5	Hegianwandweg, playground	101
6.6	Hegianwandweg, vegetable garden	101
7.1	Play in public space	116
8.1	Auckland City and case study neighbourhood	132
8.2	Participant researcher photographs of neighbourhood places	139
9.1	Well-being in museum practice	152
9.2	Bedside museum object handling session	158
10.1	Children and parents at Forest School	171
10.2	Dynamic, non-linear conceptual framework of well-being benefits gained from woodlands	179
11.1	Extract of McBeth's drawing in summer (central city)	195
12.1	The landscape/well-being continuum	216

TABLES

6.1	Self-evaluation according to SIA 112/1, Pflegi Areal, Zurich	91
6.2	Self-evaluation according to SIA 112/1, Hegianwandweg, Zurich	99
7.1	Quality of life and play compared	118
7.2	Aspects of the environment which enable and encourage access by older people	120–1
11.1	Child-researchers' questions in research project	190

CONTRIBUTORS

Erica Ander (MA) works as a museum and heritage consultant specialising in visitor studies and audience research. Her research interests include qualitative methodologies to capture cultural outcomes, health and well-being issues in the museum sector, measuring the impact of strategic funding and the development of the museum and archive profession. She was Research Assistant on the UCL Heritage in Hospitals Project.

Lanuola Asiasiga (PhD) has research interests in Pacific people's well-being and most of her research projects have touched on some aspect of this. She is based at SHORE at Massey University, New Zealand, a multidisciplinary group undertaking policy and community research and evaluation on a variety of health and social topics.

Janice Astbury is a PhD researcher in the School of Environment and Development and the Sustainable Consumption Institute at the University of Manchester, UK. Her research focuses on engaging citizens in enhancing urban sustainability and builds on previous work in Canada and Mexico. She has over twenty years of experience in applied research, programme design, management and evaluation within international organisations, philanthropic foundations, NGOs and community organisations.

Fiona Bannon is a Senior Lecturer in the School of Performance and Cultural Industries University of Leeds where she leads the 'MA Performance Culture and Context'. She holds a doctorate in aesthetic education from the University of Manchester. Teaching and research interests include collaborative practice, improvisation, collective creativity, choreography and aesthetics. Fiona is a founding member of Architects of the Invisible, a performance collective that explores experimental choreography and social interaction.

Penelope Carroll (PhD) has research interests that include social policy, housing, neighbourhoods and health, community development and child friendly cities. She is currently involved in studies investigating relationships between children's activity levels and independent mobility, neighbourhood characteristics and parental safety discourses. She has a background in journalism and communications and a strong interest in social justice.

Helen Chatterjee (PhD) is Deputy Director of Museums and Collections and Senior Lecturer in Biological Sciences at University College London. Her research focuses on the role of museum object handling as a therapeutic activity in healthcare. Helen was Principal Investigator on the AHRC funded Heritage in Hospitals project. She edited *Touch in Museums: policy and practice in object handling* and is the co-author of *Museums, Health and Well-being*.

Richard Coles is Professor of Urban Landscape and Environmental Interaction, with a background in forestry and issues relating to urban greening. He has a particular interest in examining how individuals perceive the landscape and has developed a range of theoretical perspectives which model user/environment interaction from which the current emphasis on well-being stems. His initial training in biological sciences and current work within a design school of architecture allows him to adopt a unique stance to investigation where he has received grant funding from the UK research councils and the EU. With Zoë Millman he has developed a range of well-being initiatives which target the landscape, walking, memory and cultural engagement.

Patrick Devine-Wright holds a Chair in Human Geography at the University of Exeter. Research interests include the symbolic and affective dimensions of people–place relations, social and psychological aspects of siting new energy infrastructure, and motivation for pro-environmental and pro-social actions. He has led and contributed to many interdisciplinary research projects and sits on the Social Science Expert Panel advising UK government departments.

Christina Ergler is a PhD candidate in the School of Environment at the University of Auckland, New Zealand. Her research interests span social, cultural and health geography. Her current research concerns children's well-being in vertical and suburban environments. Over the past years she has become interested in developing methodological approaches to acknowledge children's expertise in what she terms 'beyond passive participation'.

Kevin J Gaston is Professor of Biodiversity & Conservation at the University of Exeter. He was appointed inaugural Director of the Environment and

Sustainability Institute (ESI) at Exeter University in November 2010 and took up his post in May 2011. Based within the ESI, Kevin works closely with colleagues from across the university; he is a member of the bio-sciences department in the College of Life and Environmental Sciences.

Colin Hunter is professor of Sustainable Development and has been at the University of St Andrews since 2011. A natural scientist by training, he has led many interdisciplinary projects throughout his career, having held previous appointments at Leeds Metropolitan, Huddersfield, and Aberdeen Universities in planning, environmental science and geography.

Katherine Irvine is a research scientist at De Montfort University and the James Hutton Institute in the UK, examining natural resource policy, conservation behavior and environmental psychology to build bridges between human well-being, environmental quality and sustainable behaviour. Her collaborative, interdisciplinary research investigates the benefits of nature interaction for human well-being and the design/evaluation of interventions to promote sustainable environmental behaviour.

Robin Kearns (Professor of Geography) is a socio-cultural geographer at the School of Environment, University of Auckland, looking at the capacity of urban design to promote physical activity and social cohesion. He leads studies linking urban design and health, the dynamics of places and their influence on human well-being including the effects of policies and political practices on the cultural dynamics of places.

Lamine Mahdjoubi is Professor of the Built Environment at the University of the West of England. His key research interests concern evidence-based understanding of the effects of outdoor play environments on children's health, and well-being. The findings of his research helped to provide guidelines for planning, designing or retrofitting neighbourhood outdoor environments and school playgrounds.

Zoë Millman is a post-doctoral researcher at Birmingham Institute of Art & Design, with a background in museums and the history of art and architecture. She was awarded her PhD, 'Landscape narratives and the construction of meaning in the contemporary urban canal-scape' in 2012 (Birmingham City University/British Waterways). Her current research relates to how we perceive, remember, give meaning to and express our understanding of the landscape. Zoë's recent work has used creative research methods to investigate landscape perceptions, identities and well-being in partnership with community groups and national organisations.

Jake Morris joined the Social and Economic Research Group (SERG) at Forest Research in 2005 where he manages a variety of the social research projects under the 'Well-being', 'Governance', 'Society and Diversity' and 'Evaluation and Appraisal' research programmes. He has an Honours Degree in modern languages from Oxford University, a Masters from the Institute of Latin American Studies, University of London and a doctoral thesis on local participation and protected area management.

Liz O'Brien is Deputy Head of the Social and Economic Research Group (SERG) at Forest Research. Her work focuses on the well-being benefits people gain from engagement with trees, woods and forests where she is interested in the social distribution of well-being benefits gained from woodlands and barriers in accessing them. She has evaluated a number of Forestry Commission initiatives set up to improve health and well-being including the impacts on children.

Louise Reid is a lecturer in Geography and Sustainable Development at the University of St Andrews. Prior to her appointment in 2011, Louise was a post-doctoral fellow in the St Andrews Centre for Housing Research (2010–2011), and at the University of Aberdeen on the ESRC/BBSRC/MRC funded 'BeWEL' project (2009–2010).

Rachel Sara studied architecture to Doctoral level at the University of Sheffield. She contributes widely to a range of academic architectural journals, books and conferences that explore 'other' forms of architecture, 'performative architecture' and urban design, play, performance and transgression in relation to the built environment. This influences her teaching, where she runs architecture studio projects exploring the relationship between architecture and dance.

Lindsay Sowman is a PhD candidate in the School of Landscape Architecture at Lincoln University, Christchurch, New Zealand, where he has been a tutor and lecturer (on contract), contributing to a range of design and theory papers in the undergraduate and graduate programmes of the school. He began his PhD as a Teaching and Research Fellow, combining his previous background in psychology and counselling with his current interest as a landscape architect, developing current research into landscape, place and well-being.

Benedict Spencer is an urban designer with a passion for the enjoyable use of public space. Formerly Head of Education at CABE, he is now working for Sustrans promoting sustainable travel, and completing a PhD at the University of the West of England exploring the relationship between playable public space and quality of life for older people.

Nicola Tava'e has a Bachelor of Health Science degree, Postgraduate Diploma of Public Health and Masters of Public Health with Honours. She is a PhD student with SHORE and Massey University, affiliated with the 'Kids in the City' project, and is interested in Samoan parents' parenting practices, impacts on children's independent mobility and physical activity as a member of the Kids in the City research team.

Linda Thomson (PhD) was Lead Researcher on Heritage in Hospitals with articles published on this project in *Journal of Applied Arts & Health*, *International Journal of Art Therapy* and *Journal of Pain & Symptom Management*. She is currently developing a heritage-specific measure of well-being. Previously, Linda was a lecturer in biopsychology and research methods. Her research includes the role of the senses, specifically vision and touch, in enhancing memory and learning.

Sara Warber is Associate Professor of Family Medicine, University of Michigan Medical School. Before joining the faculty, she completed the prestigious Robert Wood Johnson Clinical Scholars Fellowship. Her work concerns the measurement of health and well-being outcomes on youth, aging, cancer survivorship and cardiovascular disease. She contributed to a US National Institutes of Health project to develop a validated tool to measure holistic well-being for integrative medicine research. She is a co-founder of the International Society for Complementary Medicine Research.

Katie Williams is Professor of Spatial Planning and Director of the Centre for Sustainable Planning and Environments at the University of the West of England, Bristol. She specialises in sustainable urbanism and is known for her work on neighbourhood design, sustainable behaviours, climate change adaptation, urban form and land reuse. Research is funded by UK research councils, government agencies and industry. She holds visiting lectureships in the USA, Thailand, Peru and The Netherlands.

Karen Witten has research interests centred on interactions between the physical characteristics of neighbourhoods, cities, social relationships and the health and sustainability-related practices of the people living in them. Professor Witten's current work explores children's and parents' experiences of neighbourhood environments and how these cohere to constrain or enable children's independent mobility.

Irene Yerro Vela (Pamplona, 1977) has an MA in architecture from ETSAUN Navarra-Spain and a Master of Advanced Studies (MAS) specialising in housing from ETH-Zurich. She has been employed by various international architectural offices including Aires Mateus (Lisbon) and ARTEC-Architekten (Vienna). She works as a freelance. She is a PhD candidate at the Institute of Urban Planning, Landscape Architecture & Design (Vienna University of Technology).

INTRODUCTION

Richard Coles and Zoë Millman

Over recent years there has been increasing international debate concerning the health and well-being of society. This includes attempts to understand more clearly how the qualities of the environment and access to landscapes, both natural and designed, influence health, with particular focus on physical and mental well-being. This area of enquiry includes issues regarding how we perceive and react to the landscape and the ways in which access to different landscapes can enrich people's lives, with particular attention on the role of nature, urban green spaces and how people access them. Well-being is an area of enquiry that crosses disciplinary boundaries, has multiple dimensions and is discussed using various terminologies; how we might use these variables to understand the relationship between the landscape, human experience and well-being is the focus of this book.

In *Landscape, Well-being and Environment*, we have brought together a range of material concerning the research work of those who hold a deep interest in well-being, society, the landscape and environment. The material is presented as a series of explorations in the form of chapters by our co-authors. Each chapter considers current research concerning a particular niche of enquiry, but they are also set within the broader context of investigation regarding how we respond to the environment.

We experience the landscape every day, and can readily identify favourite places, the quality of our neighbourhoods, describe our ideal landscape associations and places that we go to for relaxation. We are broadly aware of the pleasures (and fears) that the landscape holds, but a little deeper enquiry begins to uncover that the potential benefits of landscape to human health and well-being are not fully understood or appreciated. Hence we suggest the need for a more sophisticated audit of public health, physical and mental well-being in relation to the environmental qualities of different neighbourhoods and different landscape typologies. Several authors in this volume, for example, comment on the paucity of the urban environment regarding physical and mental stimulation, while others suggest a basis for developing a landscape typology which takes into account the ability of the landscape to embrace people as 'special places' in the support of well-being.

Who this book is aimed at

The chapters have been brought together as a comprehensive exploration of well-being in relation to the environment and landscape, where each chapter considers the respective authors' current research and includes the review of related literature, so presenting a substantial resource in terms of identifying further reading. Together the 12 chapters combine the extensive experience of 27 international authors, representing different disciplines ranging from environment to arts practice, including forestry, social sciences, museum studies, landscape architecture, urbanism and geography, typically involving multidisciplinary teams. From each we can gain a different disciplinary perspective, but also understand that cross-disciplinary collaboration is needed, and indeed demonstrated, to give an holistic view of the subject. The field is wide and the material is presented in such a way that it is accessible to a diverse audience, enabling the exploration of different perspectives, suitable for different levels of enquiry: personal, practice-based, academic, student or research. It is especially relevant to those interested in (studying or responsible for) the built environment, resource management, public health, responding to society or considering interventions that aim to support the well-being of individuals and communities.

The wider context

This book is informed by wider discussion surrounding the multi-dimensions of well-being in the form of two international conferences organised by the editors, Well-being 2011 and Well-being 2013, which aimed to explore the current well-being agenda. Both conferences invited a diverse audience drawn from different disciplines, sectors and organisations. Delegates included academics, architects, landscape architects, urban designers, community workers, artists and health professionals from the environment sector, social, health, housing, education, arts and humanities. Truly international in flavour, delegates attended from across the UK, mainland Europe, the USA, Canada, New Zealand and Australia, all with the aim of helping to explore and define what 'well-being' actually means in today's society. The aims of these events were to encourage open discussion, to explore the concepts of well-being and happiness, to debate what 'well-being' means to individuals and how it can be supported to advance our understanding; the same aims underpin this book. At these conferences delegates were invited to explore different facets of the well-being interface, but also encouraged to experience interventions that have been found to impact upon well-being by participating in workshops, explored within the remit of professional practice and which have already influenced teaching on courses, including those concerned with environmental design, arts and health.

Our own professional and academic agendas have been influenced and enlivened by engagement with other disciplines. For example, in looking at various environments, working with housing associations, community groups, environmental organisations, educationalists, cultural institutions, in developing models of well-being, incorporating the well-being agenda into landscape architecture and architecture courses. We see a growing interest from students in exploring well-being and society in terms of their professional practice and identity. It has informed our research agenda with doctoral research students in the fields of landscape, arts and health researching different aspects of the environment or different groups in society. We are working with practice partners to further explore approaches and impacts of interventions to apply theoretical aspects to practical situations.

Much of our work concerns examining the magnitude of the user/environment interface, the processes which underpin the formation of positive associations and lead to a positive state of mind associated with high levels of well-being. Much of this concerns the impacts of walking, testing/developing methodologies which can capture the true feelings of people, for example self-narrated walking, guided walking, walk and talk, place identity and attachment, contact with nature, memories and remembering. These facets are also discussed by the contributing authors in their individual chapters, and we hope that this volume goes some way to assisting others to develop their own approaches, expose them to a wide range of literature, and enhance investigation and practice.

Organisation of the chapters

We have tried to present chapters in some logical order moving from general aspects of well-being and landscape to a focus on different sections of society, environments or interventions. It is hoped that this will allow the reader to appreciate both broad and detailed aspects of the well-being/environment debate, identify the types of supporting literature and the specific results of the individual research. The chapters include different theoretical perspectives and summaries of current thinking, in addition to presenting new knowledge. Each chapter is a complete summary of a research study including full reference to literature, discussion and concluding remarks to enable the reader to synthesise the material presented.

Chapter 1 introduces several concepts of well-being in an examination of a unifying framework for reconciling personal well-being with wider pro-environmental behaviour, including motivations and philosophical divisions. It sets well-being within the wider context of environmental citizenship, considering personal well-being in relation to the wellness of the planet and wellness of society, bringing together disparate knowledge and methodologies.

Chapter 2 continues this theme where the reader is introduced to the actual experiences of users. Here the reader can find an overview of several theoretical well-being/health models that are presented to explain the positive impacts of landscape upon the human psyche and the body which are then explored in relation to the specific views of users. This chapter broadens our understanding of the different domains identified in the theoretical models, but considered from user perspectives to test theory. As well as providing discussion on methodologies for engaging with users, it contains informative perspectives on how well-being is expressed in everyday language.

Chapter 3 introduces the reader to the actions of engagement with the environment, specifically the experience and quality of the journey experienced through walking, drawing upon psycho-geography and related material. In this chapter the reader will find an in-depth exploration of the subject matter set within the context of a range of literature drawn from arts and related perspectives to consider an everyday aesthetic for well-being which is derived from the experience of users. It includes discussion on urban design and movement patterns which is highly informative and suggests a suite of design criteria that might be embraced. In particular, the author draws on an important range of literature dealing with aesthetic experience, with powerful arguments concerning design for living and lived experiences, well reflected in the chapter title –'Synchronising self and city'.

Chapter 4 is written from the viewpoint of the landscape architect to consider additional theoretical perspectives, to examine the relationship between environment and health, focusing on place attachment and investigating the concepts through a case study. This includes a thorough consideration of methodological approaches and the nature of experiential enquiry. Chapters 3 and 4 together provide a comprehensive consideration of issues relating to human experience of the environment/ landscape, but each focuses on different perspectives, respectively, the standpoints of 'self' and 'place'.

Chapter 5 continues the theme of people/nature interaction, but moves towards the development of a landscape typology which could be used to enhance the quality of landscapes. New ideas are introduced including the resilience of urban ecosystems, eco-sociological complexes and civic ecology. This is a particularly relevant chapter for considering the practicalities of landscape provision and management, again grounded in comprehensive literature.

Chapter 6 signals a slight change in emphasis as it considers the experience of the architect in designing residential complexes. The reader will recognise the previous discussions concerning the connections between the environment and individuals as the author considers the integration of green space as a functional resource in residential complexes. Here well-being is considered a subset of sustainability, referring to living in 'green dwellings' and 'free space' as important for everyday life, and considers the need for an architectural response.

Chapter 7 is set in the context of design of the public realm and takes an intriguing position examining playable space from the perspective of older people, quality of life and life satisfaction. In doing so, the authors add another dimension to the well-being debate and the reader is invited to make comparisons between the issues discussed in earlier chapters and the language used to describe play activities in both children and adults. Play and playable spaces are presented from both theoretical and case study examples drawing on the researchers' own work to illustrate the debate with responses from users. Once again it is fully supported by relevant literature.

Chapter 8 examines another subset of the well-being debate: the responses of children and how they react to their local neighbourhoods. Discussion raises additional concerns regarding the quality of neighbourhoods and their ability to support physical and mental well-being, specifically in children. This chapter reviews literature relating to children's activity, and decline in their mobility and independence as a setting for the authors' own research which examines children's attitudes and perceptions of their local environment, in this case in New Zealand. The authors present differing understandings of place qualities from the perspectives of locals and professionals. Readers are invited to consider the implications of the methodology, the perceptions of different groups, how we engage with children in the research process, and to relate this to professional practice and the processes by which we give voice to children.

Chapter 9 moves outside the specific context of landscape to consider an under-debated aspect of culture, inviting readers to draw on the experience of the museum sector and consider the approaches developed in their work. There are a number of issues here, since the experience of the authors shows how this sector is reacting to the well-being agenda and parallels can and should be drawn regarding the implications for other fields, specifically the critical approaches used and the outreach opportunities. The authors discuss challenges and the results of their 'Heritage in Hospitals' project, collaboration with partners and the ways in which the responses have been analysed. They focus on the well-being outcomes of handling and experiencing objects, suggesting dimensions which can be applied to encountering objects within the environment. Their work is especially significant as it uses established quality of life measures and introduces supporting literature to which the reader is referred.

Chapter 10 focuses on the natural environment and considers the work of the UK Forest Research – Social and Economic Research Group (SERG). The authors take a national perspective regarding the use of the UK forest estate, how the public relate to it and use it to realise mental and physical health benefits, considering woodlands and health in the wider remit of social, cultural and well-being values. The SERG is in a unique position to review the perceptions of woodland users and to participate with respondents to gain new insights into the management of the woodland resource. They discuss research findings in relation to aspects of governance, user engagement and activities, concluding with a conceptual framework for the delivery of well-being benefits which can be compared to the theoretical perspectives of the earlier chapters. As such this chapter informs us more generally regarding the management of natural resources with well-being in mind. The chapter is well supported by literature which specifically targets research regarding the unique social and health performance of woodlands.

Chapter 11 returns to the theme of children, emphasising that children are experts regarding their worlds. It presents ideas about engagement with children as users of the environment to develop new insights regarding the environment and well-being, and how the impacts are described and derived from a child's perspective. Notable in the discussion are the benefits of participants being active in the research process. Although this chapter focuses on children, who are under-represented in the process, there are broader implications here for engagement with a wider profile of potential users. We suggest that the reader considers the results of the authors' work, especially regarding the ways that we could improve research design.

There is a wealth of material in this book and Chapter 12 attempts to draw the various stands together, reviewing and summarising the key points in ways that hopefully are useful to the reader and thus to help consolidate the different ideas of well-being as it relates to the landscape. We invite the reader to use the information found here in their own professional or academic remits. As identified earlier we have found exploration of well-being from different professional and disciplinary perspectives to be highly informative and beneficial to our understanding and we hope that this is the case in this volume.

1
EXPLORING THE POTENTIAL FOR A 'DOUBLE DIVIDEND'

Living well and living greener

Louise Reid and Colin Hunter

Introduction

Throughout history, there has been much discussion about what it means to be well or unwell (Diener and Biswas-Diener, 2008; Mathews and Izquierdo, 2009), how these understandings of wellness relate to life experiences (Christopher, 1999), and continued debate about how personal well-being can be measured (Linley et al., 2009). Recently there has been a resurgence of political interest in personal well-being, symbolised in the UK by a request from the Prime Minister for an Office of National Statistics review of well-being measures. Such interest has been fuelled by the recognition that until the recent economic recession, the UK, like much of the Western world, experienced a prolonged period of economic growth and relative stability, which did not result in measurable improvements in personal well-being (Andreou, 2010). As Ryan and Deci (2001) have argued, such material wealth created a 'culture of surplus' through which the pursuit of improved personal well-being has involved ever greater consumption of material goods, leaving in its wake a legacy of environmental problems. Despite vociferous calls for greater conceptualisation of the relationship between pro-environmental behaviour and personal well-being, this area of research remains neglected. This chapter introduces a novel unifying framework to understand the relationship between forms of pro-environmental behaviour and types of personal well-being using the concept of a 'double dividend'.

The concept of a 'double dividend' (Jackson, 2005) holds much promise as an ideal which, if realised, may result in improved personal well-being whilst simultaneously reducing our impact on the environment. The double dividend has long been discussed within the realm of environmental economics in the context of environmental taxation, but has been borrowed by Jackson (2005) to describe 'win–win' situations where environmental and well-being outcomes may be achieved. For instance, transforming consumption may be viewed as an 'opportunity to simultaneously address disenchanting aspects of the consumerist lifestyle that undermine personal and collective well-being' (Soron, 2010). Explicit in the concept of the double dividend is an inherent reciprocity: 'what's good for us is good for the environment' (Jacob et al., 2009), improvements in one will benefit the other. However, as a desirable end point, the double dividend remains under-conceptualised, particularly with regard to the relative role of theoretically distinct types of personal well-being. Moreover, and despite vociferous calls for greater enquiry into the relationship between personal well-being and actions that protect the environment, so called 'pro-environmental behaviour' (Andreou, 2010; Cafaro, 2010; Hall, 2010; Jackson, 2005; Jacob et al., 2009; Ryan and Deci, 2001; Soper, 2007; Soron, 2010), we are no closer to understanding how we might achieve the double dividend.

This chapter is therefore an attempt to develop the double dividend and put forward a novel unifying framework in order to encourage reflection and debate on how the double dividend may be realised and what a new research agenda might entail. The chapter does so by providing an overview of debates surrounding pro-environmental behaviour and personal well-being, with a particular focus on two different notions of personal well-being, 'hedonia' and 'eudaimonia'. Bringing these together and recognising the value of existing theories, such as the 'no avail thesis', 'alternative hedonism', the 'exalted view' and 'environmental citizenship', our novel unifying framework is presented. The chapter then concludes by offering some reflections on this new conceptualisation, presenting a new research agenda.

Pro-environmental behaviour research

Much research now attributes climate change and growing environmental degradation to the way that modern societies function, leading to a flourishing of debates about environmental concern and protection (Gregson et al., 2007; Reid et al., 2009; Seyfang, 2006; Shove, 2010). Central to such debates has been discussion of pro-environmental behaviour: 'behaviour that has a reduced impact on the environment, such as reduced journeys using the car, switching off lights, and recycling' (Reid et al., 2010). In short, pro-environmental behaviour is a term used to describe actions undertaken by an individual, household or group to protect the environment (Barr and Gilg, 2005; Gatersleben et al., 2002; Lucas et al., 2008).

According to Steg and Vlek (2009b), research attempting to understand pro-environmental behaviour typically fits into a threefold taxonomy, that which is concerned with:

1   intent (deliberate or unintended) or impact (higher or lower magnitude of environmental damage/benefit) behaviours;

2   curtailment or efficiency behaviours (drying washing outside vs. using a highly efficient a-rated tumble drier); and,
3   direct and immediate (recycling) or indirect and delayed (activism) impact behaviours.

Recent work has focused on those behaviours with greatest environmental impact and how they might be changed (Reid et al., 2011). For instance, consumption is an activity recognised as particularly environmentally harmful because of the energy required for the manufacture, transport and disposal of goods, and associated greenhouse gas emissions (Steg and Vlek, 2009a). Indeed, trends indicate that consumption is continuing to grow despite advances in product design which make appliances more efficient (Steg and Vlek, 2009a), meaning that current 'developed' societies are not doing more with less, but more with more. There has thus been notable discussion about which behaviours individuals should be encouraged to change: curtailment behaviours, where consumption is limited or restricted; or efficiency behaviours. Unfortunately it appears that curtailment activities, those which promise greatest environmental benefit, but which are perceived as compromising current lifestyles, are less popular than efficiency behaviours 'manifested through buying organic or green labelled products, rather than not buying or using certain products' (Jensen, 2008).

A great deal of research has explored the motives behind pro-environmental behaviour (Joireman et al., 2004; Norlund and Garvill, 2002). For example, studies have sought to measure which factors have the most significant influence on the lengths that individuals go to protect the environment (Batley et al., 2001; Bratt, 1999; Darnton, 2008), and include knowledge, information, attitudes, personal efficacy and values. Values, and altruistic and biospheric (concern about the biosphere) values in particular, have been highlighted as being especially potent in determining how individuals view the environment and the lengths that they may go to, to protect it (de Groot and Steg, 2008). Understanding how the ways in which people feel about the environment is translated into what they do to protect it has thus been a key area of debate for those interested in exploring pro-environmental behaviour (Feng and Reisner, 2011). Research has, for example, demonstrated some inconsistency between how individuals feel and what they do (Ignatow, 2006): the 'value-action gap'. This 'gap' is a product of the difference between an individual expressing a desire to protect the environment but not actually doing so (Gatersleben et al., 2002).

Although discussion about the antecedents, precursors and predictors of pro-environmental behaviour continues, debate is no longer solely occupied with the value–action gap, and has also considered the mechanisms through which pro-environmental behaviour may become mainstreamed (Reid et al., 2010). This changing rhetoric is a reflection of criticism of approaches that suggest pro-environmental behaviour can be predicted according to a particular mixture of antecedents because individuals are autonomously acting and rational beings.

Considerable attention has thus been devoted to exploring the way in which pro-environmental behaviours are simply a manifestation of wider social, cultural, political and economic processes influenced by socio-technological transitions (Hand et al., 2005). Building on this, research has become particularly concerned with the issue of whether individuals are deliberately or accidentally 'pro' or 'anti'-environmental in their behaviours. There is now a convincing case that such behaviour is not a matter of individual choice, but is produced and reproduced over time according to the development of particular practices like heating, cooling, cooking and showering (Shove, 2010). Accordingly, the role of individual choice is only ever secondary to broader social processes, with the 'infrastructure of provision that locks consumers into materially intense consumption patterns' (Renner, 2004 in Soron, 2010).

Whilst the dialectic tension between the individualistic and socio-technological perspective is immense (see recent commentaries between Shove 2010, 2011, and Whitmarsh et al., 2011), they have been of great interest to those interested in developing policies to encourage pro-environmental behaviour (Darnton, 2008; Southerton et al., 2011). Encouraging pro-environmental behaviour is thus a vast task. In recognition of the magnitude of this challenge, it may therefore be necessary to direct attention towards reducing and preventing those most environmentally detrimental of activities (flying, driving), encouraging the curtailment of them, rather than simply developing efficient solutions (greener fuels) which may only yield marginal improvements in environmental impact.

Understanding personal well-being

As the introduction to this chapter suggested, a change in pro-environmental behaviour, whether through individual choice or not, may have consequences for personal well-being. This section of the chapter therefore delves deeper into debates surrounding personal well-being in order to consider how personal well-being may be influenced by pro-environmental behaviour. In doing so, the concepts of 'hedonia' and 'eudaimonia' are introduced, which, this chapter will contend, may be useful to consider when attempting to better conceptualise the double dividend.

One of the challenges of undertaking research on personal well-being is that rarely is it the same for all individuals, instead varying from one individual to another, and throughout the lifespan (Ryff et al., 2004). For instance, 'objective' conditions such as physical health or housing quality may be poor, but a sense of personal well-being high (Fleuret and Atkinson, 2007). Thus, having 'good' personal well-being depends not only on the everyday experiences of the individual, but also upon how those experiences and conditions are perceived (Andreou, 2010). At the core of research has been an examination of the relationship between: physical health and mental health; the absence or presence of positive and negative feelings; and, the role and effect of emotions and moods (Christopher, 1999). Whilst much research has focused on identifying and understanding the variables (objective conditions, socio-demographics, personality) believed responsible for personal well-being, it has been noted that philosophical questions about the nature of personal well-being often remain secondary to these concerns (Christopher, 1999).

One of the largest philosophical divisions in the research on personal well-being has been between hedonia and eudaimonia. As well as being two distinct theoretical constructs, hedonia and eudaimonia have lent their names to 'types' of personal well-being (hedonic and eudaimonic) and inspired a generation of methodological development which has sought to measure each of them. Personal well-being that is achieved through the absence of negative experiences, emotions and feelings relates to hedonia and constitutes hedonic well-being, whereas personal well-being which is achieved despite the presence of negative experiences or feelings is related to eudaimonia, described as eudaimonic well-being. Recently, research has begun to demonstrate that hedonic and eudaimonic forms of personal well-being may not be mutually exclusive (Huta and Ryan, 2009). Nevertheless, the majority of existing work has emphasised their dissimilarity (Huta and Ryan, 2009), reinforced by their having distinct biophysical signatures (Ryff et al., 2004), which is why we retain the separation for the purpose of this chapter.

Both hedonia and eudaimonia have their roots in ancient Greek philosophy with hedonia, or hedonism, having become more successfully mainstreamed within the popular vernacular. Commonly understood to describe feelings of pleasure and delight, hedonia is predominantly concerned with the experience of pleasure and frequently related to the concept of happiness (Christopher, 1999). Indeed, some philosophers have argued that pleasure or happiness is the most important intrinsic good, meaning that it is valuable for its own sake and therefore an end worthy of pursuit (Ryan and Deci, 2001). Eudaimonia, viewed as a concept distinct from hedonia, is seen as being closely related to the deeper principles or values guiding one's life, such that eudaimonic well-being may be described as 'acting to the best of one's ability, exercising virtues like kindness or gratitude, and developing one's potential' (Huta and Ryan, 2009). Eudaimonic personal well-being is therefore experienced through the achievement of goals that are not necessarily pleasure giving, with happiness being only ever one part of what makes individuals 'well'. An important difference between eudaimonia and hedonia is that hedonic well-being exists through the absence of negative feelings or bad life events, but that eudaimonic well-being occurs despite these. Simply put, hedonia relates to the pursuit of happiness and eudaimonia the happiness of pursuit.

The dominance of Western individualism has been blamed for the way in which more responsibility for personal well-being lies with the individual ('self-help', 'self-health') than ever before, inflating the importance of acting in one's own interest (Sointu, 2005). Such individualistic notions have given precedence to hedonic well-being, in as far as individuals pursue lifestyles that give greatest immediate personal pleasure and happiness. Similarly, the extent to which an individual acts in self-interest has been noted as a key driver of environmental problems 'as individuals pursue aims they find satisfying or pleasurable, they may create conditions that make more formidable the attainment of well-being by others' (Ryan and Deci, 2001). The importance that the pursuit of personal well-being has in shaping our relationship with the environment cannot, therefore, be understated (Jackson, 2005).

The role that the specific types (hedonic and eudaimonic) of well-being may play in our relationship with the environment has not yet been investigated. Indeed, the distinction between hedonia and eudaimonia means that there is great potential to explore how they may differently influence and be influenced by pro-environmental behaviour. Whilst both forms of well-being may be affected by policies that encourage pro-environmental behaviour, it is also likely that personal well-being has a critical role to play in encouraging such behaviour. Thus, and as will be developed further in the next section, eudaimonia or eudaimonic forms of personal well-being appear to offer greater potential in terms of simultaneously being good for us and good for the planet.

Linking personal well-being and pro-environmental behaviour: conceptualising the double dividend

Jackson's (2005) conceptualisation of the double dividend is tightly bound to the issue of consumption, which, he argues, may influence personal well-being at the same time as being a display of an individual's pro-environmental behaviour (e.g. buying environmentally friendly washing powder). Although a potentially powerful vehicle to convey the relationship between personal well-being and pro-environmental behaviour, Jackson's double dividend fails to fully acknowledge the distinctions between hedonia and eudaimonia. This section therefore seeks to introduce our novel unifying framework, building on Jackson's double dividend, but making explicit the relationship between specific forms of personal well-being and types of pro-environmental behaviour. As a precursor to this, the discussion will draw on existing theories that have looked at personal well-being and environmental behaviour, such as the 'no avail thesis' (Andreou, 2010), 'alternative hedonism' (Soper, 2007), 'the exhalted view' (Andreou, 2010), and 'environmental citizenship' (Dobson, 2010; Dobson and Saiz, 2005), considering what they may offer in pursuit of the double dividend.

The no avail thesis and alternative hedonism

The gratification of 'wants' and pursuit of personal (hedonic) well-being through consumption has, in part, been used to explain the way in which individuals are driven to consume (Sointu, 2005). An often used explanation for the consumption and therefore accumulation of material goods is the way in which individuals judge their levels of goods with those of others around them, colloquially known as 'keeping up with the Joneses' (Andreou, 2010; Hall, 2010). To paraphrase Andreou (2010), the pleasure gained from material goods is perpetuated by comparison with others: being better off and having more than others leads to greater pleasure. This becomes cyclical when, to offset the waning pleasure which follows from becoming accustomed to having more 'stuff', individuals accumulate yet more: 'people become habituated to higher standards of living, eventually returning to their original level of happiness' (Hall, 2010). The cyclical pattern of consumption behaviour is arguably linked to notions of the 'hedonic treadmill' (Diener et al., 2006), so that consumption increases to maintain feelings of hedonic well-being, in order to retain the individual's position on the treadmill.

Andreou (2010) related such thinking to the 'no avail thesis', a set of ideas premised on the concept that current 'conveniences and luxuries are not having a significant impact on our happiness, making the [environmental] costs incurred for them a waste'. An example of this is the increasing popularity of health and beauty products, which when consumed, bring the promise of, but do not guarantee, greater wellness (Sointu, 2005), despite the detrimental environmental impact of their production and transportation (van Gelder, 2004). The implication is that, over time, the environment will degrade to such an extent that current lifestyles will be compromised, with ever greater implications for personal well-being.

The no avail thesis, though pessimistic is, according to Andreou (2010), surmountable given that 'there is room for one to be as happy with much less, so long as others, particularly one's peers, also have much less', achieved by a wholesale reduction in consumption by all. The theory of 'alternative hedonism' is similarly concerned with the way in which consumption provides pleasure at the cost of the environment but moves debate forward by suggesting how the reduction may take place. Alternative hedonism proposes that when thinking about consumption, the tactile, sensual and physical pleasures of consuming differently should be considered (Soper, 2007), advancing different ways of thinking about how enhancements in personal well-being may be encouraged by alternative consumption. For example, when putting in place a policy to encourage a shift from the car to the pushbike, the sensory pleasures gained from this alternative consumption, such as enjoyment gained from cycling (feeling the wind as it rushes past) should be highlighted (Soper, 2007). Likewise, the displeasure from having to work long hours in order to afford to buy material goods is similarly important to recognise.

Both the 'no avail' and 'alternative hedonism' theories are aligned more closely with hedonic than eudaimonic forms of personal well-being given that they are concerned with the physical pleasures of consuming, and consuming differently, rather than forgoing such pleasures by not consuming at all. Moreover, and relating this to Steg and Vlek's (2009b) taxonomy, it may be argued that the 'no avail' and 'alternative hedonism' perspectives are more closely related to efficiency behaviours than curtailment behaviours, in so far as consumption is not relinquished, simply refocused or reframed. There are, therefore, limitations to such perspectives. For instance, and as suggested by the 'no avail thesis', improvements in hedonic personal well-being may be short-lived and transient. At the same time, efficiency behaviours are an extension of business-as-usual thinking, as the assumptions underlying consumption are not altered. The magnitude of change promised may therefore be restricted. If, for instance, the pleasure gained from consuming in alternative ways alters because of changes in an individual's personal circumstances, the original and environmentally harmful behaviour may be reverted to. Take, for example, the previously mentioned move from driving to cycling: the arrival of children may mean that more pleasure is gained from being with them than spending time cycling to work, meaning reversion to the original car-driving behaviour may occur. In recognition of the relatively transient nature of such shifts, it is helpful to consider if and how eudaimonia is a more promising prospect than hedonia when seeking to achieve the double dividend.

Exalted view and environmental citizenship

Developed in relation to the existence of innate or intrinsic personal values, not extrinsic or superficial ones, Andreou's (2010) 'exalted view' and Dobson's (2010) 'environmental citizenship' promote a shift towards reduced consumption (curtailment behaviours) rather than alternative consumption (efficiency behaviours). The exalted view, for example, relates to the idea that the crux of personal well-being surrounds the non-material (e.g. mental and spiritual) rather than the material realm (Andreou, 2010). The key to personal well-being may therefore lie in the moral or spiritual benefits of reduced consumption rather than physical pleasures. Indeed, instead of thinking about the relatively transient physical pleasures of alternative consumption, it may be more productive to encourage the adoption of 'virtuous lifestyles' in which reductions in consumption rather than alternative consumption are the explicit focus.

Harnessing an individual's intrinsic principles and values may instigate behavioural change that endures. This idea has also been developed in notions of environmental citizenship which 'seek to draw out latent values already harboured by an individual' in order to encourage behavioural change (Dobson, 2010). Environmental citizenship claims to encourage pro-environmental behaviour by promoting emotional connections between citizens and their environment by evoking active participation, reflection and discursive engagement. Capitalising on values around care and compassion for other humans may be one route to pro-environmental behaviour change by encouraging reflection about the effect of environmentally harmful behaviours on other members of society. There is a direct link from here to virtuous ways of living, allied to eudaimonic forms of personal well-being as, for instance, individuals feel good or virtuous by not consuming and therefore helping others. Approaches that therefore seek to utilise these innate ideals hold greater promise in seeking to encourage a society in which 'consuming less confers higher status than consuming more' (Cafaro, 2010), an altogether different approach from that advocated by the no avail or alternative hedonism perspectives. Importantly, the act of curtailing behaviour or going without may result in eudaimonic personal well-being which, as outlined above, arises despite what may be perceived as negative events or experiences (not having or doing things). This eudaimonic-based logic is a departure from approaches which simply seek to 'green' consumption or 'nudge' individuals into different ways of acting. It suggests that the fundamental assumptions around consumption and the role it has in modern society needs greater reflection.

Towards a unifying framework

As a pictorial representation of our thinking, Figure 1.1 demonstrates how pro-environmental behaviour and personal well-being may be unified. The lack of any similar device reinforced the necessity of its development and our desire to engender further investigation of ways in which the double dividend may be achieved. Indeed, and as we have argued, it is necessary to not only consider the way in which pro-environmental behaviour and personal well-being may be related, but, specifically, how particular types of behaviour and well-being may co-exist. Explaining each element of Figure 1.1 in turn, we seek to unify the disparate concepts of pro-environmental behaviour and personal well-being with the afore mentioned theories: the 'no avail thesis'; 'alternative hedonism'; the 'exalted view'; and 'environmental citizenship'.

Firstly, it is important to recognise that the figure does not suggest eudaimonic personal well-being and hedonic personal well-being are on the same continuum: that one offers more well-being than the other. Instead they are separate constructs so that the further away one moves from the central point, the greater the improvement in both. The y-axis is, however, a continuum such that the top of the axis represents greater detrimental environmental impact and vice versa. Thus, curtailment activities, which promise greater environmental protection have less environmental impact when compared with efficiency activities – reflected in their position on the y-axis.

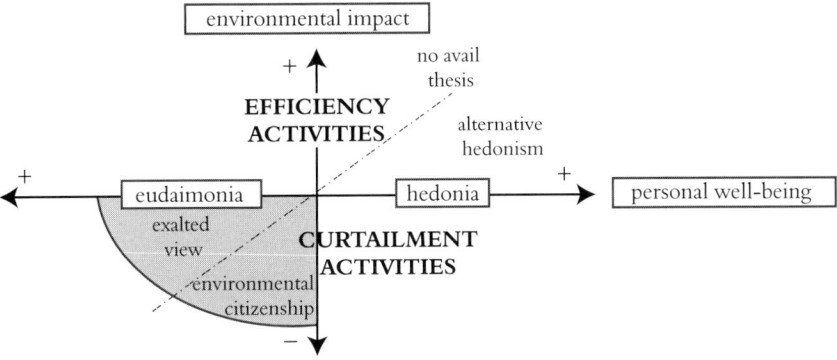

FIGURE 1.1 A unifying framework for the double dividend

The top right-hand quadrant displays the positive relationship between hedonic personal well-being and environmental impact, that is, improvements in hedonic personal well-being typically result in greater environmental impact. One example of this might be a foreign holiday which involves a long-haul air flight with high environmental impact. The same quadrant also describes the connection of the no avail thesis and alternative hedonism theories to the relationship between personal well-being and environmental impact. Importantly, the no avail thesis is placed above the dashed line and alternative hedonism below it, representing our interpretation of their relationship with material objects (the no avail thesis discusses the accumulation of material goods whilst alternative hedonism is more focused on the experiences involved in the accumulation and use of material goods).

The bottom left shaded quadrant is arguably the most important of all the quadrants as this is where we suggest the double dividend lies. Accordingly, and based on the discussion, greater eudaimonic personal well-being may potentially result in greater pro-environmental behaviour and lesser environmental impact. Examples of double dividend activities might include, for instance: local conservation volunteering, green prescriptions, green gyms and 'staycations'. This quadrant also demonstrates that the exalted view and environmental citizenship may be more likely to reduce environmental impact through the uptake of pro-environmental behaviour whilst simultaneously increasing eudaimonic personal well-being.

In summary, we hope that Figure 1.1, as a representation of our argument, has demonstrated: 1) the importance of distinguishing between efficiency and curtailment pro-environmental behaviours, in order to reflect the magnitude of their environmental impact; 2) the significance of unpicking the concept of personal well-being and exploring the theoretically distinct concepts of eudaimonia and hedonia; and 3) that the most productive relationship to consider in pursuit of the double dividend is that between eudaimonic personal well-being and curtailment pro-environmental behaviours.

Conclusions and agendas

Despite calls from eminent academics that the 'concern of greatest importance, not only for psychological theorists, but also for humanity, is the study of relations between personal well-being and the broader issues of the collective wellness of humanity and the wellness of the planet' (Ryan and Deci, 2001), progress on this front has been limited. This chapter represents an attempt to respond to such calls, presenting our unifying framework in order to encourage consideration of how the double dividend may be realised.

The double dividend holds much promise as an ideal which, if realised, may result in improved personal well-being whilst simultaneously reducing our impact on the environment. We have built upon Jackson's (2005) original contribution with greater acknowledgement of the distinction between hedonia and eudaimonia.

The main argument presented in this chapter is that eudaimonic well-being offers the greatest potential in this endeavour by encouraging the curtailment of environmentally harmful activities, exactly those behaviours regarded as most important in mitigating our impact on the environment. Thus, and as has been argued by Pelletier and Sharp (2008), messages about environmental behaviour should focus 'systematically in terms of intrinsic gains or losses (i.e. health, well-being) as opposed to extrinsic gains or losses (i.e. make or save money, comfort, prestige, and fame)', as these are more likely to influence the uptake of a wider range of behaviours over a longer duration. Such suggestions support a double dividend that builds on eudaimonia rather than hedonia and curtailment rather than efficiency, a relationship we have sought to make more explicit in this chapter.

Both the exalted view and environmental citizenship highlight the importance of reflection, discussion and the engagement of individuals in such debates. Indeed, it may be that this is encouraged by the research process itself (e.g. Hobson, 2003; Reid et al., 2011), in addition to efforts undertaken by policymakers. In the era of the 'Big Society', there are serious questions about how we might mobilise civil society to realise the (eudaimonic) benefits of protecting the environment, an agenda to which geographers could productively contribute, particularly our expertise in bringing together disparate knowledge and methodologies. In addition, we need to seize opportunities to evaluate existing activities, or interventions, which aim to achieve the double dividend, and capitalise on these in order to progress our theoretical thinking.

Acknowledgements

This chapter follows from work undertaken as part of the BeWEL project, funded by the ESRC, MRC and BBSRC through the 'Understanding Individual Behaviour: Exploratory Networks' (UIBEN) initiative (RES-355-25-0012). We gratefully acknowledge this support. We would also like to thank Alison Sandeson and Jenny Johnston, University of Aberdeen, for their help in drawing the figure.

References

Andreou, C. (2010) A shallow route to environmentally friendly happiness: Why evidence that we are shallow materialists need not be bad news for the environment(alist), *Ethics, Place & Environment*, 13(1), 1–10.

Barr, S., and Gilg, A. (2005) Conceptualising and analysing household attitudes and actions to a growing environmental problem: Development and application of a framework to guide local waste policy, *Applied Geography*, 25, 226–247.

Batley, D., Colbourne, P.D., Fleming, P., and Urwin, P. (2001) Citizen versus consumer: challenges in the UK green power market, *Energy Policy*, 29, 479–487.

Bratt, C (1999) Consumers environmental behaviour: Generalised, sector-based, or compensatory?, *Environment and Behaviour*, 31(1) 28–44.

Cafaro, P. (2010) Getting to less, *Ethics, Place & Environment*, 13(1), 11–14.

Christopher, J. (1999) Situating psychological well-being: Exploring the cultural roots of its theory and research, *Journal of Counseling and Development*, 77, 141–152.

Darnton, A. (2008) Reference report: An overview of behaviour change models and their uses, *Government Social Research* [online]. Available from: http://www.gsr.gov.uk/downloads/resources/behaviour_change_review/reference_report.pdf

de Groot, J., and Steg, L. (2008) Value orientations to explain beliefs related to environmentally significant behaviour: How to measure egoistic, altruistic and biospheric value orientations, *Environment and Behaviour*, 40(3), 330–354.

Diener, E., and Biswas-Diener, R. (2008) *Happiness, unlocking the mysteries of psychological wealth*. Oxford: Blackwell.

Diener, E., Lucas, R., and Scollon, C. (2006) Beyond the hedonic treadmill: Revisions to the adaptation theory of well-being, *American Psychologist*, 61, 305–314.

Dobson, A. (2010) Environmental citizenship and pro-environmental behavior, *SDRN Briefing*, http://www.sd-research.org.uk/wp-content/uploads/sdrn_envirocitizen_briefing_final.pdf

Dobson, A., and Saiz, V. (2005) Introduction, *Environmental Politics* 14(2), 157–162.

Feng, W., and Reisner, A. (2011) Factors influencing private and public environmental protection behaviours: Results from a survey of residents in Shaanxi, China, *Journal of Environmental Management*, 92, 429–436.

Fleuret, S., and Atkinson, S. (2007) Wellbeing, health and geography: A critical review and research agenda, *New Zealand Geographer*, 63, 106–118.

Gatersleben, B., Steg, L., and Vlek, C. (2002) Measurement and determinants of environmentally significant consumer behaviour, *Environment and Behaviour*, 34(3), 335–362.

Gregson, N., Metcalfe, A., and Crewe, L. (2007) Identity, mobility, and the throwaway society, *Environment and Planning D: Society and Space*, 25, 682–700.

Hall, C. (2010) The habitual route to environmentally friendly (or unfriendly) happiness, *Ethics, Place & Environment*, 13(1), 19–22.

Hand, M., Shove, E., and Southerton, D. (2005) Explaining showering: A discussion of the material, conventional, and temporal dimensions of practice, *Sociological Research Online*, 10(2), http://www.socresonline.org.uk/10/2/hand.html

Hobson, K. (2003) Thinking habits into action: The role of knowledge and process in questioning household consumption practices, *Local Environment*, 8(1), 95–112.

Huta, V., and Ryan, R. (2009) Pursuing pleasure or virtue: The differential and overlapping well-being benefits of hedonic and eudaimonia motives, *Journal of Happiness Studies*, 11, 735–762.

Ignatow, G. (2006) Cultural models of nature and society. Reconsidering environmental attitudes and concern, *Environment and Behaviour*, 38(4), 441–461.

Jackson, T. (2005) Live better by consuming less?: Is there a 'double dividend' in sustainable consumption?, *Journal of Industrial Ecology*, 9(1–2), 19–36.

Jacob, J., Jovic, E., and Brinkerhoff, M. (2009) Personal and planetary well-being: Mindfulness meditation, environmental behaviour and personal quality of life in a survey from the social justice and ecological sustainability movement, *Social Indicators Research*, 93, 275–294.

Jensen, J. (2008) Measuring consumption in households: Interpretations and strategies, *Ecological Economics*, 68(1–2), 353–361.

Joireman, J., Van Lange, P., and Van Vugt, M. (2004) Who cares about the environmental impact of cars? Those with an eye toward the future, *Environment and Behaviour*, 36(2), 187–206.

Linley, P., Maltby, J., Wood, A., Osborne, G., and Hurling, R. (2009) Measuring happiness: The higher order factor structure of subjective and psychological well-being measures, *Personality and Individual Differences*, 47, 878–884.

Lucas K., Brooks, M., Darnton, A., and Elster Jones, J. (2008) Promoting pro-environmental behaviour: existing evidence and policy implications. *Environmental Science & Policy*, 11(5), 456–66.

Mathews, G., and Izquierdo, C. (2009) *Pursuits of happiness: Well-being in an anthropological perspective*. Oxford: Berghahn Books.

Norlund, A., and Garvill, J. (2002) Value structures behind environmental behaviour, *Environment and Behaviour*, 34, 740–756.

Pelletier, L., and Sharp, E. (2008) Persuasive communication and environmental behaviours: How message tailoring and message framing can improve the integration of behaviours through self-determined motivation, *Canadian Psychology*, 49(3), 210–217.

Reid, L., Hunter, C., and Sutton, P. (2009) Writing it down: suggestions for a new approach towards understanding pro-environmental behaviour, *International Journal of Sustainable Development and World Ecology*, 16(6), 369–73.

Reid, L., Sutton, P., and Hunter, C. (2010) Theorising the meso level: The household as a crucible of environmental behaviour, *Progress in Human Geography*, 34(3), 309–327.

Reid, L., Hunter, C., and Sutton, P. (2011) Rising to the challenge of environmental behaviour change: A reflexive diary approach, *Geoforum*, 42, 720–30.

Ryan, R., and Deci, E. (2001) On happiness and human potentials: A review of research on hedonic and eudaimonic well-being, *Annual Review Psychology*, 52, 141–166.

Ryff, C., Singer, B., and Love, G. (2004) Positive health: Connecting well-being with biology, *Philosophical Transactions of the Royal Society of London B*, 359, 1383–1394.

Seyfang, G. (2006) Community Currencies: A New Tool for Sustainable Consumption? The Centre for Social and Economic Research on the Global Environment (CSERGE), University of East Anglia, Norwich, http://www.cserge.ac.uk/publications/cserge-working-paper/edm-2006-09-community-currencies-new-tool-sustainable-consumption

Shove, E. (2010) Beyond the ABC: Climate change policy and theories of social change, *Environment and Planning A*, 42(6), 1273–1285.

Shove, E. (2011) On the difference between chalk and cheese—a response to Whitmarsh et al's. comments on 'Beyond the ABC: climate change policy and theories of social change', *Environment and Planning A*, 43(2), 262–264.

Sointu, E. (2005) The rise of an ideal: Tracing changing discourses of wellbeing, *The Sociological Review*, 53, 255–74.

Soper, K. (2007) Re-thinking the 'good life': The citizen dimension of consumer disaffection with consumerism, *Journal of Consumer Culture*, 7, 205.

Soron, D. (2010) Sustainability, self-identity and the sociology of consumption, *Sustainable Development*, 18, 172–181.

Southerton, D., McMeekin, A., and Evans, D. (2011) International review of behaviour change initiatives, *Scottish Government*, http://www.scotland.gov.uk/Publications/2011/02/01104638/0

Steg, L., and Vlek, C. (2009a) Encouraging environmental behaviour: An integrative review and research agenda, *Journal of Environmental Psychology*, 29(3), 309–317.

Steg, L., and Vlek, C. (2009b) Social science and environmental behaviour, in Boersema, J., and Reijnders, L. (eds) *Principals of environmental sciences*, Springer: London.

van Gelder, J. (2004) Greasy palms: European buyers of Indonesian palm oil, *Friends of the Earth Report*, http://www1.milieudefensie.nl/globalisering/publicaties/rapporten/greasy_palms_buyers_final.pdf

Whitmarsh L., O'Neill, S., Lorenzoni, I. (2011) Climate change or social change? Debate within, amongst, and beyond discipline, *Environment and Planning A*, 43(2), 258–261.

2
MODELLING WELL-BEING AND THE RELATIONSHIP BETWEEN INDIVIDUALS AND THEIR ENVIRONMENTS

Sara Warber, Katherine Irvine, Patrick Devine-Wright and Kevin Gaston

Introduction

Well-being is considered fundamental to quality of life. Yet there are worldwide concerns over increasing rates of obesity, chronic diseases, stress and associated mental ill-health. In seeking novel approaches to addressing these problems there is a resurgence of interest in the influence of the environment, in particular the natural environment, on human health and well-being. Over half the world's population now lives in urban areas; in Europe and North America the predicted level of urbanisation for 2010 was 70–80 per cent (Department of Economic and Social Affairs, 2008). With these changes worldwide, there is increasing need to understand the health impacts of urban living, identify mitigating factors, and implement sustainable patterns of development (Capon, 2007; Harris et al., 2007; Thompson, 2007; Vohra, 2007). Urban green space, including parks, is beginning to be studied as a potential health resource (de Vries et al., 2003; Kaczynski and Henderson, 2007; Korpela and Ylén, 2007, 2009; Korpela et al., 2008, 2010; Maas et al., 2006, 2009; McCormack et al., 2010; Pinder et al., 2009).

Despite mounting evidence of an effect of the natural environment on human health, we are only beginning to understand the potential mechanisms underlying these interactions. Drawing from analysis of open-ended responses from urban green space users about how they feel after leaving the park and utilising theories and models within environmental psychology and health, we develop an encompassing 'conceptual framework' for considering the relationship between the natural environment and human health where existing frameworks from different disciplines, often studied in isolation, provide some guidance.

Existing environmental and health frameworks

Attention Restoration Theory

Attention Restoration Theory (ART), a dominant model within the field of environmental psychology, proposes that the natural environment is cognitively restorative (Kaplan, 1995; Kaplan and Kaplan, 1989). Fundamental to ART is the hypothesis that the capacity to concentrate on, or direct attention to, one stimulus at a time (e.g. a task) requires inhibition of other competing stimuli and that, over time, this capacity fatigues. As mental fatigue increases, the ability to concentrate decreases resulting in mistakes, failure to focus, or impatience (Kaplan, 1987). Studies of brain-damaged patients demonstrate that attention deficits are associated with damage in the pre-frontal cortex which plays an inhibitory role in high-level mental activity like problem solving, goal setting, or planning (Lezak, 1982; Mesulam, 1985; Rothbart and Posner, 1985). ART proposes that natural settings can facilitate recovery from mental fatigue.

Sense of place

Sense of place theory suggests that the experience of the place itself is psychologically important. Found across a number of disciplines (including geography: Tuan, 1974; sociology: Fried, 1963; environmental psychology: Manzo, 2003; natural resource management: Patterson and Williams, 2005), place-related theory and research focuses on place attachment, i.e., the emotional attachments or bonds that people have with a physical place (Altman and Low, 1992; Brown et al., 2003), and place identity, i.e. the contribution that a place makes to one's personal identity (Devine-Wright and Lyons, 1997; Proshansky et al., 1983).

Psychophysiologic theory

Psychophysiologic or stress reduction theory links nature experiences to human physiology (Manfredo, et al., 1996; Ulrich, 1983; Ulrich et al., 1991). Stress from life events or daily hassles induces a state in which the body is dominated by the sympathetic nervous system, i.e. the fight or flight response (Cannon, 1929; Jansen et al., 1995). The opposite, the relaxation response, described by Wallace and Benson (1972), and mediated by the parasympathetic nervous system, explains the benefits of some alternative medicine techniques such as meditation, massage, or hypnosis. Experimental research has shown that being in a non-threatening natural environment reduces measures of sympathetic outflow, such as blood pressure, heart rate, skin conductance, serum cortisol, and urine adrenaline suggesting that this might be a physical mediator of some of the health benefits of nature (Alvarsson et al., 2010; Li et al., 2009, 2010; Parsons et al., 1998; Ulrich et al., 1991; Yamaguchi et al., 2006).

Models of health

Health outcomes may be measured generally with self-reported health, mortality, and morbidity, or quite narrowly in laboratory testing as in the biomedical model that attends primarily to diagnosis and treatment of physical disease. However, an expanded model, the biopsychosocial model (Engel, 1977; Fava and Sonino, 2008), that emphasises the contribution of psychological health and social support or barriers, has been embraced more thoroughly in recent decades. Others have proposed further expansion to include the importance of the spiritual dimension, creating the biopsychosocial–spiritual model (McKee and Chappel, 1992). Still others have begun to tease apart the construct of psychological well-being and identified component parts that might be more clearly delineated as a cognitive and an emotional or affective portion (Andrews and McKennell, 1980). An expanded model including five dimensions, physical, cognitive, affective, social, and spiritual, could become a relevant framework for assessing the health effects of urban green space, but has yet to be systematically applied in current environment and health research.

Urban green space users

We saw the need for a direct appeal to urban green space users to identify, in their own words, what effects they experience after being in green spaces. Our specific research questions were:

1 To what extent can urban green spaces be considered a resource for health promotion?
2 To what degree do existing theories and models account for the perceptions and experiences of urban green space users?

The study specifically sought to analyse offered comments on the effects of being in green space to inform a weighted taxonomy representing both breadth and relative salience, which is then compared to the existing theories and supports a more comprehensive model of the health value of human interaction with urban green space.

Methods

This qualitative study was embedded within a project whose aim was to understand the contribution of urban green space for biodiversity maintenance and human quality of life (Irvine et al., 2013; Jenks and Jones, 2010).

Setting

The research was conducted in Sheffield, UK, which has a population 513,000 (Office for National Statistics, 2001). All publicly accessible green spaces of more than one hectare (15) were selected along a wedge-shaped transect from the city centre to the western suburbs. The area surrounding the study sites ranged from high-density city developments to low-density suburbs. Study sites ranged in size from 1–23 hectares and included urban parks, formal gardens, semi-natural urban areas, and school playing fields (Fuller et al., 2007).

Data collection

The open-ended question, 'And thinking about after you leave this park, what words would you use to describe how you feel after you leave here', was embedded in a semi-structured interview that included demographics, questions exploring biodiversity conservation, and closed-ended questions about sense of place, attention restoration (Fuller et al., 2007), and the soundscape (Irvine et al., 2009). The post-park feeling question was asked prior to the closed-ended sense of place and attention restoration questions. Study materials were piloted and reviewed by a university ethics committee.

Procedures

A brief project description and assurance of anonymity was provided in writing and verbally prior to interview commencement. Consent was obtained verbally. The interviews took place *in situ* with green space users from 0700 to 1830 on weekends and weekdays from July through October. In 13 of the sites every third individual was invited to participate; in the remaining two, due to low user numbers, all individuals were approached. Interviewers took notes on responses to the open-ended questions, keeping close to the words of participants. In the few instances in which participants self-completed the questionnaire, responses were verbatim. Where a participant gave multiple responses for the question asked, all were noted. Interview length for the entire questionnaire ranged from 5 to 70 minutes (average = 18 minutes).

The participants

Interviews for 312 out of 565 approached green space users were conducted (representing a 55 per cent response). The sample included 168 women, 271 participants of European ethnicity, and ages 16 to over 70 years old. Forty-seven per cent of the participants were visiting the park alone and 36 per cent considered themselves daily users. Comments from 12 individuals visiting the green space for the first time were excluded because their responses were considered speculative; seven participants did not answer the question.

Analysis

Responses were entered into Excel spreadsheets. Multiple responses were treated as separate statements rather than one single response resulting in 527 unique responses. Participant responses then underwent an iterative content analysis (Elo and Kyngas, 2008; Morgan, 1993) and subsequently were sorted into codes based on participants' language. Similar codes were clustered into descriptive or theoretical themes that were further organised into domains based on the theoretical constructs already explored, i.e. from sense of place, attention restoration theory, psychophysiologic theory, and the biopsychosocial–spiritual health model. The qualitative data were transformed into quantitative data through a counting process that provided a measure of salience. The coding process resulted in no double coding of responses allowing quantification at all three levels (code, theme, and domain) in order to gain insight into the frequency with which a given feeling state was present among the participants.

The results

Participants' comments describing how they felt after leaving the park were grouped into seven domains: *Physical, Affective, Place Attachment, Spiritual, Cognitive, Global Well-being,* and *Social* (Figure 2.1). Taken together these described a complex holistic set of states produced by being in urban green spaces. The following convention is used in reporting the results: *Domain, Theme, code*; selected participant comments have been provided in quotation marks to illustrate the states and the associated language (participants are identified by a number e.g. P82, codes, domains, and themes are shown in italics).

Physical

The *Physical* domain, with 217/527 comments (41 per cent), included the themes Relaxed, Revitalised, Depleted, Comfortable, and Uncomfortable. The domain described post-park states associated with the physical body and dominated the descriptions from green space users. This domain included the most often cited theme, Relaxed, with 126/527 comments (24 per cent), of which 85 per cent were the first mentioned comment. Most responses consisted of the single word 'relaxed' although some individuals provided greater imagery. For example, P82 felt 'wound down a bit', P30 linked relaxation and nature by stating 'bit mellow because of greenery in the city', while P310 said '… more relaxed from being away from traffic on road'. The relaxed theme represented a major outcome experienced by park users and was clearly different in tone from the 52 comments grouped into the Revitalised theme (*refreshed, energised, full of fresh air, exercised*), where the respondents seemed to be more fired up and ready for whatever was to come next. These post-park states are captured by words such as 'refreshed', 'fresh', 'recharge your battery' (P111) or '[a] sense of well-

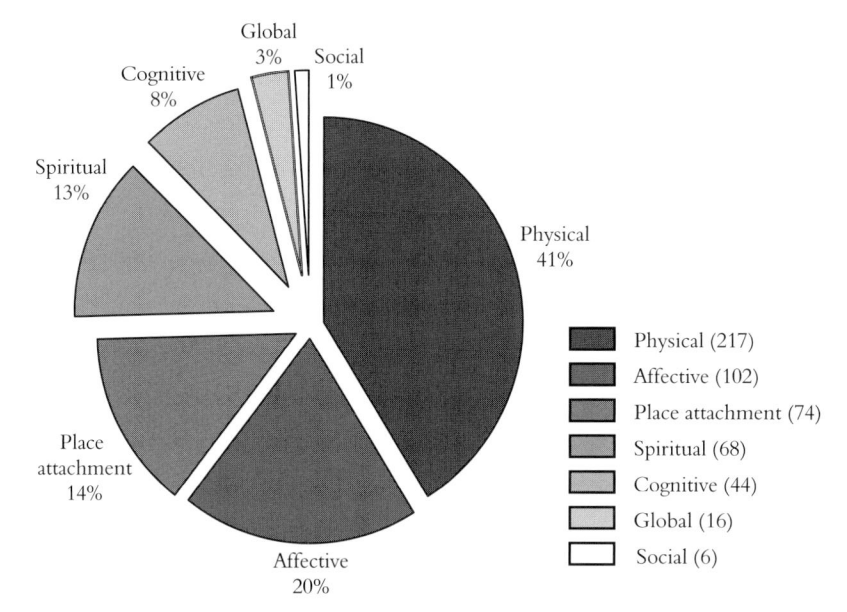

Global 3%
Cognitive 8%
Social 1%
Spiritual 13%
Physical 41%
Place attachment 14%
Affective 20%

Physical (217)
Affective (102)
Place attachment (74)
Spiritual (68)
Cognitive (44)
Global (16)
Social (6)

Note: Numbers in parentheses indicate the total number of respondent comments per domain

FIGURE 2.1 Post-park state following use of urban green space (modified from Irvine et al. 2013)

being because been in fresh air' (P98). One individual described this as '[a] bit more energised; revived having had fresh air/exercise' (P47). Some park users did feel negative physical states, such as depleted (28), because they were tired from physical pursuits ('physically exhausted as I always run around when here' (P275)), tired from being vigilant ('exhausted, glad to be going home because always feel on guard, have to watch my back literally' (P159)), hungry or thirsty; or they felt Uncomfortable (2). These comments are contrasted with those who were physically Comforted by being in the park (9) because they are *rested*, *warm*, or *well fed*, e.g. 'warm when sunny' (P161).

Affective and place attachment

The *Affective* domain (102/527; 19 per cent) and the *Place Attachment* domain (74/527; 14 per cent) taken together represented park users' emotions, whether their personal feelings within themselves or their feelings about the park. The majority (59/102; 58 per cent) of the personal feelings were Positive Emotions, described as *happy*, *good/fine/nice*, or *pleasant*. Additionally, some people (13) felt Intensely Positive Emotions, including *wonderful*, *exhilarated*, and *joyful*. In many instances participants described their positive post-park state in a single word which was reflected in the code name. For a few, the response provided additional insight into the experience, e.g. 'makes you change, feels good' (P73), or 'come up feeling fed up, leaving feeling great' (P241) or 'happy because [you] have seen wildlife [you] would not have seen at home' (P187). In the *Place Attachment* domain, the Value of the Park was highlighted by more than half (43/74; 58 per cent) of the comments. It was a *contrast from the city, a nice experience, an enjoyable space*. An exemplar of this group was the participant who described the park as 'less offensive to at least three senses' (P110). Another individual (P17) came to walk the dog and indicated '[I] considered joining a gym but realised it was more enjoyable to come to the park for walking'. Some park users (24) were moved to expressions of Appreciation, describing their feelings of being *glad, lucky, pleased, grateful*, and feeling *love* for the place, as exemplified by 'grateful to God for having this lovely place' (P26) and 'I just love it, even on cold, rainy days' (P61).

While the majority of respondents had positive feelings, there were some for whom the resultant emotional state was contingent on context, such as others' behaviour, the activity, or the weather. An example was one participant (P18) who came to 'exercise, have a picnic, and get out with the girls' and felt afterwards 'it really depends on what happens with kids, what kind of outing it was; either feel really nice or thank God that is over'.

There were also a number of people who either had not thought about how the park affected them (8 in the theme I Don't Know) or had Neutral Feelings (22) about being in the park. Some neutral responses included 'just something I do every day' (P304), 'bland' (P23), or 'not life changing, it's convenient' (P32). These participants tended to be 'passing through' (P23). In contrast, there were other examples of people passing through who experienced Positive Emotions, such as the individual walking to work who left the park feeling 'pleasant' (P129) or the participant who stated they are 'happier – purposefully change [route] to avoid road' (P143).

In addition, there were some park users who had Negative Feelings (12). These were generally based on either the deteriorated condition of the park (5) or a perception of lack of safety (7). For example, one was 'disappointed, upset by condition of park' (P34) and another felt 'relieved because it can be unsafe and isn't welcoming' (P272).

Spiritual

The *Spiritual* domain emerged as an important post-park state, fourth most commonly mentioned across all domains. Park users offered numerous comments (68/527; 13 per cent) organised into the themes of Tranquil or Interconnected. Tranquil was by far the largest theme of this domain (58/68) reflecting a sense of peace akin to being in a sacred place and was expressed by codes such as *calm, peaceful, at ease, tranquil, serene, quiet*. Many responses were expressed in a single word and were reflected in the code names. Examples of more detailed responses included 'calms you down – out of hustle and bustle' (P92) or the individual who stated 'go from peace to rat race; feel peaceful here' (P94). The other identified aspect of spiritual well-being, Interconnected (10/68), captured the experience of being part of the whole, i.e. unified with and a part of a wider reality. Some people directly stated their feeling of connection with nature as noted by '[I] left with images of green' (P138). Others spoke more about the euphoric feeling of being outside of the built environment which is necessarily in nature. The quote: 'the feeling of just getting outdoors!' (P109) is an exemplar comment for this group.

Cognitive

Cognitive effects (44/527; 8 per cent) were experienced in terms of Satisfied (26/44) and Attention Restoration (17/44). The *job done* code under Satisfied was very practical; these participants came with a specific purpose in mind, e.g. walk the dog, take the kids out for a play, pursue an activity, and accomplished that purpose. It was also a statement about satisfaction with the compatibility between the setting and one's purpose. *Satisfied/content* was a more global statement expressing a higher order sense of contentment or satisfaction with their choice. One participant (P117) indicated they came because 'off from work, lovely weather, [to] read a book' and left 'satisfied with what they did with day'. Another (P144) came to 'play football, [because of] proximity' and left 'content, achieved what came for'. Attention Restoration included codes of *had a break*, *clear-headed*, *better perspective*, and *motivated*. An example of this experience was the individual (P217) who stated 'got things in perspective because I've done a bit of mulling things over and everything is put in its place after being here'. As with the *Physical* and *Place Attachment* domains there was scant negative experience. Only a single person who was passing through felt *rushed*.

Social

The *Social* benefit of feeling more connected to others was only mentioned by 6 participants (1 per cent). For one individual (P66), who came to the park for the facilities, this effect was expressed as 'caring – feel more inclined to think about people as individuals rather than just lump together in a category, particularly in terms of teenage boys in skate park'.

Global well-being

Looking at all the post-park domains together, people described feelings representing multiple dimensions of well-being: *Physical*, *Affective*, *Spiritual*, *Cognitive*, and *Social*. In addition, a small number of participants were aware of a sense of *Global Well-being* which included two codes: *better* and *healthy*. *Better* could possibly be placed in any domain, but was unspecified giving it a global quality. One participant (P85) reported that they 'feel better – don't really know how to describe it'. Another (P276) 'feel[s] a bit better even if quite [a] subtle feeling'. *Healthy* is also a broad concept. It is interesting to note that none of the comments coded as *healthy* were the first comment given; it was as if the person, after giving other post-park state descriptions, had a gestalt realisation of the parks' contribution to their health. Examples of these groupings of comments included a person (P40) who left stating '[I] look forward to next time I will come to park, [I] feel healthy, [I've] had a walk, [and I'm] happy.' Another (P198) echoes the multiple layers of health that are affected when they indicated they felt 'ready for a sit down; mentally you feel better as well as physically; [the] good feeling lasts into day after been in park; [and you] have time to think and talk about things [you] wouldn't have time to talk about otherwise'.

To further explore the concept of multiple dimensions of global well-being or holistic health as a result of park use, we looked at participants who gave several answers to the post-park feelings question. We found that many of them described multiple aspects of health in their comments, all adding up to a holistic health benefit. For example, P208 felt physical effects of 'more relaxed, refreshed really' and mental stimulation, 'find it quite interesting – always notice something new'. P22 gained positive physical, emotional, and cognitive effects, feeling 'fresh, happy, pleasant, motivated'. Another participant (P113) experienced spiritual, physical, and emotional well-being: 'peace of mind, relaxing; listening to birds, watching wind, birds fly kind of calms me; feel fantastic, had a bit of fresh air'. Perhaps the clearest statement that summed up the holistic health effects of park use came from P20. This person's post-park state description touched on all dimensions of health: 'relaxed, quite joyful, peaceful, despite noise one hears in park, quite clear-headed actually, therapeutic – being here is therapeutic'.

Our findings, the proposed model, suggest interesting directions for future research which might be used to address additional ways of and techniques for examining user responses; for example in different settings, examining socio-demographic differences (e.g. gender, age), and different cultural contexts (e.g. United States rather than England) as well as different types of green places (e.g. wilderness setting, hospital healing garden) and which would provide insight into the universality of the findings. Future research could usefully focus on measure development, including standardised closed-ended self-report questions that reliably measure the range of identified domains as well as *in situ* measures of relaxation (both self-report and objective).

Discussion

Overall, our results derived from the comments of urban green space users *in situ*, illustrate the breadth and salience of the effects experienced. After being in the park, the majority of participants identified physical benefits of being relaxed and revitalised; relaxed was the most commonly mentioned. While most individuals felt positive physical states, a few felt depleted or uncomfortable. Also central to the post-park state of being was positive affect, both within oneself and about the green space. These were articulated as happy, joyful, enjoyable space, gratitude, and in some instance even love toward the place. A minority of individuals had neutral or, more rarely, negative feelings. Expressions of tranquility and connection to a larger reality highlighted spiritual aspects of well-being. Urban green spaces contributed to cognitive health through providing opportunities for satisfaction and a sense of accomplishment as well as attention restoration, although fewer comments directly pertained to the latter. Social connections to others were minimally mentioned and a sense of global well-being was expressed by the themes better and healthy. Taken together the domains describe a complex holistic set of states that were produced by being in an urban green space, including physical, affective (towards self and place), spiritual, cognitive, social, and global well-being.

The most common post-park state identified was 'relaxed'. This is a physiologic state in which the person experiences decreased oxygen consumption, respiratory rate, heart rate, and muscle tension along with increased brain alpha wave activity (Benson et al., 1974). Relaxation is associated with enhanced mood and improved work performance; it buffers stress and emotional problems, and improves immune system function (Gruzelier, 2002; Peters et al., 1977; Sutherland et al., 2005). Relaxation can be produced by various practices such as hypnosis or meditation, as well as by the practice of so-called nature mystics, who immerse themselves in the quiet of nature (Benson et al., 1974). In this study, our ordinary participants have informed us that this state of relaxation can be achieved just by visiting an urban green space. Relaxation may be one of the physiological mechanisms through which nature affects our physical bodies as explained in the psychophysiologic theory (Ulrich, 1983; Ulrich et al., 1991). This idea receives further support from a large scale Danish study (Nielsen and Hansen, 2007) that found an association between experienced stress levels and the distance from home to publicly accessible green space.

The next most commonly endorsed domain includes a broad spectrum of positive emotions from feeling good or happy to experiencing joy and exhilaration. The emerging field of positive psychology (Seligman, 1999) has produced empirical work that links positive emotions with resilience (Fredrickson et al., 2003), human psychosocial flourishing (Fredrickson and Losada, 2005), and even longevity (Moskowitz et al., 2008; Ostir et al., 2000). As these benefits of positive emotions become better understood, interventions to produce them are likely to become more important. Urban green space appears to be a means by which people can voluntarily increase their experiences of positive emotions and accrue multiple downstream benefits. Another affective element found in our work is place attachment. This construct includes positive statements about the green space itself or feelings towards the space, such as love or gratitude. This feeling of positive connection to the place is in accordance with Tuan's concept of topophilia (1974) and the sense of place literature (Manzo, 2003). Similarly, others have looked at the frequency of time spent in nature as predicting positive affinity towards nature (Kals et al., 1999) or how affective connection to nature predicts intention to engage with or visit nature in the future (Hinds and Sparks, 2008).

The green space users in this study identified elements of tranquility and interconnectedness as a relatively significant portion of their feelings after being in the space. We gave these themes a collected domain of spiritual. Others using qualitative analysis (Fredrickson and Anderson, 1999) have documented similar elements of spirituality experienced by women in pristine wilderness; our study found that even an urban green space can enhance these essential elements of spiritual well-being. This is related to, but different from, the spirituality factor developed from closed-ended questions by Ouellette et al. (2005) as a motivator for going on a retreat in a pristine environment at a monastery. In the current study, spiritual well-being was an unanticipated benefit of green space use.

Comments pertaining to cognitive health captured a satisfaction gained from having achieved one's aims (e.g. to walk the dog, to take children to play) and from how one has spent time. The feeling of satisfaction suggests a fit or a match between what the setting offers and one's purposes and is illustrative of the concept of compatibility, posited as an important component of a cognitively restorative environment (Kaplan, 1995; Kaplan and Kaplan, 1989). Indeed participants identified effects that would suggest a restorative experience had occurred: a sense of having had a break, of clearing one's head, and gaining perspective. A relatively small proportion of participants spontaneously volunteered restoration as a benefit; in contrast, when closed-ended questions are used, attention restoration is often identified (e.g. Kaplan, 2001). Likewise, in contrast to the important contribution of social interaction in public spaces found by others (Burgess et al., 1988; Cattell et al., 2008), social connectedness was infrequently offered spontaneously as a post-park feeling.

Wellness is 'a condition obtained when a person achieves a level of health that minimizes the chances of becoming ill. Wellness is achieved by a combination of emotional, environmental, mental, physical, social, and spiritual health' (Kent, 2006). This definition expands on Engel's biopsychosocial model (1977) and parallels the domains emerging from our data that describe the post-park state. The parks provide positive emotions, a positive environment filled with fresh air, mental satisfaction and restoration, physical relaxation and revitalisation, social connection, and elements of spiritual health. As such, being in a park improves global well-being acknowledged by participants in either a single comment about being 'healthier' or in groups of comments that tap several of the domains of health. Previous epidemiologic research on the health benefits of nature in urban environments has looked primarily at walkable green spaces (Takano et al., 2002) or proportion of nearby green space (Maas et al., 2006; Mitchell and Popham, 2007). Outcomes have included mortality (Takano et al., 2002) or a single question about general health (Maas et al., 2006; Mitchell and Popham, 2007). Maas et al. (2008) found that physical activity did not account for the relationship between green space and health, leaving open the question of what variables determine the relationship. We suggest that when we wish to quantify the health benefits of nearby urban nature, we should purposefully measure multiple dimensions of health to understand the full impact of this simple decision: to go to the park.

An Interconnected Model of Well-being

Our findings suggest a broader, more encompassing conceptual framework for considering the relationship between the natural environment and health. We propose the Interconnected Model of Well-Being (Figure 2.2) that takes into account the reports of green space users and is reflective of holistic health benefits on multiple levels: physical, emotional, spiritual, mental, and social. We emphasise that when users of urban green space are directly asked to identify how they feel after being in the space, they give many more benefits than suggested by theory or identified through the use of closed-ended checklists drawn from existing research. Our findings accommodate existing theory yet illustrate the range of effects that have yet to be explored. This is the strength of qualitative research that calls us to generate new theory or models to more fully explain the phenomena under study. The model itself can guide future research by parsing out aspects of the urban green space and human health relationship into components for study while maintaining awareness of the whole person and their interconnection with the natural environment.

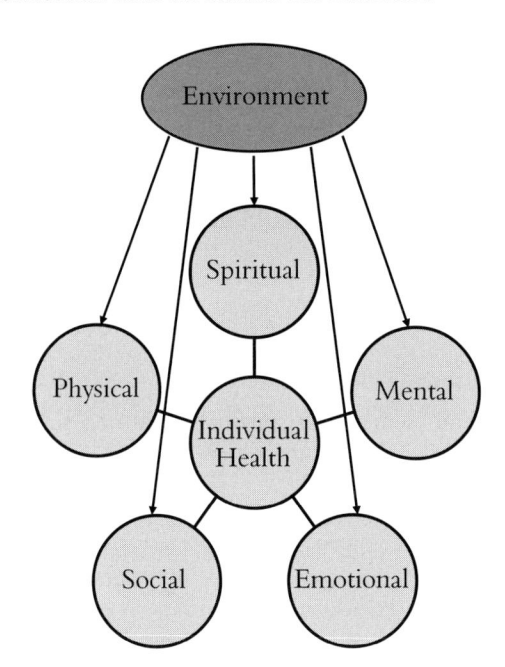

Note: Model illustrates relationship between environment and elements of human health.

FIGURE 2.2 Interconnected Model of Well-being

Implications

Against a backdrop of increasing interest in identifying novel ways to mitigate the negative effect of urbanisation on health, this research supports the notion that time spent in urban green space could be an integral part of healthy urban living. Importantly, park users' comments suggest a health value, provide crucial insight into how that value is conceptualised by the ordinary person, and could usefully guide health promotion interventions. We should anticipate that benefits will be on multiple levels of well-being: physical, mental, emotional, social, and spiritual, and could help in reducing some of our most serious health issues. As a low cost antidote for increasingly sedentary urban lifestyles, park-based physical activity could contribute to addressing the obesity and overweight epidemic for both adults and children (Bedimo-Rung et al., 2005). According to a large proportion of our participants, urban green space provides relaxation. Physical activity and relaxation together may underlie research findings of reduced cardiovascular mortality in areas with more green space (Mitchell and Popham, 2008). Our findings of improved positive emotions and spiritual well-being along with stress reduction may also have medical relevance in combating depression and anxiety (Fredrickson et al., 2003; Nakao et al., 2001; Westgate, 1996). Recent experimental work postulates a neurobiological link between stress, anxiety, and depression (Magalhaes et al., 2010) suggesting that contact with urban green space could play a role in addressing issues of mental ill-health. Our work may provide a mechanistic link to account for the observation of decreased depression and anxiety when living near green space (Maas et al., 2009). Clinically, more health care providers could consider writing 'park' prescriptions (Institute at the Golden Gate, 2010) to promote holistic well-being.

These findings also have fruitful implications for urban design and the management of publicly available green spaces. Green infrastructure, including publicly available green space (parks) has been emphasised in policy documents across the world and is considered a key dimension of the sustainable city (Bengston et al., 2004; Gomez and Salvador, 2006; Loures et al., 2007). Our participants' descriptions of post-park feelings from visits to green space provide glimmers of insight into the qualities and configurations of places that leave people feeling healthy, e.g. fresh air, feeling the sunshine, peace and quiet. We are already seeing a strand of fruitful research examining links between the proximity of green space and health status (Maas et al., 2006, 2009; Mitchell and Popham, 2007, 2008) as well physical activity (Kaczynski and Henderson, 2007). The identified presence of post-park positive emotions about the place suggests an individual-level value associated with urban green spaces. These positive attachments to place may also provide insight into collective shared meanings which have been posited as an important dimension when considering the value of the natural environment for societal well-being (Fish et al., 2011). Similarly, the presence of negative feelings associated with upkeep and safety identifies the importance of green space management.

Urban green space has the potential to provide several types of holistic health benefits including relaxation, positive emotions about self and environment, tranquility, revitalisation, and satisfaction. The dominant benefit identified is relaxation and given its demonstrated importance in health maintenance, more research is warranted to understand this process. Policy implications include promotion of urban planning and programmes to optimise utilisation of green space as a multidimensional health resource. The preservation of green space could be framed as a health benefit to humans and a motivator for environmentally sound policy decisions.

Acknowledgments

The work was supported by Engineering and Physical Science Research Council grant GR/S20529/1 to the CityForm consortium.

References

Altman, I. and Low, S.M. (1992) *Place Attachment*, New York: Plenum Press.
Alvarsson, J.J., Wiens, S. and Nilsson, M.E. (2010) 'Stress recovery during exposure to nature sound and environmental noise', *International Journal of Environmental Research and Public Health* 7: 1036–1046.
Andrews, F. and McKennell, A. (1980) 'Measures of self-reported well-being: Their affective, cognitive, and other components', *Social Indicators Research* 8: 127–155.
Bedimo-Rung, A.L., Mowen, A.J. and Cohen, D.A. (2005) 'The significance of parks to physical activity and public health: A conceptual model', *American Journal of Preventitive Medicine* 28: 159–168.
Bengston, D.N., Fletcher, J.O. and Nelson, K.C. (2004) 'Public policies for managing urban growth and protecting open space: Policy instruments and lessons learned in the United States', *Landscape and Urban Planning* 69: 271–286.
Benson, H., Beary, J.F. and Carol, M.P. (1974) 'The relaxation response', *Psychiatry* 37: 37–46.
Brown, B., Perkins, D. and Brown, G. (2003) 'Place attachment in a revitalizing neighborhood: Individual and block levels of analysis', *Journal of Environmental Psychology* 23: 259–271.
Burgess, J., Limb, M. and Harrison, C.M. (1988) 'People, parks and the urban green: a study of popular meanings and values for open spaces in the city'. *Urban Studies* 25: 455–73.
Cannon, W. (1929) *Bodily Changes in Pain, Hunger, Fear and Rage*, New York: Appleton.
Capon, A.G. (2007) 'Health impacts of urban development: Key considerations', *NSW Public Health Bulletin* 18: 155–156.
Cattell, V., Dines, N., Gesler, W. and Curtis, S. (2008) 'Mingling, observing, and lingering: Everyday public spaces and their implications for well-being and social relations', *Health & Place* 14: 544–561.
de Vries, S., Verheij, R., Groenewegen, P. and Spreeuwenberg, P. (2003) 'Natural environments-healthy environments? An exploratory analysis of the relationship between greenspace and health', *Environmental Planning A* 35: 1717–1732.
Department of Economic and Social Affairs. (2008) *World Urbanization Prospects: The 2007 Revision*. New York: United Nations.

Devine-Wright, P. and Lyons, E. (1997) 'Rembering past and representing places: The construction of national identities in Ireland', *Journal of Environmental Psycholology* 17: 33–45.

Elo, S. and Kyngas, H. (2008) 'The qualitative content analysis process', *Journal of Advanced Nursing* 62: 107–115.

Engel, G.L. (1977) 'The need for a new medical model: A challenge for biomedicine', *Science* 196: 129–136.

Fava, G.A. and Sonino, N. (2008) 'The biopsychosocial model thirty years later', *Psychotherapy and Psychosomatics* 77: 1–2.

Fish, R., Burgess, J., Church, A. and Turner, K. (2011) 'Shared values for the contributions ecosystem services make to human well-being', in *The UK National Ecosystem Assessment Technical Report*, Cambridge, England: UK National Ecosystem Assessment, UNEP-WCMD.

Fredrickson, B.L., Tugade, M.M., Waugh, C.E. and Larkin, G.R. (2003) 'What good are positive emotions in crises? A prospective study of resilience and emotions following the terrorist attacks on the United States on September 11th, 2001', *Journal of Personality and Social Psychology* 84: 365–376.

Fredrickson, B.L. and Losada, M.F. (2005) 'Positive affect and the complex dynamics of human flourishing', *American Psychologis* 60: 678–686.

Fredrickson, L. and Anderson, D. (1999) 'A qualitative exploration of the wilderness experience as a source of spiritual inspiration', *Journal of Environmental Psychology* 19: 21–39.

Fried, M. (1963) 'Grieving for a lost home: Psychological costs of relocation', in I. Dujl (ed.) *The Urban Condition*, New York: Basic Books.

Fuller, R., Irvine, K.N., Devine-Wright, P., Warren, P. and Gaston, K.J. (2007) 'Psychological benefits of greenspace increase wtih biodiversity', *Biology Letters* 3: 390–394.

Gomez, F. and Salvador, P. (2006) 'A proposal for green planning in cities', *International Journal of Sustainable Development and Planning* 1: 91–109.

Gruzelier, J.H. (2002) 'A review of the impact of hypnosis, relaxation, guided imagery and individual differences on aspects of immunity and health', *Stress* 5: 147–163.

Harris, P.J., Harris-Roxas, B.F., Harris, E. and Kemp, L.A. (2007) 'Health impact assessment and urbanisation', *NSW Public Health Bulletin* 18: 198-201.

Hinds, J. and Sparks, P. (2008) 'Engaging with the natural environment: The role of affective connection and identity', *Journal of Environmental Psychology* 29: 109–120.

Institute at the Golden Gate. (2010) *Park Prescriptions: Profiles and Resources for Good Health from the Great Outdoors*, Sausalito, CA: Institute at the Golden Gate.

Irvine, K.N., Devine-Wright, P., Payne, S., Fuller, R., Painter, B. and Gaston, K.J. (2009) 'Green space, soundscape and urban sustainability: An interdisciplinary, empirical study', *Local Environment* 14: 155–172.

Irvine, K.N., Warber, S.L., Devine-Wright, P. and Gaston, K.J. (2013) 'Understanding urban green space as a health resource: A qualitative comparison of visit motivation and derived effects among park users in Sheffield, UK', *International Journal of Environmental Research and Public Health* 10: 417–442.

Jansen, A.S.P., Nguyen, X.V., Karpitskiy, V., Metterleiter, T.C. and Loewy, A.D. (1995) 'Central command neurons of the sympathetic nervous system: Basis of the fight-or-flight response', *Science* 270: 644–647.

Jenks, J. and Jones, C. (eds.) (2010) *Dimensions of the Sustainable City (Volume 2)*. The Netherlands: Springer.

Kaczynski, A. and Henderson, K. (2007) 'Environmental correlates of physical activity: A review of evidence about parks and recreation', *Leisure Science* 29: 315–354.

Kals, E., Schumacher, D. and Montada, L. (1999) 'Emotional affinity toward nature as a motivational basis to protect nature', *Environment and Behavior* 31: 178–202.
Kaplan, R. (2001) 'The nature of the view from home: Psychological benefits', *Environment and Behavior* 33: 507–542.
Kaplan, R. and Kaplan, S. (1989) *The Experience of Nature: A Psychological Perspective*, New York: Cambridge University Press.
Kaplan S. (1987) 'Aesthetics, affect, and cognition: Environmental preferences from an evolutionary perspective', *Environment and Behavior* 19: 3–32.
Kaplan, S. (1995) 'The restorative benefits of nature: Toward an integrative framework', *Journal of Environmental Psychology* 15: 169–182.
Kent, M. (2006) *The Oxford Dictionary of Sports and Science Medicine*, 3rd ed., New York: Oxford University Press.
Korpela, K.M. and Ylén, M. (2007) 'Perceived health is associated with visiting natural favourite places in the vicinity', *Health & Place* 13: 138–151.
Korpela, K.M. and Ylén, M.P. (2009) 'Effectiveness of favorite-place prescriptions: A field experiment', *American Journal of Preventive Medicine* 36: 435–438.
Korpela, K.M., Ylén, M., Tyrväinen, L. and Silvennoinen, H. (2008) 'Determinants of restorative experiences in everyday favorite places', *Health & Place* 14: 636–652.
Korpela, K.M., Ylén, M., Tyrväinen, L. and Silvennoinen, H. (2010) 'Favorite green, waterside and urban environments, restorative experiences and perceived health in Finland', *Health Promotion International* 25: 200–209.
Lezak, M. (1982) 'The problem of assessing executive functions', *International Journal of Psychology* 17: 281–297.
Li, Q., Kobayashi, M., Wakayama, Y., Inagaki, H., Katsumata, M., Hirata, K., Shimizu, T., Kawada, T., Park, B., Ohira, T., et al. (2009) 'Effects of phytoncide from trees on human natural killer cell function', *International Journal of Immunopathology and Pharmacology* 22: 951–959.
Li, Q., Kobayashi, M., Inagaki, H., Hirata, Y., Li, Y., Hairata, K., Shimizu, T., Suzuki, H., Katsumata, M., Wakayama, Y., et al. (2010) 'A day trip to a forest park increases human natural killer activity and the expression of anti-cancer proteins in male subjects', *Journal of Biological Regulators and Homeostatic Agents* 24: 157–165.
Loures, L., Santos, R. and Panagopoulos, T. (2007) 'Urban parks and sustainable city planning—The case of Portimao, Portugal', *WSEAS Transactions on Environment and Development* 3: 171–180.
Maas, J., Verheij, R.A., Groenewegen, P.P., de Vries, S. and Spreeuwenberg, P. (2006) 'Green space, urbanity, and health: How strong is the relation?', *Journal of Epidemiology & Community Health* 60: 587–592.
Maas, J., Verheij, R.A., Spreeuwenberg, P., Groenewegen, P.P. (2008) 'Physical activity as a possible mechanism behind the relationship between green space and health: A multilevel analysis', *BMC Public Health* 8: 206–218.
Maas, J., Verheij, R.A., de Vries, S., Spreeuwenberg, P., Schellevis, F.G., Groenewegen, P.P. (2009) 'Morbidity is related to a green living environment', *Journal of Epidemiology and Community Health* 63: 967–973.
Magalhaes, A.C., Holmes, K.D., Dale, L.B., Comps-Agrar, L., Lee, D., Yadav, P.N., et al. (2010) 'CRF receptor 1 regulates anxiety behavior via sensitization of 5-HT2 receptor signaling', *Nature Neuroscience* 13: 622–629.
Manfredo, M., Driver, B. and Tarrant, M. (1996) 'Measuring leisure motivation: A meta-analysis of the recreation experience preference scales', *Journal of Leisure Research* 28: 188–213.

Manzo, L. (2003) 'Beyond house and haven: Toward a revisioning of emotional relationships with places', *Journal of Environmental Psychology* 23: 47–61.
McCormack, G.R., Rock, M., Toohey, A.M. and Hignell, D. (2010) 'Characteristics of urban parks associated with park use and physical activity: A review of qualitative research', *Health & Place* 16: 712–726.
McKee, D.D. and Chappel, J.N. (1992) 'Spirituality and medical practice', *Journal of Family Practice* 35: 201, 205–208.
Mesulam, M. (1985) *Principles of Behavioral Neurology*, Philadelphia, PA: F A Davis.
Mitchell, R. and Popham, F. (2007) 'Greenspace, urbanity and health: Relationships in England', *Journal of Epidemiology and Community Health* 61: 681–683.
Mitchell, R. and Popham, F. (2008) 'Effect of exposure to natural environment on health inequalities: An observational population study', *The Lancet* 372: 1655–1660.
Morgan, D.L. (1993) 'Qualitative content analysis: A guide to paths not taken', *Qualitative Health Research* 3: 112–121.
Moskowitz, J.T., Epel, E.S. and Acree, M. (2008) 'Positive affect uniquely predicts lower risk of mortality in people with diabetes', *Health Psychology* 27: S73–S82.
Nakao, M., Fricchione, G., Myers, P., Zuttermeister, P.C., Baim, M., Mandle, C.L., Medich, C., Wells-Federman, C.L., Martin Arcari, P., Ennis, M., et al. (2001) 'Anxiety is a good indicator for somatic symptom reduction through behavioral medicine intervention in a mind/body medicine clinic', *Psychotherapy and Psychosomatics* 70: 50–57.
Nielsen, T.S. and Hansen, K.B. (2007) 'Do green areas affect health? Results from a Danish survey on the use of green areas and health indicators', *Health & Place* 13: 839–850.
Office for National Statistics. (2001) *2001 Census: Standard Area Statistics (England and Wales)*. Manchester, England: ESRC/JISC Census Programme, CensusDissemination Unit, MIMAS; Leeds, England: Center for Interaction Data Estimation and Research.
Ostir, G.V., Markides, K.S., Black, S.A. and Goodwin, J.S. (2000) 'Emotional well-being predicts subsequent functional independence and survival', *Journal of American Geriatric Society* 48: 473–478.
Ouellette, P., Kaplan, R. and Kaplan, S. (2005) 'The monastery as a restorative environment', *Journal of Environmental Psychology* 25: 175–188.
Parsons, R., Tassinary, L., Ulrich, R., Hebl, M. and Grossman-Alexander, M. (1998) 'The view from the road: Implications for stress recovery and immunization', *Journal of Environmental Psychology* 18: 113–140.
Patterson, M. and Williams, D. (2005) 'Maintaining research traditions on place: Diversity of thought and scientific progress', *Journal of Environmental Psychology* 25: 361–380.
Peters, R., Benson, H. and Porter, D. (1977) 'Daily relaxation response breaks in a working population: I. Effects on self-reported measures of health, performance, and well-being', *American Journal of Public Health* 67: 946–953.
Pinder, R., Kessel, A., Green, J. and Grundy, C. (2009) 'Exploring perceptions of health and the environment: A qualitative study of Thames Chase Community Forest', *Health & Place* 15: 349–356.
Proshansky, H., Fabian, A. and Kaminoff, R. (1983) 'Place-identity: Physical world socialization of the self', *Journal of Environmental Psychology* 3: 57–83.
Rothbart, M. and Posner, M. (1985) 'Temperament and the development of self-regulation', in L. Hartlage, C. Telzrow (eds.) *The Neuropsychology of Individual Differences: A Developmental Perspective*, New York: Plenum Press.
Seligman, M. (1999) 'Positive social science', *Journal of Positive Behavioral Intervention* 1: 181–182.

Sutherland, G., Andersen, M. and Morris, T. (2005) 'Relaxation and health-related quality of life in multiple sclerosis: The example of autogenic training', *Journal of Behavioral Medicine* 28: 249–256.

Takano, T., Nakamura, K. and Watanabe, M. (2002) 'Urban residential environments and senior citizens' longevity in megacity areas: The importance of walkable green spaces', *Journal of Epidemiology and Community Health* 56: 913–918.

Thompson, S. (2007) 'A planner's perspective on the health impacts of urban settings', *NSW Public Health Bulletin* 8: 157–160.

Tuan, Y. (1974) *Topophilia: A Study of Environmental Perception, Attitudes, and Values*, Englewood Cliffs, NJ: Prentice-Hall, Inc.

Ulrich, R. (1983) 'Aesthetic and affective responses to the natural environment', in I. Altman and J. Wohlwill (eds.) *Behavior and the Natural Environment, Human Behavior and Environment: Advances in Theory and Research* (Volume 6), New York: Plenum.

Ulrich, R., Simons, R., Losito, B., Fiorito, E., Miles, M. and Zelson, M. (1991) 'Stress recovery during exposure to natural and urban environments', *Journal of Environmental Psychology* 11: 201–230.

Vohra, S. (2007) 'International perspective on health impact assessment in urban settings', *NSW Public Health Bulletin* 18: 152–154.

Wallace, R. and Benson, H. (1972) 'The physiology of meditation', *Scientific American* 226: 84–90.

Westgate, C.E. (1996) 'Spiritual wellness and depression', *Journal of Counseling Development* 75: 26–35.

Yamaguchi, M., Deguchi, M. and Miyazaki, Y. (2006) 'The effects of exercise in forest and urban environments on sympathetic nervous activity of normal young adults', *Journal of Internal Medicine Research* 34: 152–159.

3

SYNCHRONISING SELF AND CITY

An everyday aesthetic for walking

Fiona Bannon

> Every day life is what holds us intimately, from the inside.
> (Leuilliot, 1977)

Here Leuilliot reminds us that people live through the corporeal practices of their everyday lives, where learning and relearning is something that takes place constantly. As this chapter unfolds we will trace what it is that intimately supports us in our ongoing emplaced experiences. In this journey lie moments that may be felt to be profoundly pleasurable, although the instances from which they spring may be mundane in the extreme. The fabric of these ordinary, often overlooked, activities is effectively an interlacing of memory, evaluation, reflection and knowledge generation. The argument I propound here is that these 'moments' can be understood as an aesthetic sense of everyday, a shaping of resonant experience where each individual is a connoisseur of his or her perception and thoughts. By way of exploring this simultaneity of experiences the discussion addresses potential interconnections that exist between a number of ideas including well-being, everyday aesthetics and active spatial design. The experience of walking in the city is used as an affective meeting point to frame these ideas where being alert to our idiosyncrasies and the mutual transformations that take place between self and site help us to synchronise, *what holds us*. With Lefebvre (1991) reminding us that '… it is by means of the body that space is perceived, lived – and produced', it seems pertinent to explore what benefit might flow from the aesthetic potential of that most ordinary of acts, i.e. walking.

To start the journey it is worth considering what might be meant by 'well-being'. To engage with this I draw on experiences in movement-based somatic practice and choreography, where I have found the necessity to explore the spatial, temporal and psychological constructs that inform everyday inquiry as part of my ongoing practice. When I stumbled upon Lefebvre's (2004) attributes of a 'Rhythmanalyst' as someone who '…concerns himself with temporalities and their relations within wholes' it resonated with my work in choreography. His talk of the immersive nature of participant observation for a researcher of social interaction reverberates with choreographic habits developed over time spent organising the movement of people in space and time. Similarities lie in the combination of the social with the cultural, aesthetic and poetic, under an umbrella of phenomenological inquiry, all being sensitised to explorations that champion '…what we have to rely on first and foremost and always' (James, 1890).

When the cultural theorist de Certeau (1984) starts his essay 'Walking in the City' from a vantage point high at the top of the World Trade Center, he looks down across Manhattan, able to grasp the city in a moment, in total contrast to the complex meanderings of the street inhabitants far below. At street level is a vibrant and visceral collection of energies that touch, collide and shape the inhabitants as they negotiate the imposed geometries of the space in which they exist. It is this rhythmic motion through space that can stimulate our attention, simultaneously offering attraction and distraction, facilitating what the urban planner Virilio (2010) refers to as our 'accelerated reality' of communication and urbanism. In shifting through space we experience an ebb and flow of persistent personal and social psycho-geography, in tune with the prized harmonious succession of little joys, mingling the qualities of how we live, with what we do (Simenon, 1962). Being in-touch, or in-dialogue, with the places that we inhabit foregrounds the haptic as part of our ability to forge connections. Although this may relate more ordinarily to a sense of touch, the term also refers to our sense of kinesthesis or ability to sense our body moving in space. In this way we can come to understand perception as something concerning the whole body at a senseful level, something synaesthetic and spatially interrelated to the place/s in which we are sited.

To strive for well-being

In 1946, the World Health Organization (WHO) defined the idea of health as '…a state of complete physical, mental and social well-being, and not merely the absence of disease or infirmity'. Some may see this as overly bureaucratic and unrealistic and indeed it did take a further forty years for the WHO (1989), to suggest that '…good health and well-being require a clean and harmonious environment in which physical, psychological, social and aesthetic factors are all given their due importance'. Underneath this utopian definition lies an emphasis on a reciprocal dialogue between the external environment and internal individual experiences of persons, something that might be thought akin to an optimal sense of 'well-being'. Similar sentiments have appeared in a host of documents that address aspects of well-being, for example, a Green Paper prepared as part of 'Our Healthier Nation' (Department of Health, 1999) identifies a key aspect of health as 'a resource for enjoying life to the full' (Stuart-Brown, 1999). Myers, Sweeney and Witmer (2001) outline a wellness model framed as a 'lifespan' where they define wellness as '…a way of life oriented toward optimal health and well-being in which the body, mind, and spirit are integrated … to live more fully…'. In 2007, Arts Council England published 'The Arts, Health and Wellbeing' a national framework profiling a range of partnership projects crossing arts and health. The framework did at least acknowledge that in order to put into practice the broad view of health endorsed by the WHO and to foster healthy communities, the cooperative learning from experts ranging across fields of specialism in the arts and health sectors would be required.

Inspiration to consider what experience the arts might contribute to health and well-being can be found in an ever broadening range of literature. I find them to be expressed succinctly throughout the sentiments outlined by pragmatist aesthetician, John Dewey. In *Art as Experience* (Dewey, 1980) he argued for a rebalancing of what he saw as the compartmentalisation increasingly enforced on modes of thinking, knowledge generation and experience. His argument underscores a need to maintain interaction between sensory experiences, environments and our evaluative and critical abilities because it is the very mingling of ideas and experience that makes us distinctive. He goes on to suggest that without sufficient attention given to the complex interactions so evidently part of our ability to make sense we will only progress towards a dulling and narrowing of life experience and expectation. What is shared in these ideals is the grounding of an argument for heightening our appreciation for designs for living. This could be appreciated as something of a quest for an 'everyday aesthetic life-world', drawing together evaluations evoked by emotional response, stimulated through bodily sense and realised in transformative engagement with our contexts.

It was Husserl who introduced the metaphor 'life-world' as '…the locus of interaction between ourselves and our perceptual environments and the world of experienced horizons within which we meaningfully dwell together. It is the world as we find it, prior to any explicit theoretical conceptions' (cited in Eckartsberg, 1998).

According to Eckartsberg what is perhaps most important to take from these thoughts is the attempt to account for the fullness of experience, to purposefully attend to 'lived' experiences rather than to work to abstract or merely to quantify. This he identifies as 'experiaction', something combining everyday life experience with action. What this seems to prize is our ability to recognise, remember, report and reflect on the potential richness as a replenishing source of resonance. According to Philip (1998) it is through such resonance that we come to promote positive affirmation of ourselves, enhance our well-being and consolidate positive identification with environmental factors. It can be argued that it is this that enables us to individually and collectively interact with and make sense of our optimal life worlds. For

Norberg-Schulz (1979) and Relph (1976) who respectively focused on a phenomenological approach to situatedness and design there is sympathy with this idea. They both highlight the importance of dwelling and of becoming informed by our own human focused experience of place. Through their arguments support can be found for a renewal of interest in the intermingling of sensuous qualities of our life-experienced-environments. From their work we can come to appreciate that forging a sense of belonging to and identifying with 'place', is a vital part of our well-being. Returning to Lefebvre we find that such richness found in a 'moment' might encompass '...fleeting but decisive sensations (of delight, surrender, disgust, surprise, horror, or outrage) which were somehow revelatory of the totality of possibilities contained in daily existence' (Lefebvre, 1991).

What becomes evident is that it is the 'totality of possibilities' moving between focus on an inside feeling of individual experience and the complex realm of negotiation and compromise that we experience as we exist as social beings with 'others'. These others, we pass by as we move and negotiate our way through space. It is others who have made the decisions that have resulted in the form of our built environment, the buildings, roads, pavements, pollutions, colours, hazards and enchantments. Our individual and socially prescribed wealth of experience is manifest in the ways we behave as we inhabit, create and are immersed in space. Our behaviours necessarily include a wide range of rhythms and spatial dynamics. Together these facets coalesce as our aesthetic patterning of everyday existence.

Finding an everyday aesthetic

Generations of changing argument and positioning in philosophy, from consideration of the nature of the universe, and the place of humanity in it, to focus on the human condition and situation, have slowly but inevitably brought about shifts of emphasis in aesthetic theorising. Modifications in understanding what the term aesthetic might mean now draw on consciousness, or considered thought, promoting it as more than abstracted desire or passion, and other than taste or a placid and passive view of experience. Understanding aesthetic as enhancements of felt experience, of being moved in some way, provides a route towards the sense that we individually make of the world, resulting from our own unique form of vivid awareness or 'mind'. These are important ideas for a growing range of thinkers who consider an everyday aesthetic as a broadening of the discussion away from the more closeted arena of 'traditional' aesthetics of art and art theory. What is becoming available is an opening of discourse for a new domain of inquiry engaged with the sensuous and imaginative responses to lived experience.

However, it may be that perceived divisions in the long-standing debate are misplaced if we revisit ideals proposed by the philosopher Baumgarten, who is most often credited with first employing the term 'aesthetic'. He identified it as sensitive cognition, giving it the Graeco-Latin name *cognitio aesthetica*, the intention being to mend what he saw as the divided experience of the world, reminding us of knowledge that could be found in the world of feelings and sensation. In tracing the etymology of the word 'aesthetics', we find *aisthitikos* as the ancient Greek word for that which is 'perceptive by feeling' and from this that the primary grounding of the field of aesthetics is not art but reality-corporeal, our material nature. This physical–cognitive intermingling is 'out front' of the mind encountering the world pre-linguistically; it is prior not only to logic but also to meaning. Aesthetics in this context involves an appreciation of connections between sensual (*aestheta* – perceptions) and reasoned knowledge (*noeta* –thoughts), generated through sensual accounts of experience and the potential transformation of our implicit understandings.

Tatarkiewicz cited in Dziemidok (1986) and writing in the early 1930s, returned to this argument suggesting that many of the existing theories of aesthetics failed because they did not adequately address the range, complexity and unavoidably human interconnections involved in the concept. He describes three uniting attitudes that contribute to and form part of aesthetic experiences, those being

1   aesthetic (sensual),
2   literary (intellectual) and
3   poetic (emotional).

The literary and poetic attitudes, he explains, expand the boundary of the sensual by promoting the source of enjoyment and satisfaction experienced with the felt experience involving the whole personality. What this approach offers is an amalgamation of ideas in a pluralistic theory, which importantly allows for the impact of variations in personality, emotional sensibility and temperament, something that this discussion will return to later.

Dissanayake (1992) writing from an anthropological stance takes what, for some, is a radical point of view championing what she sees as our innate existence as aesthetic beings. Her argument is that humans are predisposed to active engagement in making sense of individual and collective experience. Perception in this case is an active process of searching for order, pattern, form and structure in a simultaneously cognitive, emotional and operational manner. There are multiple and simultaneous variations in such experiences, as there will be in the attention given to the experience by individuals. The source of the differences in experience is biological and subsequently culturally influenced. For Berleant (1970), too, acknowledging something of a biological basis for aesthetic perception is fundamental. He argues that the course of any experience is continuously altered by a stream of feedback resulting from the attention or intention of the first engagement. Through this complex networking, information, both external and internal, is filtered and in this way an aesthetic attitude can be taken towards anything.

Taking the aesthetic to be part of what we are means it is inevitably embedded in our everyday, in moments of surprise, wonder and self-realisation. The prospect of discovering the unexpected fosters a sense of excitement for situations where, as Ginsberg (1986) suggests that we should, 'Take the time to be found by what we do not know awaits us. Invest in openness. On the way to the known masterpieces one may enter experiences more gratifying aesthetically than viewing the celebrated object.'

This admittedly broad sweep of discussion concerning what might be an everyday aesthetic, aims to establish a path towards 'experiential unity', acknowledging in this the coexistence of cognitive and emotional aspects of experience. Perhaps in Berleant's (1986) description of 'empathy' there is a potential doorway to experience, drawing on both the object and the derived pleasure. For Berleant the motivation of empathy is about actively feeling your way through aesthetic experiences, not only by paying attention but being kinaesthetically immersed within the sensation. Such experiences can usefully be characterised as multi-sensory synaesthesia, forging connections with all the senses at once. Taken together these ideas offer a way to appreciate experience as an absorbed attention combining sensation and a perceptive imagination, as can be found echoed in the work of recent scholars, for example Saito (1998), Eaton (2001), Light & Smith (2005) and Papastergiadis (2006). Together they promote aesthetic appreciation as embedded in imaginative engagement with the everyday. With the argument from Dewey that aesthetic response is continuous with the practical and intellectual challenges that contribute to the flow of human experience, I am reminded that aesthetic attention can be recognised in fleeting moments, where there is a coming together of resonant sensations in a self-consciousness of felt (practical) and focused thought (logical), something of a route towards well-being.

Living design

Designing environments that might propagate resonant qualitative change for people going about their daily lives remains a significant societal challenge. What might seem most significant in the task is finding ways to capture a sense of flow, shifting continuities, purposefulness, textures and dynamic variations, even the potentialities of space. For it is people who live within and make daily use of a place, that come to shape it and be shaped by it. It may be that by focusing on the body-in-action, recognising how it might be influenced by the architecture that surrounds it, that we can come to appreciate ways to make active, engaging and versatile spaces for living.

In the following section I briefly highlight a project that came to my attention because of a personal interest in urban walking and a chanced reading of publicity for 'The High Line', a city park project in New York. An outcome of this project is a public park constructed on an elevated section of old freight train line on the West Side of Manhattan. The park project initiated in 2002 and owned by the City of New York is now maintained as an open public space. Finding my way to The High Line introduced me to the 'Active Design Guidelines' (New York City Department of Design and Construction, 2010), another New York City initiative stating in its blueprint an aim to promote physical activity and health into design through a renewed approach to creating rich and vibrant living experiences. This drive chimed well with the underlying direction of travel for a sensuous everyday aesthetic of my own walking practice, endorsing as it does the idea that we are most healthy when engaged in the fullest sense, with our location, and that our engagement with place starts with movement. Acknowledging that '…the design of the built environment can have a crucial and positive influence on improving public health' appeared to me to be a significant first step. Taking this as a starting point reverberated well with the sentiments of Malnar and Vodvarka (2004), who have asked what might our built environment be like if sensory response, sentiment and memory were critical design factors, and with Pallasmaa (2005) who reinforced the same point when arguing that '… "life-enhancing" architecture has to address all of our senses simultaneously and fuse our experience of self with our experience of the world'.

Motivated by the challenge to decrease obesity levels in public health, the Active Design Project identified that they might start to find solutions if they were to think differently and change what had become accepted approaches to design. From reading the guidelines it appears that they suggest that we should design cities and buildings informed by rhythm that encourages movement. Such a step could potentially enhance the ways people interact with their environment, including increased mobility through spaces, use of stairs and walkways instead of elevators, increased time spent in public spaces and more attention given to the design of interesting environments where people can pass through and be part of. With increasingly clear evidence that we have effectively designed physical activity out of daily life, we have secured the sedentary over the active, displacing opportunity with fixity based on route, time saving and end-gaining.

In order to envision new public spaces, they included public health professionals, architects, urban designers, and planners with a target to reverse design trends that have precipitately contributed to declining physical activity and to look again at how to design for living. This has meant creating opportunities for physical involvement as part of a daily life experience. This is something that they argue will in turn support the maintenance of health and contribute to environmental sustainability. A simple though impactful example is encouraging movement through spaces by designing prominent and attractive walkways, steps and stairs rather than reliance on elevators. Stairs and slopes have become an integrating feature of the design rather than a necessary add-on removed to the edge. In this way even the simple attention to stairs can mean that they provide a view, a context, a focal point and depth of field, adding visual interest to the design.

In the process of thinking differently and enabling new design the researchers utilise five 'D' relationship variables. In a correlation between urban design and movement patterns, they include; 'density, diversity, design, destination accessibility and distance to transit'. Their argument is that by developing and maintaining these five qualities they can promote active living through urban design and planning.

- *Density* – the concentration of people in any given urban zone.
- *Diversity* – the variety and balance of land use.
- *Design* – including the visible characteristics of an area's street network and 'streetscape'.
- *Destination accessibility* – data about the ease of travel to a central business district, concentrated area of jobs, specific attractions.
- *Distance to transit* – identifies average distances between home and work to the nearest public transport.

Supplemental to this the Robert Wood Johnson Foundation's Active Living Research Program found five design qualities to be critical in the identification of good walking environments. The characteristics relate to found physical features of environments and link well with the earlier discussion concerning everyday aesthetic qualities and the opportunity to experience a living sense of inquiry as a connoisseur of feeling, perceiving and thinking. According to the research findings, retaining appreciation of the following five qualities in the process of designing new spaces will offer the potential for an enhanced realisation and perception of the public realm and consequently the lives lived in relation with the environment. The key qualities include:

- *Imageability* – the quality of a place that makes it distinct, recognisable and memorable. A place can be said to have high imageability when the arrangement of physical elements captures attention, evokes feelings and creates a lasting impression.
- *Enclosure* – how the streets and public spaces come to be defined visually by the buildings, walls, trees and other vertical elements.
- *Human scale* – attention given to the size, texture and articulation of physical elements as they correspond with the size and proportions of humans. Equally important here is a corresponding relationship with the passage through a place in relation to the speed at which humans walk.
- *Transparency* – how people get a sense of moving through a place, what they can see or perceive as objects or activity. This is especially the case in reference to human activities taking place beyond the edge of a street.
- *Complexity* – the visual richness of a place. This quality depends on variety, detail and articulation of the physical environment

Walking a city

The discussion outlined earlier highlighted de Certeau's (1984) association of acts of mobility with the way a city comes into existence; he reinforces the need to remember that it is the interrelatedness between people and city that completes 'place'. For de Certeau, places result from an intermingling mobility, something unpredictable that effectively comes into existence through continuous improvisation in space. In this way we might appreciate that there is potential in the relationships forged through walking as a creative, sensuous, kinaesthetic response, where the everydayness of walking can enhance realms of individual and communal interrelations. As Halttunen (2005) rightly argues a sense of place '… is about being in the world, about pausing and resting, belonging and becoming involved'.

Walking continues to experience a resurgence of interest across a range of arts practices from Hamish Fulton (2002), Richard Long (1997, 1998); the audio walks of Janet Cardiff (Schaub, 2005); the New Walking Culture proposed by the Wrights and Sites Collective (Hodge et al., 2006); to Simon Whitehead's (2006) 'Walks to Illuminate'; as well as literary projects, for example Rebecca Solnit's (2002) *Wanderlust*. The popularity of tourist walking tours, architecture walks, city walks, guided tours, themed walks from heritage to fashion to food suggests that there is something valuable being identified in the idea of getting to know and unlock the richness of places by walking through and around them.

In the discussion that follows, consideration is given to work by two theorists who blend rhythm, mobility and kinaesthetic sensibility that effectively chart an appreciation of everyday aesthetics with our habits of sociality when walking. Firstly 'Rhythmanalysis' framed by Henri Lefebvre and Catherine Regulier (2004a, b) and secondly 'Laban Movement Analysis' (LMA) initiated in work by movement theorist Rudolf Laban. Both models recognise bodily understanding as felt experience that exists in combination with created and shared temporal environments. Lefebvre's suggestion that to '…capture a rhythm one needs to have been *captured* by it' (Lefebvre, 1996) endorses the idea that the Rhythmanalyst thinks through their body. 'He does not neglect therefore… smell, scents the impressions that are so strong in the child and other living beings, which society atrophies, neutralises in order to arrive at the colourless, the odourless and the insensible' (Lefebvre, 2004). Here he addresses the idea that it is through sensation that we can access the possibility of perception, as a starting point for our knowledge making. These sensations always exhibit a sense of totality, something that forges interrelatedness between things. He goes on to argue that if we were to neutralise such opportunity to the point of becoming insensitive to the places we inhabit then we would effectively forego a vivacity for life that we can ill afford to be without.

Within the concept of 'dressage', Lefebvre and Regulier (2004a, b) identify what they saw as a form of socialisation, of 'breaking-in' or training in rhythmic awareness. They argue that such activity is part of a social project that patterns cultural habits of movement, through the use of space and the management of time. Lefebvre (2004) warns what he perceives as a compromise might arise in attempts to control such performance of measured display and perhaps most significantly that as individuals we may risk becoming 'dispossessed of our body'. It is worth noting similar thoughts by Laban who encouraged the exploration of movement in order to appreciate what he thought of as the fullest individual range of kinetic and dynamic possibilities. Only then, he suggests, can a selection be made of what might seem most suitable in any given situation and for each individual alone (Laban, 1966). Lefebvre, like Laban, argues that it is through our own rhythms that we are inserted into the complexity of the world that we inhabit. What becomes evident in aspects of their theorising is that by heightening an individual's appreciation of the interdependencies existing between their physical, intellectual and emotional selves, we might come to more fully appreciate the plurality of the rhythms by which we live.

In the study of human movement and 'effortanalysis' initiated by Laban, an appreciation for different 'attitudes', 'efforts' or dynamic rhythms were identified. The proposal was that these dynamic qualities exist along a series of continuums including space, weight, time and flow and that they always operate in combination. It is through the use and identification with these combinations of qualities that the inner impulse of the individual is revealed (Bartenieff & Lewis, 1980; North, 1972). In the constant flux of learning to cope with our environment we move between stability and tentative instability, what Lefebvre calls a complex rhythmic assemblage. In learning to appreciate these rhythms/ efforts we come to understand more about ourselves in relation to how we shape experiences of our surroundings. What is perhaps most informative about these thoughts is acknowledgement that for most of us life occurs, 'on the move', and that it is through movement that we come to know of ourselves and of others.

In the paper 'Articulations: Walking as Daily Dance Practice' (Bannon, 2011), my aim was to explore choreographic possibilities in response to ideas unearthed walking in the city of Leeds. The results of engaging in this walking project over a period of four years included gathering a range of interrelating ideas, that folded and became enmeshed as a memory map of multiple journey's walking to work, something Ingold (2004) succinctly captures as a kind of sedimentary activity, iteratively impressed on the ground. In Leeds these memories became juxtaposed with the grand narratives of weight, permanence and grandeur that old cities seem to assume and work to retain as part of their own landscape of inheritance.

By focusing in on the movement of moments whilst walking through the city, I effectively entered an ongoing dialogue between my very human interaction and the rhythms of the designed space. In a daily walk such as this there is opportunity to become immersed in an everyday of possibility between forms. As this particular walk progresses it is shaped by a slow climbing gradient that twists along the now irregular pathways that have resulted from the layered decisions of generations of city planners. The journey is punctuated by collisions with fast moving streets that, like arteries, secure the fluid movement of vehicles through this motorway-encircled city. The buildings stand close together, mirroring distorted views of walkers who slide across the glassed walls. The mass of varied levels, gradients, angles, colours and textures break the otherwise calm horizon.

Walking with my back to the train station, and facing forward toward the office blocks of the academic quarter, the central business district lies to my right and the open space of the Pennine Hills to my left. It is the ground beneath that supports each step with the open sky lifting each moment passing between each building. This dimensional cross section secures me as I meet the successive waves of walkers each plotting an individual course. As individuals cross my path we create discrete spatial tensions building a unison or rhythmic counterpoint. Suddenly I am aware of a flock of people taking an unexpected turn to the right, opening enough space for me to weave, to dodge or slide sideways between bench and lamp post. I stride forward, creating an ever-increasing vacuum behind me, squeezing the possibilities of the space that lies ahead.

What made this continued exploration seem worthwhile was exploring ways to tap into an aesthetic simultaneity existing in the fleeting, embodied transitions found in movement. Traditional notions of choreography may be invisible in these unplanned and often unpredictable patterns, but in the process of identifying rhythmic flow through space there was opportunity to explore engagement, interaction and a senseful appreciation of a changing daily practice. I came to understand this as something social as much as individual, a mutual inscription of something life-enhancing. In the process I found myself integral to the unfolding events of the liveliness of place, a participant, active initiator, respondent and observer, not abstract at all (Careri, 2002; Massumi, 2002).

Acknowledging walking to be a fundamental and necessary daily practice, offered opportunity to explore the irregular, the coincidence and the impermanence of everyday cityscapes. Walking presented opportunity to observe the functional and seemingly neutralising activity of living for the people who seem intent on getting from A to B, alive to ensuring the least interference in what outwardly appears to be a dulled pattern. This dulling mode is evident in the shuffle of feet across pavements designed to reduce the need to lift and step, where ground is smooth, even, flat and hard, something that effectively increases our 'groundlessness' (Ingold, 2004). This habit of establishing only the 'end gain' of a destination diminishes the potential richness of lived experience along the way. It is this that the Active Design team seem to have been acutely aware of in looking at how we design for living.

What I found out about walking was the possibility of making tangible experiences of place as a self-realising form of 'living inquiry'. It has come to be a practice of re-sensualising the everyday, each walk a revelation of the multiplicity of assembling experiences. The task remains to combine the sensation and cognition of the passage through place, time and space in a way that fosters the 'experiential unity' of the experience. After all it is about feeling a way into an experience, which engages your attention as well as kinaesthetic sensations. To isolate one, from another, would diminish each, and lessen the wealth of the whole.

So the practice is one of scoring a range of walking tactics, observing designed adaptive responses and incorporating them into an evolving personal sense of mobility. Walking remains a complex, full body activity operating as constant variation between stability and instability. A walk is an adaptive activity, responding to the altering internal and external factors that influence each step and enable us to gain access to our physically sensed way of being. This is something Laban explored in his research to understand non-verbal aspects of communication and modes of knowledge generation, when he noted that, 'Words expressing feelings, emotions, sentiments or certain mental and spiritual states will but touch the fringe of the inner responses which the shapes and rhythms of bodily action are capable of evoking' (Laban, 1960).

It is the synchronicity of this activity rich with spontaneity, at once live, socially interactive and reactive that guides my own practice of walking as an orchestration of body–mind. As I choreograph impromptu walks, combining nuance and chance with the felt dynamic of the transference of weight I am reminded that an aesthetic of everyday is founded in our senses and actualised through our engagement with daily life. It presents:

- a continuous slow unfolding of tangible built and bodily architecture;
- a vibrant sensory somatic self;
- a fluid dialogue, that throws knowing off-balance (Bannon, 2011).

Synchronising self and the city

The chapter has concentrated on recognition of relationships that exist between individuals and the locations they inhabit. With a city conceived, designed and produced to facilitate and support human activity there is chance for it to become a network of unrelated social, economic, political activities, where people and city can have little but contingent relations. It is the case that the form, structure and functions of the city influence people, controlling rhythm, flow, time and emotional response. How in this context might we design affective lives remains a valid question with the need to acknowledge the rhythms of people as a key ingredient in planning. What I have come to appreciate through this process is the multiple sensory experiences to be found in the immediacy of our 'locatedness', and the relationship forged, as Will Self (2006) suggests, in the possibility to capture '…the transitory deliberations of the human psyche'.

What is explored here is a call for a sense of place as 'being in the world', something of an aggregate of our sensory somatic selves, desires, decision and technologies. The synchronicity of our mobility means that we are in constant flux, adopting and adapting to the rhythms, and emotional determinations of others and ourselves. Synchronising with self and city means being responsive to the sight, sound, smell, feel and taste of the places we move through, and create. It means dealing with an entanglement of multiple pathways and trajectories that together forge our sense of place-making. Together the very human practices of everyday life, including sensorial responses, imagination and creativity, contribute to a phenomenological sense of meaning-making. This in turn nudges us closer to appreciating what Howes (2005) refers to as a 'sensuous interrelationship of body-mind-environment' and closer to championing an aesthetic sensibility for active design of our everyday.

For many people, arguing for a sense of location has little if any resonance, a position worsened by the increased sensory impoverishment of the surroundings in which many people live. We are in a period of accelerated change, embraced as we are by a host of 'out of body' experiences. The large digital screens that dress our city squares beam images of distant places as a backcloth to the 'here and now'. With people set adrift, many oblivious of the places they physically occupy and the waves of technological change impacting on how they live, what is crucial is to explore what it is to live well. In current walking practices you can find a resurgence of the meander and value in the mis-guide, which provide opportunities to deviate from the customised sense of place.

There may be a need to return to the work of architectural theorist Norberg-Schulz (1979) and his call for a realisation of the 'concretization of existential space'. Through his central theme exploring a heightening of our awareness of the genius loci or 'spirit of place' we might foster the generation of cooperation in design, practice and policy that will afford a positive impact on the way that people design for living. What underpins much of the thinking at the centre of the argument is the degree of control placed on the richness of these orchestrations by the controlling visions of designers. In this argument lies a seminal thought: that by re-energising environments and thinking again about how people might interact with planned and unplanned places we might convert what has become a continuity of the drab into a place with more vitality and life. At the beginning of the chapter I identified an interest in supporting a daily practice of 'self', sense and surroundings. The intent remains the same that by revisiting the ideals of walkers who stepped out in defence of a right to roam, caught up in the shared rhythms of the city we might come to appreciate more fully the well-being afforded by living life on the move and know ourselves more fully in the process. Ultimately if we can foster enhanced interaction, participation and communication in designs for living we might go some way to meeting the recognised aims of the WHO as it continues to strive toward global health and well-being in the twenty-first century.

References

Arts Council England (2007) The arts, health and wellbeing, http://www.artscouncil.org.uk/media/uploads/phpC1AcLv.pdf

Bannon, F. (2011) 'Articulations: Walking as Daily Dance Practice', *Choreographic Practices*, 1, 97–109.

Bartenieff, I. & Lewis, D. (1980) *Body Movement: Coping with the Environment.* The Netherlands: Gordon and Breach Science Publishers.

Berleant, A. (1970) *The Aesthetic Field: A Phenomenology of Aesthetic Experience.* Springfield, IL: Charles, C. Thomas.

Berleant, A. (1986) 'Experience and Theory in Aesthetics'. In M. H. Mitias (Ed), *Possibility of Aesthetic Experience.* Dordrecht: Martinus Nijhoff, 91–106.

Careri, F. (2002) *Walkscapes, Walking as an Aesthetic Practice.* Barcelona: Gustavo Gill.

de Certeau, M. (1984) *The Practice of Everyday Life.* Berkeley, CA: University of California Press.

Department of Health (1999) Saving Lives: our healthier nation. London, Stationary Office, July, Volume 4386 of Cm Series.

Dewey, J. (1980) *Art as Experience.* Originally published in 1934. New York: Perigee Books.

Dissanayake, E. (1992) *Homo Aestheticus: Where Art Comes From and Why.* New York: The Free Press.

Dziemidok, B. (1986) 'Controversy about Aesthetic Attitude. Does Aesthetic Attitude Condition Aesthetic Experience?' In M. H. Mitias (Ed) *Possibility of Aesthetic Experience.* Dordrecht: Martinus Nijhoff, 139–158.

Eaton, M. (2001) *Merit, Aesthetic and Ethical.* Oxford and New York: Oxford University Press.

Eckartsberg, R, von. (1998) 'Introducing Existential Phenomenological Psychology'. In Ron Valle (Ed) *Phenomenological Inquiry in Psychology.* New York: Plenum Press.

Fulton, H. (2002) *Walking Journey.* London: Tate Publishing.

Ginsberg, G. (1986) 'Experiencing Aesthetically, Aesthetic Experience and Experience in Aesthetics'. In M. H. Mitias (Ed) *Possibility of Aesthetic Experience.* Dordrecht: Martinus Nijhoff.

Halttunen, K. (2005) 'Groundwork: American Studies in Place'. Presidential Address. American Studies Association 4. *American Quarterly*, 58(1), 1–15.

Hodge, S., Persighetti, S., Smith, P. & Turner, C. (2006) 'A Manifesto for a New Walking Culture', *Performance Research,* 11(2), 115–122.

Howes, D. (Ed) (2005) *Empire of the Senses: The Sensory Culture Reader.* Oxford: Berg.

Ingold, T. (2004) 'Cultures on the Ground: The World Perceived Through the Feet', *Journal of Material Culture*, 9, 315–340.

James, W. (1890) '*Principles of Psychology'.* New York: Holt. Cited in E. G. Boring (1953). 'A History of Introspection,' *Psychological Bulletin*, 50, 169–189.

Laban, R. (1966) *Choreutics.* Annotated and edited by L. Ullmann. London: Macdonald and Evans.

Laban, R. (1960) *The Mastery of Movement.* London: Macdonald and Evans

Lefebvre, H. (2004) *Rhythmanalysis: Space, Time and Everyday Life.* Translated by Stuart Elden and Gerald Moore. London: Continuum.

Lefebvre, H. (1996) *Writing on Cities.* Translated and edited by Eleonore Kofman and Elizabeth Lebas. Oxford: Blackwell.

Lefebvre, H. (1991) *The Production of Space.* Translated by Donald Nicholson-Smith. Oxford: Blackwell.

Lefebvre, H. & Régulier, C. (2004a) 'Attempt at the rhythmanalysis of Mediterranean cities'. In H. Lefebvre (Ed) *Rhythmanalysis: Space, Time and Everyday Life.* Trans. Stuart Elden, Gerald Moore. London, New York: Continuum, 85–100.

Lefebvre, H. & Régulier, C. (2004b) *The Rhythmanalytical Project.* In H. Lefebvre (Ed) *Rhythmanalysis: Space, Time and Everyday Life.* Trans. Stuart Elden, Gerald Moore. London, New York: Continuum, 71–83.

Leuilliot, P. (1977) Preface to Guy Thuillier, *Pour une histoire du quotidien au XIXe siècle en Nivernais*. Paris and The Hague: Mouton, 1977, xi–xii.
Light, A. & Smith, J. M. (Ed) (2005) *The Aesthetics of Everyday Life*. New York: Columbia University Press.
Long, R. (1998) *Mirage*. London: Phaidon.
Long, R. (1997) *A Walk Across England*. London: Thames Hudson.
Malnar, J. M. & Vodvarka, F. (2004) *Sensory Design*. Minneapolis, MI: University of Minnesota Press.
Massumi, B. (2002) 'Navigating Movements', http://www.brianmassumi.com/interview/navigatingmovements.pdf (accessed 12 August 2009).
Myers, J. E., Sweeney, T. J. & Witmer, J. M. (2001) Optimisation of human behavior: promotion of wellness. *The Handbook of Counselling*. Thousand Oaks, CA: Sage Publications, 641–652.
New York City Department of Design and Construction. (2010) 'Active Design Guidelines: Promoting Physical Activity and Health in Design'. New York: City of New York, http://www.nyc.gov/html/ddc/html/design/active_design.shtml (accessed 16 February, 2011).
Norberg-Schulz, C. (1979) *Genius Loci*. New York: Rizzoli International.
North, M. (1972) *Personality Assessment Through Movement*. London: Macdonald and Evans.
Pallasmaa, J. (2005) *The Eyes of the Skin: Architecture and the Senses*. New York, John Wiley.
Papastergiadis, N. (2006) *Spatial Aesthetics: Art, Place and the Everyday*. London: Rivers Oram.
Philip, R. (1998) 'The Association of Tourist Health with Aesthetic Quality and Environmental Values'. Unpublished report for the WHO.
Relph, E. (1976) *Place and Placelessness*. London: Pion Limited.
Saito, Y. (1998) 'The Aesthetics of Unscenic Nature', *Journal of Aesthetics and Art Criticism*, 56(2), 101–111.
Schaub, M. (2005) *Janet Cardiff: The Walk Book*. Köln: Verlag der Buchhandlung Walther König.
Self, W. (2006) 'Will Self: PsychoGeography. Motorway Madness', *The Independent*, 25 February, www.independent.co.uk/opinion/columnists/will-self/will-self-psychol geography_526072.html.
Simenon, G. (1962) *Pedigree*. Translated by Robert Baldick. London: H. Hamilton.
Solnit, R. (2002) *Wanderlust: A History of Walking*. London: Verso.
Stuart-Brown, S. (1999) 'One step forward or two steps back?', *The Newsletter of the Faculty of Public Health Medicine*, 1(1), 3.
Virilio, P. (2010) 'After Architecture: A Conversation [with é Sylvére Lotinger]', *Grey Room*, 3, 32–53.
Whitehead, S. (2006) 'Walks to Illuminate', http://www.untitledstates.net/walksto illuminate/simon.htm (accessed 17 May 2013).
World Health Organization (1946) Preamble to the Constitution of the World Health Organization as adopted by the International Health Conference, New York, 19–22 June, 1946; signed on 22 July 1946 by the representatives of 61 States (Official Records of the World Health Organization, no. 2, p. 100) and entered into force on 7 April 1948. The Definition has not been amended since 1948.
World Health Organization (1989) *European Charter on Environment and Health, 1989*. First European Conference on Environment and Health, Frankfurt-am-Main, Germany, 7–8 December, http://www.euro.who.int/__data/assets/pdf_file/0011/116012/WA3095.pdf

4

TOWARDS A LANDSCAPE OF WELL-BEING

The role of landscape and perceptions of place in human well-being

Lindsay Sowman

Introduction

The relationship between the environment and human well-being is at the centre of human existence and experience. It is an infinitely complex relationship, about which we have an equally infinite range of personal and collective social intuitions, but at the same time, and perhaps rather surprisingly, it is one about which relatively little is known in any systematic or empirical sense. There is an enduring recognition and understanding of the impacts of various environmental parameters such as clean air and water, nutritious food, appropriate shelter and the like, on physical health and well-being. Likewise, the organised endeavours of human cultures throughout history to design living environments based on this understanding is well established as one of the most fundamental of human preoccupations. Even the earliest designed landscapes reflect a sophisticated sensitivity to the healthful, restorative and spiritually nourishing aspects of gardens and human-scale landscape spaces. What is less well understood, however, are the myriad operative and causal factors which delineate these impacts and explain the complex relationships between them. The fundamental question, succinctly put by Stephen Kellert, is this: 'What do we know about the relationship between natural systems and human physical and mental wellbeing? The truth is, not much' (Kellert, 2005).

Historically, much of the literature on this subject had its origins in the field of environmental health, and focused on the hazards of exposure to toxic substances and malignant conditions. That pollution of air, water and soil has had negative impacts on well-being is undoubted. The inverse proposition is also held to be true, and at an intuitive level. The geographer Will Gesler asserts that 'there is a long tradition that healing powers may be found in the physical environment, whether that entails materials such as medicinal plants, the fresh air, pure water of the countryside, or magnificent scenery' (Gesler, 1992).

More broadly, and based upon an established literature in the field of environmental psychology, a robust research energy through the 1970s and 80s was directed toward examining the relationship between the physical, psychological and spiritual dimensions of 'quality of life' and the quality and configuration of living environments. A range of investigations have explored the effects on health and well-being of exposure to and interaction with certain landscape types, typically those in which 'natural values' are high, and where open green space, vegetation, trees and water feature prominently.

Some key theoretical threads

There have been a number of analyses from within a varied disciplinary milieu, including the health-related sciences, human geography, environmental psychology and architecture, which have examined the fundamentals of the human–environment interface. These have been diverse in conceptual basis and experimental content, but all strive toward an explanation of the drivers of human behaviour and experience.

Jay Appleton's widely regarded Prospect Refuge Theory is one example. In *The Experience of Landscape*, Appleton (1975, 1987) draws on habitat theory to examine ideas about the primitive (by which he means deep-seated) bases of human behaviour and aesthetic experience. He suggests that human imagery and symbolism reflect fundamental propensities to engage with and react to certain landscape types, and that the preferences humans show for these landscapes are driven by these primitive bases.

Another theoretical construct which seeks to develop explanatory mechanisms for this relationship is that proposed by Wilson (1984), and Kellert and Wilson (1993). The Biophilia Hypothesis posits that innate tendencies mediate the way in which people interact with and respond to the natural environment, which reflect bio-cultural processes rooted in the evolutionary origins of the human species. It argues that these processes have shaped bio-philic (affiliative) and bio-phobic (aversive) responses to particular landscape configurations, and that this tendency has become inextricably woven into aspects of human psychology, culture and society. This preference has become encoded as a pre-cognitive response to environments that include or provide for prospect and refuge.

Other experimental approaches have sought to describe the relationship between landscape and human behaviour and aesthetic preference by examining the content of preferred landscapes. Preference theory articulates the view that groups of human respondents have relatively coherent and predictable aesthetic preferences for particular landscape types and clusters of landscape features. This area of research activity looks at preference as a particular human construct, and essentially at landscapes as typologies, rather than at human 'experience' of landscape. While it makes little specific reference to well-being, there are a number of studies in this domain which demonstrate that the general well-being of participants can be increased significantly by contact with landscapes and environments with high aesthetic value.

Other fields of research have sought more explicitly to examine the relationship between the environment and health. One of the most seminal discussions of this relationship is Restorative Environments Theory (Kaplan, 1992, 1995), developed by Stephen and Rachel Kaplan and set out in their book *Experience of Nature* (Kaplan and Kaplan, 1989). The focus of this field of research has been on the nature of human experience within the context of 'the' environment, and of specific environments, and represents a significant touchstone for environmental psychologists examining the idea of psychological well-being through aesthetics. Subsequent studies have looked explicitly at the link between environmental preferences and restorative potential (Galindo and Corraliza Rodriguez, 2000; van den Berg and ter Heijne, 2005).

In other research, urban green space and naturalistic environments are increasingly recognised as significantly contributing to human health and well-being. Many studies in environmental psychology support the contention that people are aesthetically attracted to the natural components of landscapes, and to landscape configurations which are predominantly natural or naturalistic (Browne, 1992; Ulrich, 1979, 1983; Ulrich and Parsons, 1992; de Vries, 2010).

There is recent research activity into the relationship between physical environments and psychological health (Graf, 2006), augmenting an expanding body of research evidence supporting an increasingly comprehensive argument that viewing green space and scenes of nature provides not only aesthetic pleasure and stimulation, but enhances emotional well-being, contributes to the reduction of stress, and otherwise facilitates improved health outcomes (Ulrich, 1979; Kaplan, 1995; Herzog et al., 2003; Hartig and Staats, 2006; Maas et al., 2006; Hartig, 2007; Nielson and Hansen 2007).

Theory in landscape architecture

Across many disciplines, emerging concepts about the environment and human health and well-being have been formed and reformed. This has created something of a theoretical maelstrom within which smaller, less well evolved disciplines scramble to find conceptual frameworks and theoretical principles which have a relatively unqualified application and utility to them, and upon which they can confidently rely to base their disciplinary actions. Landscape architecture is one such discipline.

It is relatively easy to establish broad parameters for a worldview of landscape architecture as a discipline. James Corner argues that the central mission of the profession of landscape architecture resides in 'imaging the world' (Corner, 1999), but beyond this apparently straightforward mission statement for practice, 'landscape' is actually a profoundly complex intellectual construct. It encompasses a multiplicity of meanings and associations with every aspect of the physical and cultural environment (Meinig, 1979), and is steeped in symbolic meaning (Jackson, 1989). Landscape is also about 'experience', and an encounter with the phenomenal world. Bowring and Swaffield (2010) write 'Landscape architecture is a profoundly phenomenological enterprise, and its most compelling and significant achievements are often intangible, experiential and multi-sensory.'

We can argue that as a theoretical construct, 'landscape' represents the interface, the fulcrum of human culture and the environment. The profession and practice of landscape architecture expresses the way in which the designed or modified environment represents human belief, behaviour and aspiration – in short, all of the complexities of human agency in the physical world. It is at once aesthetic, functional, behavioural and experiential. Corner also argues that the idea of 'landscape' is an active instrument in the shaping of modern culture. In his view, it expresses the essence of culture, embracing both naturalistic and phenomenological experience, and the theory and practice of the art and science of landscape architecture releases energies and interactions that enable us to engage with and comprehend the world in a unique way.

What is evident from searches through traditional landscape orientated literature, however, is the relative paucity of research into the environment/well-being relationship which is responsive to the particular needs of the discipline. Murphy (2005) points out that the design based sciences, among which landscape architecture might be included, lack a sufficient knowledge base which reflects their own theoretical and practical concerns, upon which to propose changes to the environment. He argues that 'Little or no time is being directed to acquiring knowledge or research methods to determine what or how best to design, or what relationships provide the most desirable conditions in the environment' (Murphy, 2005).

Fortunately, in recent years a more focused research effort has been made in the area of landscape and health – predominantly focused on open space/green space parameters. Further work is yet needed in landscape research toward an integrating theory which identifies the fundamental parameters of 'landscape' as an environmental, social and psychological construct, and its relationship and contribution to human well-being. For example, Catherine Ward Thompson reiterates the call for 'qualitative approaches, sensitive methods ... and careful interpretation to tease out any relationship between landscape and well-being' (Ward Thompson, 2010). We seek 'a joined up approach' (Bell, 2010) to understanding this relationship – and by extension, one which informs our design thinking and decision making.

The concept of 'place'

There are many discussions about 'place'. It is a concept of interest and fascination to many disciplines, but the exclusive possession of none. It is a central idea to human geography and to the studies of perception and recognition of the environment in environmental psychology, and it also appears in philosophical discourse. It is a polymorphic idea though, and as Tim Cresswell puts it: 'It is also a problem as no-one quite knows what they are talking about when they are talking about place' (Cresswell, 2004).

As a construct, it is often simply defined: 'Most fundamentally, place is simply a portion of geographic space' (Gesler and Kearns, 2002). This is a definition rooted in location – a stable, situated entity, bounded geographically, with a particular identity, and which has historical antecedents and an ongoing continuity between past and present. Beyond this starting point, however, 'place' is also understood as a construct of human experience. It is a notion of the human body in time and in environmental space, as well as the way in which humans influence the environment and, in turn, are influenced by it. In this way, place is a cultural phenomenon, spatially referenced, but experiential in character, and drenched in the meanings that give form and content to human engagement with the world. This classical understanding of place is particularly expressed in the ideas of Tuan Yi-Fu (1974, 1977, 1979a, b) and Edward Relph (1976, 1985, 1992, 1997). For example, Tuan (1979a, b), suggests that location becomes 'place' when people ascribe meaning to localities that attach a more intense emotional value to that location in such a way that elevates it above being merely a point in space or a functional node. At this point, location stands as a literal idea, while place becomes an experiential one. Places can be said to be 'particular' – that is to say, they are differentiated in conceptual and experiential terms from other locations; places assume or reflect a personality that is unique, recognisable and durable (Tuan 1979a, b).

Place is fundamentally about meaning – the coincidence of the physical world and man's conception and interaction with it. Places have meaning – they are the focus of human 'being', and are characterised by the beliefs of people and human culture (Relph, 1976, 1985). Place is also inherently about human experience – indeed, it is the essential experiential quality of 'place' that differentiates it from space, and from a purely geophysical notion of landscape. It is through the lens of human experience, as both a cognitive and emotional affective construction, that space becomes place. Places 'are constructed in our memories and affections through repeated encounters and complex associations. Place experiences are necessarily time deepened and memory qualified' (Relph, 1985).

For many landscape architects, the concept of 'place' is a central theoretical construct in landscape theory. As early as the nineteenth century, the forefathers of landscape architecture were articulating the view that a sense of place, or 'spirit of place', was fundamentally concerned with a secure and satisfying relationship with one's physical and cultural environment, and how this is converted into a personality or spirit within landscape (Olmsted, 1870) – and of course the spirit of the place, or 'genius loci', is the centrepiece of Norberg-Schulz's (1980) work, *Genius loci: Towards a phenomenology of architecture*.

Place identity, place attachment and rootedness

'Place identity', 'place attachment' and 'rootedness' are all related notions, which may also have significant insights to offer landscape architecture. Place identity is regarded by theorists as being a substructure of self-identity. It consists of intellectual, affective and attitudinal ideas about the physical world in which people live. According to Proshansky et al.

> These cognitions are memories, ideas, feelings attitudes, values, preferences, meanings and conceptions of behaviour and experience which relate to the variety and complexity of physical settings which define the day-to-day existence of every human being. At the core of such physical environment-related cognitions is the 'environmental past' of the person; a past consisting of places, spaces, and their properties, which have served instrumentally in the satisfaction of the person's biological, psychological, and cultural needs.
>
> (Proshansky et al., 1983)

Place attachment is characterised as a multifaceted idea which describes the way in which individuals bond or 'attach' to places that they perceive to be important or significant in their own personal experience (Low and Altman, 1992; Giuliani, 2003; Scannell and Gifford, 2010). It is a particularly useful construct as it emphasises the tripartite nature of the bond between people and place. It specifically identifies 'person' (or group), 'cognitive and affective processes', and the environmental dimension of 'place' as a specific object.

Philosophical discourse also considers the relationship between place and human experience. The respected French philosopher Simone Weil proposed the concept of 'rootedness', a notion of 'connectedness', which she thought of as a deep-seated psychological/spiritual construct related to well-being. 'To be rooted is perhaps the most important and least recognised need of the human soul' (Weil, 1955). For Tuan, rootedness also implies a sense of home, or at least, of being 'at home' – of being completely at home 'in an unselfconscious way' (Tuan, 1980). This sense of being completely 'at home' enables a state of being unencumbered by the demands of context and by curiosities about place and time.

The concept of well-being

In popular conversation, the term 'well-being' is often taken to be a synonym for the word 'health', and conceptually the two ideas are often talked of with reference to each other. Within the milieu of traditional Western medicine, and arguably among the general population at large, health has typically been thought of as an instrumental measure of bodily states, both physical and psychological. However, contemporary views are focused on a more holistic and integrating conceptualisation, whereby 'health', in the sense of a bodily state of repair, might be regarded as a constituent part of well-being, but it cannot stand to represent either the content or essence of well-being. In this discussion, I will keep at arm's length the definitions of well-being which focus on illness measures, such as disease status and management, and on instrumental environmental factors like clean water, clean air, safe food and freedom from violence or physical threat.

Fleuret and Atkinson (2007) describe three distinct theoretical approaches to understanding well-being. The first is a 'theory of needs', based on Maslow's Hierarchy of Needs (Maslow, 1943, 1970). Maslow represented needs in a hierarchical structure. In the bottom layer are the basic needs, universal and unrelated to culture, which preserve and sustain life – air, food, shelter. At the top are those needs, thought to be distinctly human, which have to do with self-actualisation – the need to understand ourselves and our place in the world, and to strive for the highest form of consciousness. In contrast to those needs at the bottom of the hierarchy, these needs become acquired, and reflect culture, time and place.

The second approach is referred to as 'relative stands theory', where well-being is considered to have relative and subjective dimensions. In this view, well-being is linked to individual happiness and conditioned by the individual's perception of the context in which he or she is living (Fleuret and Atkinson, 2007). Crisp (2008) argues that the term 'well-being' is typically used to refer to what is 'good' for a person, and to a collecting notion of how well a person's life is going. At a profound level, it refers to that which contributes to happiness, but it is more than this, and is distinct operationally and conceptually from happiness. In the common parlance, happiness might be regarded as a transient state of mood – an affect that arises from and responds to an event or condition in life at a given space and time. Seligman (2011) has proposed a theory of authentic happiness, which he develops as a theory of well-being. He theorises that well-being consists of five elements: positive emotion, engagement, meaning, accomplishment, and positive relationships.

The third approach is defined as a 'capabilities approach' (after Sen, 1992), whereby well-being is thought of as a freedom or a capacity to live a flourishing life.

Well-being might most usefully be thought of as a dynamic process and a state of 'being' that gives people a sense of how their lives are going, through the interaction between their circumstances, activities and psychological resources or mental capacities. It is thus a combination of objective and subjective factors – an overarching and integrating concept that encompasses all aspects of a person's life, including physical health, psychological health, social well-being, financial security, interpersonal relationships, work, leisure and so forth. Haworth and Hart (2007) summarise it in this way:

- well-being is a complex and multifaceted state and a process
- well-being includes personal, interpersonal and collective needs, which influence each other

- well-being may take different forms across different societies, and over the life course of any given individual
- well-being is intimately intertwined with the physical, cultural, and technological environment
- interventions to enhance well-being may take different forms, and are conducted at individual, community, and societal levels.

In an instrumental sense, well-being may reflect or be expressed as a 'bodily' state of being – a physical and psychological measure of fitness. At a more fundamental level, it may be thought of as an 'existential' state of being, and a fundamental basis for human existence.

The theoretical proposition

The concept of 'well-being' expresses a holistic and integrated idea about human experience – about the wholesomeness of human existence, and about what is good for being. The idea of 'place' provides us with a substantive theoretical framework for defining and understanding particular ideas of location and culture within the broader construct of 'landscape', and for the connectedness that people feel with the world around them, through place identity and attachment. At an intuitive level, the two concepts seem to be intimately and fundamentally related. For example, in a series of seminars entitled Wellbeing: Social and Individual Determinants, organised by the Economic and Social Research Council (ESRC) in 2001, speakers outlined some of the key dimensions of well-being as currently discussed in the research literature. These included social relationships, flourishing communities, landscapes of well-being, historical and biographical continuity, and the promotion of healthy lifestyle outcomes. As part of this series, Gesler and others presented research and theoretical discussion which emphasised the idea that 'place matters to well-being' (Gesler, 2001), and in his work on therapeutic landscapes, he identified the meaning of places (in terms of experience, feelings, social support and sense of community) as a significant dimension of this relationship. Further discussion asserted the idea that places could have multiple meanings – as in dwelling places, visited places, places that affect people, and are affected by people – and emphasised the significance of places of attachment and their relationship to identity.

The Well-being and Place International Conference 2009 brought together these two key ideas about the human–environment interface, which has stimulated a new interest and invigorated a refreshed research energy into this relationship. This energy was also manifest in the Well-being 2011 Conference, Birmingham, 2011.

Historically, the theoretical literature contains many good discussions about place and its relationship to identity, and to the definition and transmission of culture, but little on its relationship to well-being as a specific concept. The relationship between place identity and well-being has received some attention from researchers working at the interface of environment behaviour and design (Proshansky et al., 1983; Sarbin, 1983; Korpela, 1989; Low and Altman, 1992; Cuba and Hummon, 1993; Edwards, 1998). Much of this work focuses on the role of favourite places in the reduction of stress, and the mediation and regulation of affect (emotional mood).

Ideas about emotion and general well-being provide a means by which it is possible theoretically to integrate the concept of place identity with ideas about restorative environments. It must be said, however, that little in landscape architectural theory as it currently exists provides such a mechanism for integrating concepts of 'sense of place' and 'place identity' together with human well-being and landscape design. We might want to ask then, within the general framework of a landscape theory of 'place', what do we know about the way in which place impacts upon and defines human experience? In so far as we might speculate that the relationship between the environment and human well-being is a central one to human experience, we might more particularly ask what contribution might 'sense of place' make to human well-being?

Research into place and well-being

This discussion reports ongoing research about place and connectedness, and about the relationship of place to human well-being. It seeks to contribute to the development of a cohesive framework for understanding this relationship, in order to assist the profession of landscape architecture to design and manage landscapes in such a way as to promote well-being as a fundamental dimension of the design response. Research in this domain sits within the context of calls for the 'construction of a multidisciplinary conceptual framework of environmental quality and quality of life… [in order to]… advance the field of urban development, environmental quality and human wellbeing' (van Kamp et al., 2003). These writers go on to argue that such a framework would assist in the development of more substantial and meaningful theory-based tools for evaluating aspects of landscape and environmental quality, and to expand our understanding of the implications of spatial planning and design policies and decisions. Such an understanding is critical in the development of an integrated theory of landscape, place, and human well-being.

This ongoing research is based on two theoretical propositions:

1. that well-being, as a personal and social construct, and as a holistic concept encompassing psychological, physical and spiritual dimensions, is related to sense of place and place identity, and the way in which humans define, create and interact with the environment
2. that sense of place and place identity contribute at an ontological level to personal and community identity, to place identity, to rootedness with the environment and thus to human well-being

This research consists of a qualitative exploration of the subjective and individually constructed meanings and experiences of the participants. The research methods are directed toward allowing these meanings to be wholly expressed, rather than seeking to predetermine either the specific content or the general response classes of participant responses. As Shotter (1985) puts it, these methods seek a contextual form of knowledge which comes from within a situation, rather than a knowledge which is obtained from an external observer. In this way, it is intended to be a hermeneutic exploration – 'An attempt to understand and interpret the experiences people have within the context of their daily lives – see[ing] the world through the point of view of others' Gesler, 2001).

There are three key objectives of this research. The first is to explore the constructions of meaning a group of research participants have about the places in which they live, and to search for clues about the dimensions of their experience of 'place'. This exploration might reveal understandings about what and how various environmental and landscape characteristics and qualities contribute to their sense of place, and the degree to which the participants identify and attach themselves to place.

The second objective is to explore these people's understanding of the concept of well-being, specifically their own well-being, and to identify how they perceive their well-being within the overall context of their life choices, with specific reference to decisions about 'place' – place of residence and place of being. The study aims to explore what meanings these people attach to the role or importance of place in defining or contributing to their well-being, and to illuminate the subjective views of these participants of how the place in which they live affects their health and well-being. The study also aims to explore what impacts participants identify as significant in the face of changes in 'place', in terms of land use, physiognomy of locality, landscape character, and population density and profile.

The third objective is to discuss and develop ways of thinking about and evaluating design responses in such a way as to assist design professionals to design landscapes of well-being as a fundamental parameter of the art and science of landscape architecture.

The example of Gore Bay

Specification and identification of case study site

Research explores the perceptions, experiences and constructed meanings of place and well-being in a selected population, in a specific location via a case study site. The choice of case study site was guided by several imperatives, including the need for an accessible population or community which is clearly defined in numeric and/or geographic terms; and strong and identifiable characteristics in terms of landscape character that make it an identifiable place which members of the community are able to 'recognise' in perceptual and experiential terms.

The site: Gore Bay

- Physically, Gore Bay is a shallow coastal indentation on the Canterbury coast of the north-eastern South Island of New Zealand. It consists of a narrow coastal strip of relatively flat land, bordered by the Pacific Ocean on one side and low cliffs on the other, beyond which are broad stretches of rolling rural farmland. It features steep shingle beaches and broad sweeps of sand, and a low inland escarpment. At the south end eroding cliffs tower over tidal rock pools.
- Culturally, Gore Bay is a small coastal beach community of approximately two dozen permanent residents and a number of holiday homes occupied or tenanted on a part-time basis throughout the year. In essential character, it is part retirement village, part holiday resort. It is at once a rural and somewhat isolated community, as well as a transient mixed profile community of long term visitors, short term visitors, surfers, fishers and holidaymakers.

Further, the community faces the potential of landscape change over time. Anecdotal evidence suggests that there is considerable disquiet about a range of issues which are perceived as being threats or challenges to prevailing landscape character. These issues include the development of new subdivisions within the environs of the bay, changes of character as a result of new dwellings replacing traditional 'baches' (small weekend or vacation houses or shacks), and threats to the beach and cliffs as a result of sea level rise and erosion.

- The participants. Participants for this project have been drawn from the various communities which make up the permanent and temporary population of Gore Bay. These include long terms residents, renters, regular and infrequent visitors.

The research methods and sequence

The investigation is based on a quadrangular structure involving semi-structured thematic interviews, photo-diary keeping (images and text), mapping and drawn exercises, and participant-centred *in situ* dialogue with object-referencing components. The research data consist of attitudes, perceptions and constructions of meaning, as expressed in verbal and graphic responses gathered through these techniques.

- Interviews. The 'semi-structured interview' is intended to gather background data on the participant, and to explore perceptions of 'place', sense of identity with and attachment to Gore Bay as place, as well as ideas of emotional and physical well-being.
- Mapping. The 'maps of meaning exercise' is a drawn mapping technique and is intended to provide graphic representations of space, spatial

relationships and spatial character, and to give graphic clues to hierarchies of spatial experience, meaning and experience of place.
- Diaries. The 'photo-diary' records moments, experiences, thoughts and events. The intent is to provide an opportunity for participants to identify and elaborate on broad landscape character, and on specific elements within landscapes which have particular meanings for them. It may also reveal more about the emotional (affective) and cognitive constructs of their connection with place.
- Dialogue. '*In situ* dialogue' is an opportunity for dialogue in particular contexts in time and space as defined by individual participants, which either have special meaning for them, or are able to help express and convey experience. The intent is to provide an opportunity for a more embodied and existential experience of landscape to be felt and communicated, not just through word and the drawn medium, but through sound, taste, smell and the kinaesthetic components of sensory perception.

Interviews and *in situ* dialogue are recorded using a digital audio recorder. Photo-diary exercises and mapping exercises are undertaken by individual participants in the field, by means of digital or film camera, logbook and sketchbook.

Based on the act of 'communicating' through language and text, these methods elicit descriptions of experience, and construct these into meaning. These methods are generally considered to be appropriate research tools for exploring subjective meanings and perspectives, and particularly for experiences of health and well-being (Ballinger and Payne, 2000). They have the potential to explore the way in which participants construct meaning about environmental perceptions and preferences, and how these might contribute to a sense of place and rootedness to one's living environment in such a way as to reflect an understanding of well-being as an integrated and holistic concept, beyond just being the sum of the multiple dimensions of physiological health and wellness. Some examples of critical discussion on these approaches include Wetherell (1999); Ballinger and Payne, (2000); Latham (2003); Bijoux and Myers (2006).

Research discussion at the ESRC Seminar Series emphasised the importance of human experiential aspects of our understanding of place, and by extension it is logical to conclude that the experiential context of the engagement with participants must also be of importance. As Gesler puts it, this 'necessitates immersion into their activities and thoughts' (Gesler, 2001). These methods combine formal, semi-formal and casual social engagement. It is thought to be particularly important that the experiential context for discourse be given full weight in the research investigations. At this point, it must be said that the nature of the investigation in a grounded sense, as well as the research hypothesis itself, is continuing to evolve through the research process. It is an example of the 'not yet fully worked through' question (Pryke et al., 2003). The inherently subjective nature of this question and the degree to which it both reflects an intuition and consists of interpersonal engagement requires that this be so. We cannot truly know in advance how to elicit constructions of meaning without predetermining the framework within which those constructions will emerge. Such is the character of this sort of research. As Doreen Massey puts it, the research question itself is a speculative element – thus is the nature of fieldwork as a form of human engagement (Massey, 1994).

The research analysis and discussion

In itself, the research question and the way it is asked is a speculation, and is ongoing. In the first instance, this research is intent upon looking at what we already know about place, and about well-being, and reflecting the light of the knowledge of one upon the other. This process itself highlights questions, ambiguities, contrasting concepts and interesting associations which become the stuff of further thematic analysis.

Crang and Cook (2007) argue that the analysis of qualitative data lies within the creative act of writing. They argue that analysis of interview data using thematic analysis consists in identifying narratives and coherent stories, and that this act is in itself an act of theory building. They regard this act of writing as a way of imposing a discipline upon the data, assembling ideas and expressing the montage of thoughts, ideas meanings and experiences that are contained within it. Following the German philosopher Walter Benjamin, Crang and Cook argue for analysis as a search for new conjunctions, collisions and re-contextualisations – taking what might be (or might have been) common and unremarkable, and putting it into a new context so as to reveal new dynamics and hitherto undiscovered possibilities.

Beyond that, the research is exploring what meanings the participants themselves construct about these concepts in their own lives and experience, and to what extent they conceive of these ideas as being related. The research seeks to allow the voices of the research participants to speak, rather than to rigidly prescribe both a process and an analysis. I accept, however, that a truly singular expression of the voice of the participant is perhaps not possible (nor even desirable) in this sort of research. A thematic analysis, reflecting a search for those conjunctions, collisions and coincidences of ideas, of itself suggests a filter, a framework of implied meaning, which quickens the researcher's sensitivities, and guides the analysis of data. In this way then, the research is an essential act of collaboration between the researcher and the 'researched'. Isabelle Stengers (2000) writes of the idea of 'co-fabrication' – working together with those whom we are researching, and mapping into knowledge their constructions of meaning within the overarching context of the fundamental research question.

The research aims to address the question of utility for the theory and practice of landscape architecture. Further discussion will be framed around how this research might assist landscape architects to develop ways of thinking about and evaluating design responses, and what directions and implications for future research reside in this investigation.

Problems and pitfalls

Qualitative social science research of this sort is not without its problems and pitfalls, and this current project has encountered its fair share of these, both methodologically, and in execution. In seeking to identify appropriate case study sites for a qualitative investigation of 'sense of place', it has been difficult to tease out the need for choosing a locality and a study population for which dimensions of place and place attachment are likely to be significant, without prejudicing both the content and the intensity of the responses of potential participants. It could be said that the act of defining or choosing a site for this project has inherently implied 'place' by definition – and in that sense, the data are already presaged and pre-framed. This is a potentially confounding factor.

Further, the design of this investigation is built around an interpersonal engagement between the researcher and the researched, and it relies heavily on the quality of this engagement for its success. Caine, Davison and Stewart (2009) introduce the idea of 'preliminary fieldwork' as an essential stage in successful qualitative research. They highlight the necessity for a formative period of relationship building, both with place and people, which precedes the fieldwork proper. This is a process of mutual exchange, a reflective engagement over time upon which the relationships which facilitate the research can be based. It is based on building sufficient trust and rapport to enable a flexible, low-key, participant-based model of engagement, where the researcher is participant, actor, stakeholder in the same way as those who are being researched.

There are tensions, however, that can arise between an authentic and enthusiastic representation of 'self', and the need to recruit participants into the study in a way that neither coerces them nor predetermines the nature of their participation. I am by nature a generally gregarious and passionate personality, characteristically expressive of my thoughts and emotions once an interpersonal connection has been established. I have found it a palpable challenge to maintain the balance between an authentic representation of myself as a person (and a passionate devotee of Gore Bay by virtue of my own engagement with it) and what might otherwise be regarded as a 'professional distance' sufficient to enable a truly idiosyncratic and authentic response by my participants. Heron and Reason argue that '... good research is ... conducted *with* people rather than *on* people' (Heron and Reason, 2006; italics theirs). This implies an authentic engagement, but there is also another implication – the risk that this engagement becomes a 'defining' act, which creates context and potentially predetermines content. The nature of experiential inquiry therefore requires a careful balance – a non-alienated research process (Rowan, 2006) and the application of a critical sensitivity (Heron and Reason, 2006) to the interpersonal interaction between the parties.

Perhaps of most significance to this project, however, has been the advent of a series of earthquakes in Canterbury – the earthquakes of 4 September 2010; 22 February 2011; 13 June 2011; and 23 December 2011. These earthquakes caused widespread damage and destruction, and the February event killed 181 people. Together, they have been deeply disruptive to the lives of all Cantabrians (indeed to all of New Zealand), and despite being geographically remote, the study population of this project has also been experientially and materially affected, and are not exempt from this disruption. Of course, the earthquakes in themselves can be seen as the most fundamental of challenges to well-being, and the destruction that has ensued represents very a direct compromise to place. Many participants have been so significantly affected by the earthquakes as to be unable either to continue to engage in the research process altogether, or to fully meet and complete the requirements of it. At the least, it is a significant challenge to any project when the pool of respondents and research data evaporates before one's eyes.

This has in itself presented an entirely new 'scape' within which this project sits – a new direction for thinking about the research – and has given rise to the need for a reflexive response to the dynamic nature of place and well-being. Qualitative research is by definition about human experience – both 'observed' as the focus of the research interest, and 'lived', as an expression of an embodied engagement with the world. The two are intertwined and inseparable. The implications of the earthquakes have yet to be fully realised or played out, both for Christchurch and for this study. The passage of time will see that particular drama played out.

Yet for all the death and destruction, the post-quake aftermath has revealed an enduring – some might even say a stubborn – spirit, reflected in an attachment to Christchurch as place. If nothing else, it has become clear that people will 'choose' to live in localities, even in the face of danger and risk, when they can recognise place and are responsive to it. Christchurch as a city, as 'landscape', is a scape of grief and loss, yes... but it is also about memory, identity and renewal. It is about place.

Towards a Theory of landscape well-being

This chapter reports on an ongoing research project. From the first, it arose out of a deeply personal engagement with a particular place, from which grew an emerging sense that place and well-being were related. Initial analysis of the data suggests that place can indeed be related to a perceived sense of well-being. In the first instance, this relationship between place and well-being is grounded on an emotional attachment, a bond formed between person and place, which is beyond aesthetic, and underscored by a sense of localism and belonging. This attachment develops over time, strengthened and reinforced by repeated engagement and experience (reiteration). Time embeds this experience in memory, and thus arises a sense of place. Place is continually being made and unmade – coalescing and evaporating as it is confirmed and deepened by experience, and then legitimated or lost in the memory.

There also seems to be a sense that people recognise an essential 'it-ness' in place – a sense that '*this is it*', which demarcates the place from any other, and is palpable enough to know or be known. Perhaps it is based on an internal psychological schema about what some sort of idealised place might be, and which is triggered by or recognised in a particular location.

This relationship is also characterised by a positive regard (a liking and/or appreciation) for the aesthetic qualities and characteristics of the place – visual in the first instance, but not exclusively so, and not necessarily based on or derived from a first impression.

Places of well-being are also places where physical and psychological needs are met or fulfilled. They are places of restoration and release, where energies are either renewed or maintained, and which enable a sense of emotional and spiritual escape into another world or plane of being, where fantasies and daydreams are possible.

Place-making is more than a geographic function – it is a gestalt, a perceptual, affective and cognitive whole. Well-being as an existential 'state of being' is a fruit of place-making. It is the consequence of finding one's 'place' in the material and phenomenological world.

References

Appleton, J. (1975). *The experience of landscape*. Chichester: Wiley & Sons.
Appleton, J. (1987). Landscape as prospect and refuge. In J. Jackle. *The visual elements of landscape*. Amherst, MA: University of Massachusetts Press.
Ballinger, C., and Payne, S. (2000). Discourse analysis: Principles, applications and critique. *British Journal of Occupational Therapy*, 63(12), 105–111.
Bell, S. (2010). Challenges for research in landscape and health. In C. Ward Thompson, P. Aspinall, and S. Bell (Eds). *Innovative approaches to researching landscape and health*. Abingdon: Routledge.
Bijoux, D., and Myers, J. (2006). Interviews, solicited diaries and photography: 'New' ways of accessing everyday experiences of place. *Graduate Journal of Asia-Pacific Studies*, 4(1), 44–64.
Bowring, J., and Swaffield, S. (2010). Diagrams in landscape architecture. In M. Garcia (Ed). *The diagrams of architecture*. Chichester: Wiley.
Browne, C. (1992). The role of nature for the promotion of well-being of the elderly. In D. Relph (Ed). *The role of horticulture in human well-being and social development. A national symposium*. Arlington, VA, 1990; Portland, OR: Timber Press.
Caine, K., Davison, C., and Stewart, E. (2009). Preliminary fieldwork: Methodological reflections from northern Canadian research. *Qualitative Research*, 9(4), 489–513.
Corner, J. (Ed). (1999). *Recovering landscape: Essays in contemporary landscape architecture*. Sparks, NV: Princeton Architectural Press.
Crang, M., and Cook, I. (2007). *Doing ethnographies*. Los Angeles, CA: Sage.
Cresswell, T. (2004). *Place: A short introduction*. Malden, MA: Blackwell Pub.

Crisp, R. (2008). Well-being. In *Stanford encyclopedia of philosophy*. Retrieved from http://plato.stanford.edu/entries/wellbeing/
Cuba, L., and Hummon, D. (1993). A place to call home: Identification with dwelling, community and region. *The Sociological Quarterly*, 34(1), 111–131.
de Vries, S. (2010). Nearby nature and human health. In C. Ward Thompson, P. Aspinall, and S. Bell (Eds). *Innovative approaches to researching landscape and health*. Abingdon: Routledge.
Edwards, J. (1998). The need for a 'bit of history': Place and past in English identity. In N. Lovell (Ed). *Locality and belonging*. London: Routledge.
Fleuret, S., and Atkinson, S. (2007). Wellbeing, health and geography: A critical review and research agenda. *New Zealand Geographer*, 63, 106–118.
Galindo, M.P., and Corraliza Rodriguez, J.A. (2000). Environmental aesthetics and psychological wellbeing: Relationships between preference judgements for urban landscapes and other relevant affective factors. *Psychology in Spain*, 4(1), 13–27.
Gesler, W. (1992). Therapeutic landscapes: Medical issues in light of the new cultural geography. *Social Science and Medicine*, 34(7), 735–746.
Gesler, W. (2001). Therapeutic landscapes. A seminar presentation at the 'Well-being: Social and Individual Determinants' Seminar Series. Economic and Social Research Council, Manchester Metropolitan University. Retrieved from http://www.haworthjt.com/Wellbeingesrc/seminars.
Gesler, W., and Kearns, R. (2002). *Culture/place/health*. London: Routledge.
Giuliani, M. (2003). Theory of attachment and place attachment. In M. Bonnes, T. Lee, and M. Bonaiuto (Eds). *Psychological theories for environmental issues*. Aldershot: Ashgate.
Graf, B. (2006). *Positive emotions in residential environments. Workshop 5 – The residential context of health.* Conference Paper to ENHR Conference: Housing in an expanding Europe. Urban Planning Institute of the Republic of Slovenia.
Hartig, T. (2007). Three steps to understanding restorative environments as health resources. In C. Ward Thompson, and P. Travlou (Eds). *Open space: People space*. London: Taylor & Francis.
Hartig, T., and Staats, H. (2006). The need for psychological restoration as a determinant of environmental preferences. *Journal of Environmental Psychology*, 26(3), 215–226.
Haworth, J., and Hart, G. (Eds). (2007). *Well-being: Individual, community and social perspectives*. Palgrave: MacMillan.
Heron, J., and Reason, P. (2006). The practice of co-operative inquiry: Research 'with' people rather than 'on' people. In P. Reason, and H. Bradbury (Eds). *Handbook of action research. Participative inquiry & practice*. London: Sage.
Herzog, T., Maguire, C., and Nebel, M. (2003). Assessing the restorative components of environments. *Journal of Environmental Psychology*, 23(2), 159–170.
Jackson, P. (1989). *Maps of meaning: An introduction to cultural geography*. London: Unwin Hyman.
Kaplan, R., and Kaplan, S. (1989). *The experience of nature: A psychological perspective*. New York: Cambridge University Press.
Kaplan, S. (1992). The restorative environment: Nature and human experience. In D. Relph (Ed). *The role of horticulture in human well-being and social development. A national symposium*. Arlington, VA, 1990; Portland, OR: Timber Press.
Kaplan, S. (1995). The restorative benefits of nature: Toward an integrative framework. *Journal of Environmental Psychology*, 15, 169–182.
Kellert, S. (2005). *Building for life*. Washington, DC: Island Press.
Kellert, S., and Wilson, E. (1993). *The Biophilia Hypothesis*. Washington, DC: Island Press.

Korpela, K. (1989). Place identity as a product of environment self-regulation. *Journal of Environmental Psychology*, 9, 241–256.
Latham, A. (2003). Research performance and doing human geography: Some reflections on the diary-photograph, diary-interview method. *Environment and Planning A*, 35, 1993–2017.
Low, S., and Altman, I. (1992). Place attachment: A conceptual inquiry. In I. Altman, and S. Low (Eds). *Place attachment. Human behaviour and environment. Advances in theory and research. Vol 12*. New York: Plenum Press.
Maas, J., Verheij, R., Groenewegen, P., de Vries, S., and Spreeuwenberg, P. (2006). Green space, urbanity, and health: How strong is the relationship?, *Journal of Epidemiology and Community Health*, 60, 587–593.
Maslow, A. (1943). A theory of human motivation. *Psychological Review*, 50, 370–396.
Maslow, A. (1970). *Motivation and personality*. New York: Harper & Row.
Massey, D. (1994). *Space, place and gender*. Cambridge: Polity Press.
Meinig, D. (1979). Reading the landscape. An appreciation of W.G. Hoskins and J.B. Jackson. In D. Meinig (Ed). *The interpretation of ordinary landscapes*. New York: Oxford University Press.
Murphy, M. (2005). *Landscape architecture theory. An evolving body of thought*. Long Grove, IL: Waveland Press.
Nielson, T., and Hansen, K. (2007). Do green areas affect health? Results from a Danish survey on the use of green areas and health indicators. *Health and Practice*, 13, 839–850.
Norberg-Schulz, C. (1980). *Genius loci: Towards a phenomenology of architecture*. New York: Rizzoli.
Olmsted, F.L. (1870). *Public parks and the enlargement of towns*. Cambridge, MA: Riverside Press.
Proshansky, H., Fabian, A., and Kaminoff, R. (1983). Place identity: Physical world socialization of the self. *Journal of Environmental Psychology*, 3, 57–83.
Pryke, M., Rose, G., and Whatmore, S. (2003). *Using social theory; Thinking through research*. London: Sage.
Relph, E. (1976). *Place and placelessness*. London: Pion.
Relph, E. (1985). Geographical experiences and being-in-the-world. In D. Seamon, and R. Mugerauer (Eds). *Dwelling, place and environment*. Dordrecht: Nijhoff.
Relph, D. (Ed). (1992). *The role of horticulture in human well-being and social development. A national symposium*. Arlington, VA, 1990; Portland, OR: Timber Press.
Relph, E. (1997). Sense of place. In S. Hanson (Ed). *10 geographic ideas that changed the world*. New Brunswick, NJ: Rutgers University Press, 205–226.
Rowan, J. (2006). The humanistic approach to action research. In P. Reason, and H. Bradbury (Eds). *Handbook of action research. Participative inquiry & practice*. London: Sage.
Sarbin, T. (1983). Place identity as a component of self: An addendum. *Journal of Environmental Psychology*, 3, 337–342.
Scannell, L., and Gifford, R. (2010). Defining place attachment: A tripartite organizing framework. *Journal of Environmental Psychology*, 30(1), 1–10.
Seligman, M. (2011). *Flourish: A visionary new understanding of happiness and well-being*. New York: Free Press.
Sen, A. (1992). Capability and well-being. In A. Sen, and M. Nussbaum (Eds). *The quality of life*. Oxford: Clarendon Press, pp. 30–53.
Shotter, J. (1985). Accounting for place and space. *Environment and Planning D. Society and Space*, 3, 447–460.
Stengers, I. (2000). *The invention of modern science*. Minneapolis, MN: University of Minnesota Press.

Tuan, Y.-F. (1974). *Topophilia: A study of environmental perception, attitudes, and values*. Englewood Cliffs, New Jersey, NJ: Prentice-Hall.
Tuan, Y.-F. (1977). *Space and place: The perspective of experience*. Minneapolis, MN: University of Minnesota Press.
Tuan, Y.-F. (1979a). Space and place: Humanist perspective. In S. Gale, and G. Olsson (Eds). *Philosophy in geography*. Dordrecht: Reidel Publishing.
Tuan, Y.-F. (1979b). Thought and landscape. The eye and the mind's eye. In D. Meinig (Ed). *The interpretation of ordinary landscapes*. New York: Oxford University Press.
Tuan, Y.-F. (1980). Rootedness versus sense of place. *Landscape*, 24(1), 3–8.
Ulrich, R. (1979). Visual landscapes and psychological well-being. *Landscape Research*, 4(1), 17–23.
Ulrich, R. (1983). Aesthetic and affective response to natural environment. In I. Altman, and J. Wohlwill (Eds). (1983). *Human behaviour and environment. Advances in theory and research. Vol 6: Behaviour and the natural environment*. New York: Plenum Press.
Ulrich, R., and Parsons, R. (1992). Influences of passive experiences with plants on individual well-being and health. In D. Relph (Ed) *The role of horticulture in human well-being and social development. A national symposium*. Arlington, VA, 1990; Portland, OR: Timber Press.
van den Berg, A., and ter Heijne, M. (2005). Fear versus fascination: An exploration of emotional responses to natural threats. *Journal of Environmental Psychology*, 25(3), 261–272.
van Kamp, I., Leidelmeijer, K., Marsman, G., and de Hollander, A. (2003). Urban environmental quality and human wellbeing. Towards a conceptual framework and demarcation of concepts; a literature study. *Landscape and Urban Planning*, 65(1–2), 5–18.
Ward Thompson, C. (2010). Landscape quality and quality of life. In C. Ward Thompson, P. Aspinall, and S. Bell (Eds). *Innovative approaches to researching landscape and health: Open space: People space 2*. Abingdon: Routledge, 230–255.
Weil, S. (1955). *The need for roots*. Boston, MA: Beacon Press.
Wetherell, M. (1999). Discourse analysis. In C. Davidson, and M. Tolich (Eds). *Social science research in New Zealand: Many paths to understanding*. Auckland: Longman.
Wilson, O. (1984). *Biophilia: The human bond with other species*. Cambridge: Harvard University Press.

5

INTERACTIVE URBAN LANDSCAPES FOR WELL-BEING AND SUSTAINABILITY

Janice Astbury

Introduction

More than fifty per cent of the world's population now lives in cities and cities contribute significantly to global environmental problems. Urban dwellers both suffer the effects of these problems locally and are well positioned to contribute to solutions (Grimm et al., 2008). Both people's involvement in environmental stewardship and the results of their efforts have the potential to contribute significantly to human well-being (Kaplan, 2000) and although the majority of people now call a city home, many urban landscapes convey messages that are negative in terms of supporting the well-being of their populations, especially that the city is beyond the control of ordinary citizens. The large fixed structures that dominate these landscapes communicate resistance to change or 'obduracy' (Hommels, 2005). In addition, they tend both to limit direct contact with nature and conceal the ecosystem services[1] that sustain life (Hough, 2004; Miller, 2005). As such, our urban landscapes are often disempowering, sometimes induce despair and generally represent a missed opportunity for people to play an active role in enhancing their individual well-being, where stewardship, contact with nature, control and respect form underpinning facets of supportive citizen-focused urban centres.

Within this context, this chapter will explore well-being from the perspective of people–nature interaction and outline some characteristics of urban landscapes that invite people to become stewards of ecosystem services. These characteristics are then translated into a set of guidelines that can be used by local government, business, community organisations and individuals to create urban landscapes that invite ecosystem-enhancing interactions.

The experience of visibly transforming the places where we live can create a virtuous circle of empowerment and the creation of quality places, which are further empowering. Coupled with the community building that usually accompanies hands-on collective efforts, this should contribute substantially to well-being (Duxbury, 2002). Experiencing that engagement with people and place, as opposed to consumption, is a source of happiness which may in turn contribute to rethinking economic goals in ways that are at the heart of the social change necessary to achieve sustainability (Bacon et al., 2010).

Conceptual framework

Resilient social–ecological systems

In describing problems associated with the design of most built environments, biologist Laura Jackson states, 'chronic ailments including asthma and allergies, animal-transmitted diseases, obesity, diabetes, heart disease, and depression are on the rise. These diverse illnesses join with forest fragmentation, stream degradation, wetlands destruction, and the concomitant loss of native species' (Jackson, 2003). What is striking about this statement is not the list of human and environmental ills, which are unfortunately all too familiar, but rather that they are mentioned together. Discussions of human and ecological health tend to happen in different fields, which limit opportunities to explore the connections between both problems and possible solutions.

In response to this challenge, efforts are underway to reframe cities as 'social-ecological systems' (Evans, 2011), which are systems of people and nature that interact in a range of complex ways. Knowing that social–ecological systems are subject to constant change with often unpredictable outcomes, an emphasis is placed on how to make them more 'resilient', i.e. able to absorb disturbance and reorganise while undergoing change so as to retain essentially the same (usually more desirable) function, structure, identity and feedbacks (Walker et al., 2004).

Seeing the system through landscape

If we can understand how people and nature interact in urban social–ecological systems, we can begin to think about how to facilitate interactions that would benefit both and increase resilience. The concept of 'landscape' is helpful for this purpose. Landscape is understood somewhat differently across disciplines but it generally integrates human and natural elements and it refers to a certain scale (Bastian, 2001). It is a unit of environment that a human being 'can make sense of', be it in an aerial photograph, a scene in a picture frame or the view through a train window. Combining thinking about the ecological landscape and the cultural landscape can help to understand at a landscape level:

- how ecosystem functions (which maintain ecosystem health) translate to ecosystem services (which support human health and well-being) (Termorshuizen & Opdam, 2009) and

- how people perceive or fail to perceive these functions and services as well as their own roles in maintaining them.

This understanding can then be applied to making urban landscapes that reveal the workings of ecosystem functions/services and invite people to steward them, generally through the development and maintenance of 'green infrastructure'.

Green infrastructure

In cities, the relationship between people and nature is rarely direct. It is mediated by social–technological systems, commonly referred to as 'infrastructure' (Kaika & Swyngedouw, 2000). In addition to the pipes and roads that most quickly come to mind, infrastructure includes systems that facilitate cleaner air and recreational spaces, as well as hydrological and climate regulation. Due both to the scale of provisioning and to its role as a defining framework in how other goods and services are supplied, infrastructure is a key factor in sustainability.

Most existing infrastructure in cities is not designed to maximise the possible benefits of available ecosystem services; it tends instead to work against natural processes (Ndubisi, 2002). In addition, it does not take advantage of the energy and creativity of local populations and often inhibits citizen involvement in working with natural cycles and energy flows (Orr, 1994). In the current context of crumbling infrastructure, limited resources and uncertain environmental and energy futures,

> …it would be desirable to design human physical and social infrastructure that is efficient in its use of the throughput of material, runs off solar energy, increases in diversity and productivity, enhances the water cycle and builds soil. Such ecologically sound infrastructure would offer many niches for other species. It would have a high capacity to adapt to changing circumstances, whilst maintaining a historical thread in its structure and interactions with its place.
>
> (Tippett et al., 2007)

Green infrastructure 'can be considered to comprise all natural, semi-natural and artificial networks of multifunctional ecological systems within, around and between urban areas, at all spatial scales' (Tzoulas et al., 2007). It provides a host of ecosystem services such as air filtering, microclimate regulation, noise reduction, rainwater drainage, sewage treatment, and recreational and cultural values (Bolund & Hunhammar, 1999). Particularly promising is its multifunctionality. Unlike conventional infrastructure, which tends to serve only one purpose, the same green space that offers drainage, air filtering and microclimate regulation can also provide habitat to support biodiversity conservation, and is a place to play or relax.

Greening infrastructure and the link to well-being

Contact with nearby nature is linked to a range of benefits for human health and well-being. Barton and Pretty (2010), Nurse et al. (2010) and Tzoulas et al. (2007) provide recent summaries of a rapidly growing literature that documents the many positive impacts on both mental and physical health. They also cite the multiple benefits at the community level including reduced crime and violence (Kuo & Sullivan, 2001a, 2001b) and increased neighbourliness (Kim & Kaplan, 2004; Kuo et al., 1998). Most important for the current discussion is evidence of the added individual and community benefits of engagement in activities that develop green infrastructure (Austin, 2002; Inerfeld & Blom, 2001). The result of Nurse et al.'s review of the literature is a proposal for an ecological approach to understanding health that applies a social–ecological system perspective: 'There is a growing awareness that human societies and their social and economic systems, as well as other organisms and the environment, interact and have complex, interdependent relationships. This deep-seated connectedness has implications for human health and development' (Nurse et al., 2010). Similarly, Tzoulas et al. sum up their review by stating, 'With the great variety of benefits attributable to Green Infrastructure in relation to the urban ecosystem and human health and well-being, it is not surprising that integrative frameworks have been developed to link human and ecosystem health' and they conclude by offering their own 'Conceptual framework linking Green Infrastructure, ecosystem and human health and well-being' (Tzoulas et al., 2007).

The many positive impacts on well-being have diverse roots, including a sense of 'connectedness to nature' (Mayer & Frantz, 2004). Some authors have traced this to a 'biophilic need' rooted in the history of the human species, which has for the most part been spent in natural environments (Kellert & Wilson, 1995). As a result, being in nature tends to lower stress and has a range of restorative effects (Kaplan & Kaplan, 1989). These effects are most often studied in relation to activities where nature is enjoyed in a passive way. It is, however, worth bearing in mind that the traditional relationship is more interactive, involving foraging, hunting, cultivation and various forms of stewardship of ecosystem services. There is currently some evidence of an evolution in the types of interaction that people seek with nature. A shift from consumptive or utilitarian values to mutualistic and protective values (for example, many people are now more interested in feeding birds than shooting them) has been noted across diverse countries (Teel et al., 2007). While the benefits of gardening are frequently extolled, insufficient attention has been paid to the diversity of human–nature interactions (Fuller & Irvine, 2010).

There are many ways that citizens can interact with nature that will contribute to the development and maintenance of green infrastructure. Activities might include planting and looking after trees; introducing more permeable surfaces; restoring streams and wetlands; greening vacant lots and roofs; growing food; building a community solar oven; constructing adventure playgrounds that reconnect children to nature; and making footpaths and cycle routes more attractive to promote active transportation. The possibilities are wide-ranging and the idea is not to dictate, but rather to invite, actions that are driven by the skills and interests of the people involved, and the characteristics of the place with which they engage. This will hopefully initiate a virtuous circle of social learning,[2] skill development and deeper engagement, which will lead to further action. As the landscapes in which these activities unfold communicate strong messages about what should happen there, it raises the question of how to stimulate citizen-led greening of infrastructure using the medium of landscape. Unfortunately, most urban landscapes currently send a rather uninviting message.

Uninviting landscapes

Humans are different from other species in a social–ecological system because our responses to stimuli are less biologically predetermined. We make decisions (consciously or unconsciously) based on a complex array of emotions and information, and these decisions have the potential to make a social–ecological system more or less resilient. Transforming the role of humans in a social–ecological system requires that we understand how people formulate the ideas that drive actions.

People act, and therefore impact, on their environments according to cultural constructs (Kirk, 1952; Relph, 1989), either their own or those of others to which they are motivated or obliged to adhere. Landscapes are understood to be both result and driver of these constructs (Mitchell, 1994; Smith, 2006).

The power of landscape to construct reality, including our ideas about the natural environment and our role in it, is a key concept in cultural geography (Cosgrove & Daniels, 1988; Duncan, 1993). The appearance of solidity and naturalness that is inherent to landscape gives it a particular power to 'make real', to naturalise and to normalise (Cosgrove, 1984). The concepts of 'landscape as text' and 'intertextuality' (where messages from landscapes interact with those from other media) seek to explain how landscapes communicate (Duncan & Duncan, 1988). The fence around a park, for example, is integrated with regulations and cultural norms. Not only do these 'texts' of fence and rules reinforce one another, they often combine to create a seamless single message. The fence signifies 'keep off' because we are taught not to 'trespass' and the ubiquitous presence of fences in the landscape naturalises ideas of private property and exclusion. It is therefore clear that in keeping with an understanding of the city as a social–ecological system, we must understand cultural landscapes as integrating physical forms and processes with social institutions.

Although cities may be social–ecological systems, the separation of people and nature is still a dominant narrative within the urban landscape; 'the urban becomes "naturalized", as if it has always been there on the one hand, and as distinct and separate from nature on the other' (Kaika & Swyngedouw,

2000). As the city itself is often portrayed as evidence of the damage caused by humans, it seems right that the 'countryside' or 'wilderness' should exist apart and, as much as possible, safeguarded from human activities (Cronon, 1996).

As nature is understood to be absent from the city, so the city is also seen as disconnected from natural systems (Heynen et al., 2006). This is a message that is relayed very forcefully by the urban landscape; most contemporary built environments are particularly effective at hiding the workings of the natural world underneath the pavement, and belying the connections to regional and global processes (Hough, 2004; Kaika & Swyngedouw, 2000). This contrasts with preindustrial cities where the visible infrastructure of irrigation revealed the workings of nature (Strang, 1996).

In addition to communicating a separation of people and nature, urban landscapes tend to convey the sense that citizens can have no role in shaping them. Modern cities are often not built on a human scale (Gehl, 2010) and appear susceptible only to institutional interventions involving planners and technological modifications, rather than through citizen action (Gandy, 2006). Most urban landscapes give the impression of being very resistant to any kind of change, i.e. they display 'obduracy' (Hommels, 2005). Beyond having the capacity to make change, sometimes even the right to be in an urban space seems questionable. The perimeter of the space where most people feel they belong and can exert some control has gradually shrunk from a public/community space to a privately owned house (Harvey, 2003). The erasing of local narratives so that local residents are no longer part of the story – or there is no story – also contributes to loss of a sense of place and belonging (Tuan, 1977). This is particularly true where the landscape signals corporate or commercial space (Hou, 2010).

In summary, urban landscapes convey some key messages that affect people–nature interaction:

- Empowerment to change the city:
  - The city and its infrastructure are not susceptible to change (obduracy).
  - Ordinary citizens do not have the power to make change; it is the domain of politicians, planners and the private sector (exclusion, disempowerment).
  - The city does not belong to citizens (one's place/home is limited to one's house at most) and therefore citizens have no right to change it.
- Nature in the city:
  - There is no nature in the city.
  - Nature does not belong in the city.
  - The functioning of the city is not dependent on natural processes.
  - Nature must be controlled.
  - Humans impact negatively on nature.

Clearly our cultural constructs, which landscapes play an important role in determining, 'can contain inconsistencies, and may or may not accurately model the properties of a social-ecological system' (Trosper, 2005). This raises the question as to whether it is possible to make landscapes that tell a different story, one where people and nature co-exist in cities, where ecosystem services support human well-being and people have a role to play in stewarding these services and the underlying ecosystem functions. As Howett's history of ecological values in twentieth-century landscape design makes clear: landscape design has often obfuscated the roles of people and nature but it has a capacity to clarify (Howett, 1998).

Invitation by design

> …insofar as the landscapes we create refract back to us a very powerful naturalization of the social assumptions that sculpted such landscapes in the first place, a revolution in our thinking may be intimately bound up with a revolution in how these landscapes are made. Seeing the world differently probably depends on making a different world from which the world itself can be seen differently.
>
> (Smith, 2006)

The challenge now is to reconnect cities to people and nature. This can be facilitated by creating landscapes that visibly integrate natural processes and teach us how these processes work, that show us how urban sustainability might look. Our urban landscapes should help us to recognise that we are living in a constantly changing social–ecological system and have an active role to play in enhancing its resilience. These 'inviting landscapes' could provide opportunities for citizens to get involved in designing and physically making places in ways that allow for creative input, community building and education, thus enhancing both natural and social capital.

Although this approach is a departure from most current practice in the built environment, the actions of some citizens and urban professionals attest to its potential and offer some indication of how it might be developed. Two emerging citizen movements, for example, demonstrate that there is both citizen interest and capacity to take on roles as stewards of nature and re-arrangers of cities.

The first, 'civic ecology' is a practice that reflects:

> the linked social and ecological systems implications of participatory environmental restoration and management initiatives in cities and elsewhere. Civic ecology emerges from the actions of local residents wanting to make a difference in the social and natural environment of their community and is recognizable when both people and the environment benefit measurably and memorably from these actions.
>
> (Krasny & Tidball, 2010)

The second comprises a variety of forms of citizen-led urbanism, where actors engage in 'unintended' use of public space (Hou, 2010). This has been described as 'everyday urbanism' (Chase et al., 1999), 'DIY urbanism', 'pop-up urbanism' and 'tactical urbanism' (Lydon et al., 2010) as well as 'insurgent urbanism' or 'guerrilla urbanism'. Having coined the latter, Hou labels the various types of intervention as: appropriating, reclaiming, pluralising, transgressing, uncovering and contesting (Hou, 2010). The effect of these unintended uses is the creation of what Franck and Stevens have called 'loose space' where the dominant meanings of sites are 'loosened' (2007), allowing the text of the cultural landscape to be re-scripted. These authors note several characteristics of loose space, some of which are likely to be shared by 'inviting landscapes'.

These citizen-led initiatives evolve in tandem, and sometimes overlap, with the work of urban design professionals. There is long line of urbanists, planners, architects and landscape architects who have designed urban landscapes that send different messages about the place of people and nature in cities. For example, Olmstead, Jensen, Halprin, McHarg and Spirn (Howett, 1998) and Hough (2004) have designed with nature. Alexander identified a 'pattern language' common to good built environments for people (Alexander et al., 1977) and Lynch emphasised the importance of 'legibility' that gives identity to a place (Lynch, 1960) and can thus encourage people to engage. Jacobs identified the links between urban design and community (Jacobs, 1961) and Gehl has been involved in designing 'cities for people' all over the world (Gehl, 2010). These are just a small sample of a large and diverse group that has laid the groundwork for a new generation of emerging urbanists (Naik & Oldfield, 2010) and design activists (Fuad-Luke, 2009) whose roles as professionals and citizens often blur. Some of them are attending to the potential of the unfinished landscape (Potteiger & Purinton, 1998).

In search of inviting landscapes

The ninety-nine 'Actions: What You Can Do With the City' that were catalogued and exhibited by the Canadian Centre for Architecture in 2008–2009 (Borasi & Zardini, 2008) provided a window onto the great variety of things people could do with cities once they decided to act. Many of these actions were orientated toward enhancing sustainability and building community. This provided an initial sample of the kind of initiatives that might have been stimulated by and/or produced inviting landscapes and which might therefore shed some light on their characteristics.

The 'Actions' mentioned above were the starting point for a scan of initiatives involving volunteers physically changing their environments in ways that enhanced social–ecological resilience in cities. The identification of common characteristics across these initiatives was the first step in the development of a typology of 'inviting landscapes'. It laid the groundwork for a series of site visits, interviews and, finally, participant observation with citizens engaging with green infrastructure in North West England[3] and which give rise to a typology of inviting landscapes with characteristics that appear to invite people to interact with nature in a way that enhances social–ecological resilience.

An emerging typology of inviting landscapes

1 *Safe*: feeling safe in a space is the first condition for being there and initiating change; perceptions of safety vary considerably based on characteristics of actors and the conditions in which they enter the site (e.g. time of day, their companions, 'authority' to be there); feeling safe for some may require excluding others who are perceived as threatening.

2 *Permission to enter*: (includes permeability) as in the case of safety, perception varies depending on actor and conditions with sub-criteria which include the space available – places that are vacant/unoccupied to some degree; no fences – the area is not fenced off or otherwise implicitly or explicitly prohibiting entry; it could even invite entry as was attempted with a sign that unusually listed all of things that people could do in a space (Potteiger & Purinton, 1998); fluid tenure – land can be either publicly or privately owned but appears unclaimed or there is formal or tacit agreement by the owner that it can be used and possibly altered by others; open to all – inclusive (although again, inclusive for some may require exclusion of others); connected – accessible from other sites that people can and do frequent.

3 *Interesting*: including the diversity of features; opportunities for engaging in favoured activities or generally having fun; opportunities for learning; responding to biophilic tendencies and curiosity about nature.

4 *Feels like home*: areas that have more of a residential rather than a corporate or institutional feel; 'defensible space' (Jacobs, 1961) such as alleyways or the pavement in front of houses; community-claimed – places that local community members have already staked a claim to in some way; play space – places that children play; nearby or en route – places close to people's homes or that they often pass though on foot or bicycle; welcoming host – a community member (usually a neighbour) takes initiative and welcomes others into the space or invites them to join in some way.

5 *Change is possible*: intervention is not prevented – either explicitly permitted or not explicitly permitted but possible to varying degrees; signs of human habitation – evidence of 'non-formal' interventions by other people in the area; positive change – existing interventions are generally perceived as positive and non-threatening; in progress – such interventions appear to be ongoing; legible – interventions are self-explanatory or explanations are given; attention-getting – interventions are innovative or humorous in some way that draws attention and shifts thinking about what is possible

in the space; temporary alterations – interventions like PARK(ing) where parking meters are fed to create temporary parks (Borasi & Zardini, 2008) change the space temporarily and fuel ideas about changes in permanent use; seeing other citizens in action – and having opportunities to talk to them; replication opportunity – has similar characteristics to a place where positive change has occurred and has been witnessed or documented and shared.

6 *Challenge-posing*: places that present problems to be solved or projects to be fixed or finished in ways likely to call on the skills or imagination of potential stewards.

7 *Needs defending*: space that is threatened by existing or potential other uses; neglected but not unloved – obviously needs care but does not show signs of excessive neglect (such as is manifested by large amounts of rubbish or vandalism).

8 *Community venue*: social spaces – places where people might meet; intersections, places to sit; comforting 'props' – places where people meet in the presence of comforting 'props' such as children and dogs or where common activities like buying and selling (e.g. car boot sales) are going on (Mean & Tims, 2005); inviting activities – space where community activities take place, such as informal sport or neighbourhood celebrations where people feel invited to join in; worthy of comment – where the 'attention-getting' interventions mentioned above give people cause to stop in the place and talk about them, as was the case with the surprising appearance of an eight-foot metal pig that was a comment on unsustainable consumption (Hou, 2010).

9 *In the presence of nature*: nature can be apprehended using human senses (can be seen, heard, smelled); nature is attractive (flies around rotting food, for example, is not inviting), interaction with nature is possible, it can be touched, smelled, tasted, collected or recorded, fed or watered, celebrated or protected, incorporated into art, changed in some tangible way. That natural elements are made legible either through the landscape alone and/or through interpretation, e.g. waterways are visible or the possibility of 'de-culverting' (where channelled waterways are brought back to the surface and naturalised) is suggested or routes that underground waterways follow are mapped and marked so as to make people aware of their presence. Ecosystem processes are visible – landscapes are not artificially maintained in an unchanging state; the continuous change that characterises resilient ecosystems is facilitated and celebrated. Potential natural resources are present, such as fruit trees (or other trees), good soil or a body of water. Ecosystem services are highlighted, for example through labelling edible elements; using art to celebrate the benefits of trees; implementing and interpreting experiments that show the advantages of different kinds of ground cover; nature shows some signs of being tended or other signs of stewardship are in evidence; nature appears to need protecting.

In turn these give rise to guidelines for facilitating the emergence of inviting landscapes which emphasise a range of characteristics:

- Physical form and governance are considered, designed and implemented in an integrated fashion.
- Recognises potential for innovation at the margins and thus explicitly accepts uncertainly and relinquishes control (while negotiating safe boundaries).
- Adopts minimum specification regulations to allow for creativity and adaptation to local conditions.
- Focuses on enabling the good and not just preventing the bad.
- Identifies and prioritises support for efforts already underway.
- Takes full advantage of ecosystem services and local natural and human resources.
- Emphasises inclusion (and is attentive to the tremendous challenges of actually creating shared space within heterogeneous communities).
- Stimulates and integrates resilience thinking in all aspects.
- Facilitates social learning, adaptive experimentation[4] and adaptive management.[5]
- Attends from the outset to documentation and communication for scaling up and/or sharing lessons learned.
- Aspires to the following site characteristics: permeable, safe, legible, human-scale.
- Eco-revelatory: revealing both local ecological processes and connections to larger systems.
- Unfinished: conveying the sense of an eternal work in progress or a garden growing.
- Open and flexible: multi-use and adaptable to different uses at different times of the day and different seasons.
- Signals inclusion.
- Incorporates existing ecological and community narratives and makes space for new ones.

This preliminary typology and the resulting guidelines can be adapted and used by individuals, community organisations, government agencies and businesses. They are tools that will likely have practical applications for efforts already underway and they will continue to be refined as they are applied in different places by different people. There may never be a definitive version. Complex and ever-changing social–ecological systems require an adaptive experimentation approach where the city is seen as a living laboratory (Evans, 2011). In the broader context, this research may encourage more discussion about the role of urban landscapes in inviting citizens to engage directly with their environments in ways that enhance social–ecological resilience.

This research project grew out of an idea that both cultural landscapes and hands-on citizen stewardship were important elements in moving toward urban sustainability. Working titles have included 'interactive landscapes' and 'engaging landscapes'. 'Inviting' began to creep in as a way to specify that this is about creating opportunities for people to do things that they want to do, as opposed to educating, motivating or obliging people to undertake prescribed actions. 'Inviting landscapes' has begun to seem increasingly apt as indicative examples accumulate demonstrating the importance of a sense of belonging to incite resilience-enhancing interventions in urban landscapes. Belonging matters because it includes us, motivates us and empowers us. It makes us feel we are part of a community, with all of the benefits of social interaction and the sense of commitment to the group. It also makes us feel that we are in our home, for which we care and are responsible. This matters for sustainability: homes get looked after and people feel at home in nature, especially when we are the gardeners. It also matters for our well-being in an increasingly urbanised world. Feeling 'at home' is a core need and it is important that we re-establish a home in a natural world, which will henceforth more often than not be located in cities.

Notes

1 Ecosystem services are the benefits that people get from nature. They can be roughly divided into four categories: provisioning, such as the production of food and water; regulating, such as the control of climate and disease; supporting, such as nutrient cycles and crop pollination; and cultural, such as spiritual and recreational benefits (Ranganathan et al., 2008).
2 Social learning is the collective learning through action and reflection that results in enhancing a group's ability to change its underlying dynamics and assumptions (Tippett & Searle, 2005).
3 The results of this research, including a more detailed description of the characteristics of inviting landscapes and guidelines for supporting their emergence, are the subject of the author's PhD thesis.
4 Experiments carried out in complex real world systems that allow humans to adapt inside the experiment and alter its parameters (Evans, 2011)
5 Adaptive management is an explicitly experimental approach to managing where interventions are tested through implementation, analysed and adapted accordingly. It is assumed that as the system is constantly changing, the process of adaptation is ongoing (Salafsky et al., 2001).

References

Alexander, C., Ishikawa, S., Silverstein, M., Jacobson, M., Fiksdahl-King, I., & Angel, S. (1977) *A pattern language: Towns, buildings, construction*, New York: Oxford University Press.
Austin, M. E. (2002) 'Partnership opportunities in neighborhood tree planting initiatives: Building from local knowledge', *Journal of Arboriculture* 28, 4: 178–186.
Bacon, N., Brophy, M., Mguni, N., Mulgan, G., & Shandro, A. (2010) *The state of happiness: Can public policy shape people's wellbeing and resilience?* London: Young Foundation.
Barton, J., & Pretty, J. (2010) 'Urban ecology and human health and wellbeing', in K. Gaston (ed.) *Urban ecology,* Cambridge: Cambridge University Press, 202–229.

Bastian, O. (2001) 'Landscape ecology – towards a unified discipline?', *Landscape Ecology* 16, 8: 757–766.
Bolund, P., & Hunhammar, S. (1999) 'Ecosystem services in urban areas', *Ecological Economics* 29: 293–301.
Borasi, G., & Zardini, M. (2008) 'Actions: What you can do with the city', Montreal: Canadian Centre for Architecture.
Chase, J., Crawford, M., & Kaliski, J. (1999) *Everyday urbanism*, New York: Monacelli Press.
Cosgrove, D. (1984) *Social formation and symbolic landscapes*, Madison, WI: University of Wisconsin.
Cosgrove, D., & Daniels, S. (1988) *The iconography of landscape: Essays on the symbolic representation, design and use of past environments*, Cambridge: Cambridge University Press.
Cronon, W. (1996) *Uncommon ground: Rethinking the human place in nature*, New York and London: W.W. Norton & Co.
Duncan J., & Duncan, N. (1988) '(Re)reading the landscape', *Environment and Planning D: Society and Space* 6, 2: 117–126.
Duncan, J. S. (1993) 'Landscapes of the self/landscapes of the other(s): Cultural Geography 1991-2', *Progress in Human Geography* 17, 3: 367–377.
Duxbury, G. (2002) 'Groundwork at 21', *Landscape Design* 306: 21–23.
Evans, J. P. (2011) 'Resilience, ecology and adaptation in the experimental city', *Transactions of the Institute of British Geographers* 36, 2: 223–237.
Franck, K. A., & Stevens, Q. (2007) *Loose space: Possibility and diversity in urban life*, London: Routledge.
Fuad-Luke, A. (2009) *Design activism: Beautiful strangeness for a sustainable world*, London: Earthscan.
Fuller, R. A., & Irvine, K. N. (2010) 'Interactions between people and nature in urban environments', in K. Gaston (ed.) *Urban ecology*, Cambridge: Cambridge University Press, 134–171.
Gandy, M. (2006) 'Urban nature and the ecological imaginary', in N. C. Heynen, M. Kaika, & E. Swyngedouw (eds.) *In the nature of cities: Urban political ecology and the politics of urban metabolism*, London: Routledge, 63–74.
Gehl, J. (2010) *Cities for people*, Washington, DC: Island Press.
Grimm, N. B., Faeth, S. H., Golubiewski, N. E., Redman, C. L., Wu, J., Bai, X., & Briggs, J. M. (2008) 'Global change and the ecology of cities', *Science* 319, 5864: 756–760.
Harvey, D. (2003) 'The right to the city', *International Journal of Urban and Regional Research* 27: 939–941.
Heynen, N. C., Kaika, M., & Swyngedouw, E. (2006) 'Urban political ecology: Politicizing the production of urban natures', in N. C. Heynen, M. Kaika, & E. Swyngedouw (eds.) *In the nature of cities: Urban political ecology and the politics of urban metabolism*, London: Routledge, 1–20.
Hommels, A. (2005) *Unbuilding cities: Obduracy in urban sociotechnical change*, Cambridge, MA and London: MIT Press.
Hou, J. (2010) *Insurgent public space: Guerrilla urbanism and the remaking of Contemporary cities*, London: Routledge.
Hough, M. (2004) *Cities and natural process: A basis for sustainability*, 2nd edn, London: Routledge.
Howett, C. (1998) 'Ecological values in twentieth-century landscape design: A history and hermeneutics', *Landscape Journal* 17, 2: 80–98.

Inerfeld, R. B., & Blom, B. B. (2001) 'A new tool for strengthening urban neighborhoods', *Journal of Affordable Housing and Community Development Law* 11: 128–134.

Jackson, L. (2003) 'The relationship of urban design to human health and condition', *Landscape and Urban Planning* 64, 4: 191–200.

Jacobs, J. (1961) *The death and life of great American cities*, New York: Random House.

Kaika, M., & Swyngedouw, E. (2000) 'Fetishizing the modern city: The phantasmagoria of urban technological networks', *International Journal of Urban and Regional Research* 24, 1: 120–138.

Kaplan, R., & Kaplan, S. (1989) *The experience of nature: A psychological perspective*, Cambridge: Cambridge University Press.

Kaplan, S. (2000) 'Human nature and environmentally responsible behavior', *Journal of Social Issues* 56, 3: 491–508.

Kellert, S. R., & Wilson, E. O. (1995) *The Biophilia Hypothesis*, Washington, DC: Island Press.

Kim, J., & Kaplan, R. (2004) 'Physical and psychological factors in sense of community: New urbanist Kentlands and nearby Orchard Village', *Environment & Behavior* 36, 3: 313–340.

Kirk, W. (1952) 'Historical geography and the concept of the behavioural environment' *Indian Geographical Journal, Silver Jubilee*, 152–160; reprinted in F. W. Boal & D. N. Livingston (eds.) (1989) *The Behavioural Environment: Essays in Reflection, Application and Re-evaluation*, London and New York: Routledge, 18–32.

Krasny, M., & Tidball, K. (2010) 'Civic ecology: Linking social and ecological approaches in extension', *Journal of Extension* 48, 1: 1–5.

Kuo, F. E., & Sullivan, W. C. (2001a) 'Environment and crime in the inner city: Does vegetation reduce crime?', *Environment and Behavior* 33, 3: 343–367.

Kuo, F. E., & Sullivan, W. C. (2001b) 'Aggression and violence in the inner city: Effects of environment via mental fatigue', *Environment and Behavior* 33, 4: 543–571.

Kuo, F., Sullivan, W., Levine Coley, R., & Brunson, L. (1998) 'Fertile ground for community: Inner-city neighborhood common spaces', *American Journal of Community Psychology* 26, 6: 823–851.

Lydon, M., Bartman, D., Woudstra, R., & Khawarzad, A. (2010) Tactical urbanism (vol. 1) Available: http://www.scribd.com/doc/51354266/Tactical-Urbanism-Volume (accessed 24 January 2013).

Lynch, K. (1960) *The Image of the City*, Cambridge, MA: MIT Press.

Mayer, F., & Frantz, C. (2004) 'The connectedness to nature scale: A measure of individuals' feeling in community with nature', *Journal of Environmental Psychology* 24: 503–515.

Mean, M., & Tims, C. (2005) *People make places: growing the public life of cities*, London: Demos.

Miller, J. R. (2005) 'Biodiversity conservation and the extinction of experience', *Trends in Ecology & Evolution* 20, 8: 430–434.

Mitchell, W. J. T. (1994) *Landscape and power*, Chicago, IL and London: University of Chicago Press.

Naik, D., & Oldfield, T. (2010) *Critical cities: Ideas, knowledge and agitation from emerging urbanists*, London: Myrdle Court Press.

Ndubisi, F. (2002) *Ecological planning: A historical and comparative synthesis*, Baltimore, MD: JHU Press.

Nurse, J., Basher, D., Bone, A., & Bird, W. (2010) 'An ecological approach to promoting population mental health and well-being – A response to the challenge of climate change', *Perspectives in Public Health* 130, 1: 27–33.

Orr, D. W. (1994) *Earth in mind: On education, environment, and the human prospect*, Washington, DC: Island Press.

Potteiger, M., & Purinton, J. (1998) *Landscape narratives: Design practices for telling stories*, New York: John Wiley and Sons.

Ranganathan, J., Raudsepp-Hearne, C., Lucas, N., Irwin, F., Zurek, M., Bennett, K., Ash, N., & West, P. (2008) *Ecosystem services: A guide for decision makers*, Washington, DC: World Resources Institute.

Relph, E. (1989) 'A curiously unbalanced condition of the powers of the mind: Realism and the ecology of environmental experience', in F. W. Boal, & D. N. Livingstone (eds.) *The behavioural environment: Essays in reflection, application and re-evaluation*, London and New York: Routledge, 277–288.

Salafsky, N., Margoluis, R., & Redford, K. (2001) *Adaptive management: A tool for conservation practitioners*, Bethesda, MD: Foundations of Success.

Smith, N. (2006) 'Foreword', in N. C. Heynen, M. Kaika, & E. Swyngedouw (eds.) *In the nature of cities: Urban political ecology and the politics of urban metabolism*, London and New York: Routledge, xi–xv.

Strang, G. (1996) 'Infrastructure as landscape', *Places* 10, 3: 8–15.

Teel, T., Manfredo, M., & Stinchfield, H. (2007) 'The need and theoretical basis for exploring wildlife value orientations cross-culturally', *Human Dimensions of Wildlife* 12, 5: 297–305.

Termorshuizen, J. W., & Opdam, P. (2009) 'Landscape services as a bridge between landscape ecology and sustainable development', *Landscape Ecology* 24, 8: 1037–1052.

Tippett, J., & Searle, B. (2005) 'Social learning in public participation in river basin management – early findings from HarmoniCOP European case studies', *Environmental Science & Policy* 8: 287–299.

Tippett, J., Handley, J., & Ravetz, J. (2007) 'Meeting the challenges of sustainable development – A conceptual appraisal of a new methodology for participatory ecological planning', *Progress in Planning* 67, 1: 9–98.

Trosper, R. (2005) 'Emergence unites ecology and society', *Ecology and Society*, 10, 1: 14. Available: http://www.ecologyandsociety.org/vol10/iss1/art14/ (accessed 24 January 2013).

Tuan, Y. (1977) *Space and place: The perspective of experience*, Minneapolis, MN: University of Minnesota Press.

Tzoulas, K., Korpela, K., Venn, S., Ylipelkonen, V., Kazmierczak, A., Niemela, J., & James, P. (2007) 'Promoting ecosystem and human health in urban areas using Green Infrastructure: A literature review', *Landscape and Urban Planning* 81, 3: 167–178.

Walker, B., Holling, C. S., Carpenter, S. R., & Kinzig, A. (2004) 'Resilience, adaptability and transformability in social-ecological systems', *Ecology and Society* 9, 2: 5. Available: http://www.ecologyandsociety.org/vol9/iss2/art5/ (accessed 24 January 2013).

6

THE CONTRIBUTION OF GREENERY IN MULTI-FAMILY HOUSES AS A FACTOR OF WELL-BEING

Irene Yerro Vela

Introduction

This chapter explores a key factor of well-being: the social and ecological contributions made by greenery in the semi-private outdoor spaces of multi-family houses, involving the analysis of two case studies of innovative and experimental housing projects in Zurich (Switzerland). It presents these studies in the context that the social contribution of green spaces should concern offering possibilities for use and comfort in relation to well-being, rather than imposing social behaviour. These semi-private, outdoor spaces are framed in a dense, urban context where issues like access to nature, free space for children to play (Hübscher and Kohler, 2007), car-free areas and open-air places for informal meetings constitute a palette of elements to achieve a better quality of life. The social contribution of green spaces is about offering different possibilities of use, user identification, and social belonging; each component forming constructs of well-being. Moreover, the research presents a palette of elements in outdoor spaces which can help to achieve a better quality of life and add extra value to a housing development. Discussion is set within the wider context of sustainable urban development where well-being is often an implied component, but one which is not always made explicit within design criteria or prescribed regarding the inclusion of 'free space'. To address this I explore the issue from an architect's perspective to examine the role of greenery in a framework of sustainable design which embraces well-being in addition to other facets of design performance.

The problem

Evidence of the need to rethink urban development models can be found in the next century's global human challenges including urbanisation, poverty, climate change, and destruction of natural resources. The new sustainable design of cities is a complex and multidimensional topic that involves different issues such as infrastructure, mobility, energy balance in buildings, water and waste treatments, urban green, and citizens' well-being. Cities whose residents sustain a relatively high quality of life, like Vienna and Zurich, share common features: small-scale distances, good infrastructure, security, cultural offerings, and green spaces. The environmental benefits of greenery are broadly known[1] and proven, but the question is how do we include vegetated structures at different scales (cities, neighbourhoods, buildings) and how can greenery contribute to a more sustainable human development in all dimensions: ecological, social, and economic?

If we consider the city as a possible solution to upcoming challenges, the role of the green, in a literal sense, has to be redefined. Environmentalists and ecologists have started to work together with architects to provide new kinds of architectural solutions. The changing boundaries between disciplines create new fields of knowledge that will shape future inquiries into architecture and urban design.

Because our cities' main urban fabric consists of housing complexes, including greenery in buildings could make an important contribution to sustainable urban development. In order to make our cities more liveable, should we include landscape requirements for green-factor systems in housing complexes? Green factor systems are landscape requirements designed to increase the quantity and quality of planted areas in some cities while allowing flexibility for developers and designers to meet development standards. Recent history shows us how European cities have a tradition of incorporating greenery. In 1994, Berlin (Germany) introduced the Biotope Area Factor (BAF), which was intended to incorporate green landscaping throughout the city environment. Ten years later, Malmö (Sweden) implemented a similar programme as Malmö's Green Space Factor system (GSF). Some North American cities have emulated Swedish and German practices demonstrating that urban landscaping requirements provide numerous ecological, economic, and social benefits. Seattle, Washington (USA) has implemented a strategy called Seattle Green Factor. The Green Factor, which is a scoring system, is designed to encourage larger plants, permeable paving, green roofs, vegetated walls, preservation of existing trees, and layering of vegetation along streets and other areas visible to the public. In addition to being attractive, green elements in the landscape improve air quality, create habitat for birds and beneficial insects, and mitigate urban heat-island effects. They also reduce storm-water run-off, protecting receiving waters and decreasing public infrastructure costs.

Approach

This research aims to demonstrate and confirm why greenery is important in the outdoor spaces of multi-family housing projects. At the same time, the benefits of including greenery will be explained mainly in social and ecological terms. Furthermore, it will suggest the key factors that result in the more than satisfying performances of the two analysed projects. Another important issue is to examine whether the architects and planners have fulfilled the owners' concepts and expectations. Finally, the case studies will support arguments for the proposal of municipal policies to promote the inclusion of greenery in private residential projects. Some cities have already done this for other kinds of spaces such as commercial and public ones, for example, green factor systems.

Two housing complexes located in Zurich (Switzerland) are presented as case studies. The first is Pflegi Areal (2002) designed by Gigon & Guyer Architects and Schweingrüber Zulauf (landscape architects), and the second is Hegianwandweg, which was planned by EM2N Architects, also in collaboration with the landscape architects Schweingrüber Zulauf.

In each case greenery placed in the outdoor spaces plays a central and attracting role in the design layout. A landscape architect in collaboration with the architects is responsible for the design of the outdoor spaces. The innovative and experimental housing projects presented here have already been recognised. The Pflegi-Areal housing complex was awarded an 'Auszeichnung für gute Bauten' (award for architectural excellence) by the city of Zurich in 2005. The Hegianwandweg Housing Project was awarded the same prize in 2006 with an additional mention for the complex's community centre. Swiss architecture is respected worldwide, with admiring international scrutiny particularly fixed on Swiss residential construction (Elser and Rieper, 2009).

Both cases are located in Zurich and were analysed in detail with interviews with the owners and personal observations beyond the detailed bibliographic research. Since 1998, the municipal government has invested, in particular, in housing construction. Public lots are leased to cooperative building associations for the construction of houses or housing developments with family apartments. These cases were selected on the basis that they are both recent projects (built in the last 10 years), from a multi-family house typology and comprise between 20 and 100 dwellings. Finally, the projects have different ownership patterns: a private and a cooperative association. This selection was done to study the different requirements and concepts that lay behind a property owner's intentions.

Analytical method

The following analytical method covers the different levels of complexity of each project: from physical or tangible aspects to cultural levels involving social behaviours and backgrounds. The two multi-family housing complexes have been analysed on five different levels:

- The architecture level of the project is explained by plans, diagrams, and descriptions of the architectural concept and idea.
- The sustainability level is assessed through the building's social, economic, and ecological performance. This is a subjective analysis following the SIA 112/1[2] recommendation and is displayed in a self-assessment card for each building.

- The landscape level of analysis considers green spaces: layout of the greenery in regards to plans, diagrams and images that shape the disposal, distribution and description of the green areas. The ecological impact of the green areas is also explained.
- The qualitative level of the analysis is drawn from the results obtained from expert interviews, clients' assessment, and inhabitants' experiences. All this information will be included in the social level: usage of the greenery.
- Finally, the main contribution of greenery in each project and the most remarkable features will be described.

Findings

Case study 1: Pflegi Areal, Zurich

Architectural level

The buildings in the former 'Pflegerinnenschule Zürich' hospital allowed a clear development within the existing building complex and the newly constructed buildings for the new office and housing functions. The buildings in the south-west portion of the parcel, designed by Pfister Architects from 1933/34, were retained and were converted to offices, while the hospital building in the north-east portion of the parcel, heterogeneous with regard to use, construction area, and authorship, was converted to housing.[3] Despite the partial replacement of the existing complex, the project retained the large-scale facility's spatial character. Analogous to the building complex of the former hospital, on the one hand, and the neighbouring buildings with solitary apartment houses, on the other hand, the new buildings 'oscillate' between a closed block development and individual building volumes.

The apartments in the newly constructed buildings primarily cover an entire floor with generous floor plans. A total of 48 apartments with 22 different floor plan types are divided into 2.5 to 6.5 room apartments. In addition, nine ateliers at courtyard level were built. Placing the ancillary and wet spaces at the centre of the apartments generates an important and enriching sense of unfettered roundabout movement in the apartments. The wet-room core allows minimal and conventional room divisions in the apartments.

Some apartments (7 from 48) have exterior spaces in the form of terraces. Most apartments, however, possess a kind of 'outer-air, inner space', also called a 'seasonal room'. Their size varies from 8 to 12m^2 and they are fully heated. They transform into an open loggia in good weather and can be used as a normal interior space during the rest of the year. Concrete is used for the basic construction as well as for the interior flooring. Powerful window openings lend the apartments generous daylight and breadth. The highly perforated wall surfaces become skeleton-like structures and give the apartments, analogous to the existing buildings, a matter-of-fact, urban expression (A+U No.11, 2006).

The colours, in the form of mineral-based, high-matter pigments, contrast with the unpretentious, common expression of the architectural language. The use of colour was developed in collaboration with the artist Adrian Schiess. Specific 'signature colours' were identified for the external surfaces enclosing each of the outside spaces (Carmen Court and garden) in order to express precisely their atmosphere. Light yellow, beige, orange, and red tones presented the first choice on the competition level. In the end, different colours were used. A yellow–green tone and white are the colours of the facades of the Carmen Court. A blue paint was chosen for the garden-side facade.

Sustainability level

Table 6.1 contains an evaluation of Pflegi Areal against SIA 112/1.

TABLE 6.1 Self-evaluation according to SIA 112/1, Pflegi Areal, Zurich

		Relevance	*Conformance*
Social			
Community	Integration, social intermix	Not relevant	Achieved
	Social contacts	Not relevant	n/a
	Solidarity, fairness	Not relevant	n/a
	Participation	Not relevant	n/a
Design	Spatial identity, mixed uses	Highly relevant	Best practice
	Individual design, personalisation	Highly relevant	Best practice
Use, development	Basic supply, mixed uses	Highly relevant	Best practice
	Slow traffic and public transport	Highly relevant	Best practice
	Accessibility/usability for everyone	Highly relevant	Best practice
Well-being	Security	Highly relevant	Best practice
	Light	Highly relevant	Best practice
	Compartment air	Highly relevant	Best practice
	Radiation	Not relevant	n/a
	Thermal protection in summer	Highly relevant	Best practice
	Noises, vibration	Relevant	Achieved

(continued)

TABLE 6.1 Self-evaluation according to SIA 112/1, Pflegi Areal, Zurich (continued)

Economy			
Building fabric	Location	Highly relevant	Best practice
	Building fabric	Highly relevant	Best practice
	Building structure/alteration	Highly relevant	Best practice
Building costs	Life cycle costs	Highly relevant	Best practice
	Financing	Highly relevant	Best practice
	External costs	Relevant	Best practice
Operation/maintenance	Operation and servicing	Highly relevant	Achieved
	Repair	Highly relevant	Achieved
Ecology			
Building materials	Resources, availability	Highly relevant	Best practice
	Environmental impact	Highly relevant	Best practice
	Harmful substances	Highly relevant	Best practice
	Deconstruction	Highly relevant	Best practice
Operational energy	Heat (cold) for indoor environm.	Highly relevant	Best practice
	Heat for warm water	Highly relevant	Best practice
	Electricity	Highly relevant	Best practice
	Coverage of energy demand	Highly relevant	Best practice
Soil and land	Site area	Highly relevant	Best practice
	Outdoor installations	Highly relevant	Best practice
Infrastructure	Mobility	Highly relevant	Best practice
	Waste from operation and use	Highly relevant	Best practice
	Water	Not relevant	Not achieved

Landscape architecture level

Together with the existing buildings, the new housing development demarcates and defines three large exterior areas: the garden (Patientenhof), the Samaritan Court (Samaritenhof) and the Carmen Court (Innenhof).

Patientenhof: As indicated by the name, this was the former garden for patients. The landscape architects decided to make some small improvements and left it almost entirely unchanged. The garden has a main grass area where some Japanese reed bushes were planted (Figure 6.1). This solution preserves the space as a playground and contributes to the creation of a quiet, serene, and pleasant ambience. The big, old, beautiful trees make this space the most vegetated with a strong, literally green character. Extensive shade created by trees makes the area ideal for summer recreation activities. In addition, the blue colour of the building facade intensifies the old atmosphere of the garden. In a corner, a playground for children includes sandboxes and a water gutter (Figure 6.1). This space is not only used by the children who live in Pflegi Areal but also by children belonging to a close-by kindergarten (Spielgruppe).

Innenhof: The Carmen Court is the place of the former nurses' garden; a new parking garage has been built under it. The court stretches across the entire length of the parcel (150m long and 23m wide). This outdoor space connects and provides access to the buildings' entrances. This space has a specific layout; materials, colours, and plants were carefully chosen to create a special atmosphere. The ground consists of fine gravel as well as large, poured-concrete slabs, which form a wide access-path to the apartments' entrances. Rebar baskets filled with pebbles and earth form a nutritional ground habitat and space for roots as well as a counterweight for trees over the garage slab (Silverwene trees). The trees here work like artificial ones and are placed on the ground as 'pieces of furniture' to provide the desired privacy to the inhabitants and to create a special atmosphere. The colours of the building's facade (light yellow and white) in combination with the rebar wire baskets reflect the sunlight and create a special atmosphere (Figure 6.2).

Samaritenhof: As the smallest outdoor space at Pflegi Areal, Samaritenhof serves as a new access for the underground parking garage and offers drop-off and parking spaces for the health centre. Large concrete slabs provide the materialisation of this car-circulation area. In some parts, the slabs are fixed to the ground and in some they are macadamised. Some existing and new trees are additionally framed by a wire grid to set them off from the vehicular area. This outdoor space has a clear concept, with contrast between the light, concrete floor slabs and the rust-red fence as a prominent feature of this space (Figure 6.3).

FIGURE 6.1 Pflegi Areal, green spaces, Patientenhof

FIGURE 6.2 Pflegi Areal, green spaces, Innenhof

FIGURE 6.3 Pflegi Areal, green spaces, Samaritenhof

Social level: the use of greenery

INHABITANT ASSESSMENT

Appreciation: The Innenhof is usually described as the most beautiful part of the Pflegi Areal complex. The elegant and Mediterranean-style layout with the trees in the stone baskets is highly appreciated by the residents who feel it has a special and calm atmosphere and they are generally able to identify with the space (Hürlimann and Frey, 2006). The owners also greatly appreciate the Patientengarten. The harmony between the park and the playground was most frequently mentioned as a pleasant element. The conservation of the old trees makes this space quite respected. 'It is quite nice to live in a central and urban location and at the same time enjoy the view of the changing seasons reflected in the old trees'.[4] Residents seldom mention the Samaritenhof. Its parking function makes it less popular, mainly just serving a practical function.

Use: Most tenants very seldom use the outdoor spaces and some tenants never engage in activities in the outdoor spaces. The Innenhof functions as a circulation and communication space between the apartments and the streets. Only a few residents go for a walk, read, or play with their children in the outdoor spaces of Pflegi Areal. Due to the mostly professional jobs of the residents and the lack of families with children, the spaces do not need to serve any special function. Some tenants were a little critical of the outdoor spaces and pointed to some problems. For example, some find the Innenhof to be an anonymous and inanimate space with a cold atmosphere. The trees of the Innenhof do not provide enough shade on hot summer days. The metal furniture becomes hot in the summer sun, making it unusable on summer days. These are not very practical solutions. The Patientengarten is used by some tenants as a recreational space.

Greenery in the outdoor spaces: Most tenants think that the outdoor spaces contain enough plants, but would like more trees. The Patientenhof's old trees provide good and cool shade especially on hot, sunny summer days. Residents appreciate the layout of the old Patientengarten with the old trees and the new Japanese reeds. Some people find the trees in the stone baskets from the Innenhof a little artificial. The changing and living aspect of the Patientenhof is much appreciated by the tenants whose windows face this green space. The appearance of the Japanese bushes in winter, when they are cut and look almost invisible, contrasts greatly with their appearance during summer, when they are tall and create a vivid field of different textures.

Places for children: In Pflegi Areal, only a few families have children. They frequently use the outdoor spaces despite limited possibilities for varied activities. The Patientenhof is not perceived as a place to play football, or to play or to run. The families would prefer spaces with weaker aesthetic concepts and more practical solutions for everyday life: for example, the Innenhof could be more than a meeting point or their children could play football in the Patientenhof.

A positive aspect is that the parents allow their children to play in the outdoor spaces without security issue concerns.

Rules: The outdoor spaces at Pflegi Areal are well maintained and tidy. A caretaker is responsible for the whole complex and for enforcing the rules for use, ensuring the appropriate functioning of the place. Most tenants appreciate this degree of order, but some do not. A person from the ateliers once tried to use the Innenhof in an alternative way by bringing her own chairs to the outdoor space (Rigutto, 2004). This action was not allowed because private furniture is not permitted in the outdoor space, as they disturb the style and aesthetics of the space.

OWNER ASSESSMENT[5]

The owners wanted to create an attractive urban space that matches the modern design of the buildings. Thus, they assumed that tenants would prefer to not have to undertake any garden maintenance. They sought to develop a space that could be strongly influenced by architectural lines. This space should invite a dialog between buildings and space and add a value to the whole housing complex. 'Exclusive' design is the keyword which defines the outdoor spaces and which justifies the high cost of the rents.

In this project, the aims and needs of the owners were very specific and the final result fulfilled their wishes. They were not especially concerned about any social concept. The project was fully realised as proposed by the architects and landscape architects.

The owners were not particularly concerned about concepts of ecology and participation. In the same way, the owners did not place a high importance on the use of the outdoor spaces, therefore, they were not expecting many activities to take place there.

The tenants' level of use of the space was not important. The owners wanted the inhabitants to identify and appreciate its aesthetic value. Its exclusive design makes it a very appealing space for creative professionals (such as authors, designers, and architects).

The expenditure on semi-private outdoor spaces accounted for 10% of the total cost of the development. This was considered quite a good investment because the project obtained added value. The rental prices in Pflegi Areal are high; few people can afford to pay 2,000 CHF for an apartment with 2.5 rooms or 8,400 CHF for the biggest dwelling, which has 6.5 rooms and a terrace (Hürlimann and Frey, 2006).

A gardening company is contracted to fully maintain the outdoor spaces. A single part-time worker is responsible for lawn maintenance, irrigation, weeding, pruning, and cleaning. Water and electrical maintenance, paving, drainage, and fencing are not included in this service.

Case study 2: Hegianwandweg, Zurich

Architectural level

Concept: The Hegianwandweg is located on land that the Zurich municipal government sold to the housing cooperative FGZ.[6] This cooperative focuses on providing housing for families at a subsidised price; this is its 24th project. The new owners were required to run a design competition in order to build high-quality housing at a reasonable price. The commission was awarded to the young architectural office EM2N that collaborated with landscape architects and some artists. Five compact buildings, with four and five floors, are joined by a hard-surface podium that defines a space accessible for everybody but clearly belonging to the community. The blocks are organised in a composition that preserves the views beyond and to the city and where outdoor spaces play a leading role in the concept of the housing development (Figure 6.4). These blocks are situated on a podium that gives the impression of a large complex related to the neighbouring rows of houses.

Ground floor: The competition brief set out a detailed mix of apartment sizes and number of units, which were interpreted by EM2N to become a flexible matrix of rooms, kitchens and sanitary units. The apartments vary in size between 64m^2 and 139m^2. With the exception of the exterior walls and the massive core, all the division walls can be removed. This allows limitless ground-floor organisation: from a loft space to an apartment with 4.5 rooms and many possibilities in between. Another sign of quality in the apartments is the orientation to the light: all dwellings are lit on two sides and half of the apartments have windows on three sides.

FIGURE 6.4 Hegianwandweg, semi-private outdoor space

Art: Following the Zurich Municipality competition's rules, the project features the artwork of four Swiss artists, which must also have a practical value for the inhabitants. Loris Hersberger designed a fluorescent neon tube installation to create a light sculpture on the ceiling (which has practically no pipes) and marked the entrance to the houses with red rectangles. Private outdoor spaces are provided in the form of individual balconies (2m deep and up to 15m long). Carl Leyer designed a highly recognised, bright-green, pixel-patterned awning. Lang and Bauman contributed by transforming the platform into a playing field. In the staircases, Stefan Altenburger proposed a mirror installation situated on the stair railings.

Construction, colours, facades: Because of technical and construction issues, the building materials are a mix of a concrete core with timber floors and walls. This solution has advantages in terms of flexibility and environmental impact. This innovative approach increased the project's total costs, but the benefits were high; for example, the building period was quite short, only 18 months. Fire protection was important. The fire wardens (Kantonale Feuerpolizei) had a challenging task: a residential building with these dimensions and characteristics had not been built previously but, through consultation, they developed a concept that fits the regulations subsequently implemented as a new standard. The outside appearance of the buildings is not wood but a simple grey plaster facade. Nevertheless, the complex seems very light and warm because of the colourful textile sunblinds placed on the balconies. The facade facing these balconies is also painted in a light-green colour. This combination of colours and materials gives a friendly atmosphere to the whole project and softens the relatively cool treatment of the architecture. This project holds the Swiss energy-efficient, certification label MINERGIE.[7]

Sustainability level

Table 6.2 contains an evaluation of Hegianwandweg against SIA 112/1.

Landscape architecture level

This project follows, in a pioneering way, the philosophy of the FGZ cooperative related to outdoor spaces. The building cooperative's strategy aims to preserve the character of the Friesenberg garden city by keeping the same number of residents and the neighbourhood lifestyle (Schmid and Karn, 2008). Cultivation without chemical products, conservation of the old trees, and common compost methods are some examples of the cooperative's techniques to conserve green spaces.[8]

Central asphalt platform: The central hard-asphalt platform (17m x 135m), which links the five buildings, connects the houses, not only physically as a circulation space, but also as the 'stage' where residents can communicate and have contact with each other. At the same time, escape routes allow people to

The contribution of greenery in multi-family houses 99

TABLE 6.2 Self-evaluation according to SIA 112/1, Hegianwandweg, Zurich

		Relevance	*Conformance*
Social			
Community	Integration, social intermix	Highly relevant	Best practice
	Social contacts	Highly relevant	Best practice
	Solidarity, fairness	Highly relevant	Best practice
	Participation	Highly relevant	Best practice
Design	Spatial identity, mixed uses	Highly relevant	Best practice
	Individual design, personalisation	Highly relevant	Best practice
Use, development	Basic supply, mixed uses	Highly relevant	Best practice
	Slow traffic and public transport	Highly relevant	Best practice
	Accessibility/usability for everyone	Highly relevant	Best practice
Well-being	Security	Highly relevant	Best practice
	Light	Highly relevant	Best practice
	Compartment air	Highly relevant	Best practice
	Radiation	Not relevant	n/a
	Thermal protection in summer	Relevant	Best practice
	Noises, vibration	Relevant	Best practice
Economy			
Building fabric	Location	Highly relevant	Best practice
	Building fabric	Highly relevant	Best practice
	Building structure/alteration	Relevant	Achieved
Building costs	Life cycle costs	Highly relevant	Best practice
	Financing	Relevant	Not achieved
	External costs	Not relevant	n/a
Operation/maintenance	Operation and servicing	Relevant	Achieved
	Repair	Relevant	Achieved

(continued)

TABLE 6.2 Self-evaluation according to SIA 112/1, Hegianwandweg, Zurich (continued)

Ecology			
Building materials	Resources, availability	Highly relevant	Best practice
	Environmental impact	Highly relevant	Best practice
	Harmful substances	Highly relevant	Best practice
	Deconstruction	Highly relevant	Best practice
Operational energy	Heat (cold) for indoor environm.	Highly relevant	Best practice
	Heat for warm water	Highly relevant	Best practice
	Electricity	Highly relevant	Best practice
	Coverage of energy demand	Highly relevant	Best practice
Soil and land	Site area	Highly relevant	Best practice
	Outdoor installations	Highly relevant	Best practice
Infrastructure	Mobility	Highly relevant	Best practice
	Waste from operation and use	Not relevant	Not achieved
	Water	Not relevant	Not achieved

avoid meeting others in case they do not want contact. The artists Lang and Bauman interpreted the space in the frames of sports fields and traffic circulation by placing a pattern of different lines; the yellow and light-blue lines guide the inhabitants and children who enjoy playing in the area. The orthogonal lines with round corners connect the building's entrances and they cross the fields of different colours placed at the centre of the platform (Moll, 2006). This space serves several functions: as a street, vestibule, backyard, playground, and neighbourhood square. It also allows children to play on roller skates, scooters, and skateboards.

Green areas: family vegetable gardens and playground: The landscape architects Schweingruber und Zulauf collaborated with the Zurich University of Applied Sciences (Zürcher Hochschule für Angewandte Wissenschaften) to follow the tradition of the 'garden cities' and create the project's large green areas (9500m^2). The plot had been used as a clay pit and later in-filled to create the family gardens. The open spaces are laid out to enclose the platform. Seven different 'islands' are placed between the houses. They connect to the main platform with different shaped paths of small stones, which generate a variety of spaces. The islands have three main functions: playground (Figure 6.5), vegetable garden (Figure 6.6), and compost areas. The vegetable gardens can be rented by inhabitants from Hegianwandweg or from people who live near there. They are much appreciated; some families, even after moving away from Hegianwandweg, still remain attached to a small piece of land and come regularly to take care of it.

FIGURE 6.5 Hegianwandweg, playground

FIGURE 6.6 Hegianwandweg, vegetable garden

Natural meadow (Magerwiese): The rest of the outdoor space is treated like a natural meadow. The concept was very clear: to restore the original landscape and indigenous plants located at the bottom of the Uetilberg. Due to the special substrate, which does not contain any humus and is mainly made of stones, the different plants needed time to bloom. The landscape architects intelligently mixed fruit trees with bright spring flowers and trees with coloured autumnal leaves that displayed a different colour atmosphere. This organisation and layout emphasises the colourful intervention: parallel colour stripes using a range of species including *Tulipa greigii* (Wildtulpen) originally from the Caucasus Mountains. As a compositional element, *Salix alba* (Silber-Weide) brings a reserved grey-green accent to the whole area (Moll, 2006). This kind of meadow is quite rare in urban spaces and allows specific plant and animal communities to develop as a distinctive local habitat. The research project BiodiverCity belongs to a national research programme 'Forschungsprogramms NFP 54 – Nachhaltige Siedlungs- und Infrastrukturentwicklung'[9] and deals with biodiversity in urban areas. An analysis of the outdoor spaces of Hegianwandweg suggests the keywords 'diversity' and 'multiplicity', as the needs of the users can be combined with its natural qualities to work sustainably for a better ecology. Users are concerned about maintenance and security, where the meadows are maintained as long grass, having the advantage that they require little maintenance: only two cuts per year are sufficient and the low cost of maintenance makes the meadow economically worthwhile. The children can play in the grass fields of Hegianwandweg without worrying about vehicles as underground car parking is accessed directly from the street, making the whole ground-level area car-free.

Social level

INHABITANT ASSESSMENT

Appreciation: Inhabitants identify with and react very positively to the outdoor spaces. Some look at the spaces from a practical perspective and particularly appreciate the freedom and security offered to their children. Other tenants are more concerned about aesthetic issues and find a harmony and beauty in the entire housing-complex design. The diversity of outdoor spaces with a strong ecological feature satisfies most residents since Hegianwandweg outdoor spaces have been designed to provide different scales of access to nature: directly with vegetable gardens and a natural meadow, but also indirectly with wide views of Uetilberg and its surroundings.

Use: The spaces are used in different modalities. The central asphalt platform works like a stage where the outside life of the complex is played. Most activities happen there: children playing, couples talking, neighbours meeting informally, or simply people entering the buildings. At the weekend and in the afternoon, the two playground islands are also often full of children playing. In particular, the central location of the playground for younger children (1 to 6 years old) allows parents to sit on a bench and talk to each other while they watch their little ones. The vegetable gardens are one of the most remarkable and distinctive features of the complex and offer an excellent opportunity for the inhabitants to informally meet and to keep in contact with each other. They find 'something to do' beyond their dwellings and the garden provides the perfect motivation to go out, sometimes helped by their children, and to meet their neighbours. Without these gardens, their contact would probably be less.[10]

Greenery in the outdoor spaces: Apart from the vegetable gardens, which are the distinctive feature of the complex, the natural meadow is also a highlight in the landscape concepts. Residents find it special and valuable. They appreciate and love the changing of the colours during the day, for example blue in the morning. They understand well the importance of wild nature. One resident who has lived in Hegianwandweg for seven years and greatly appreciates and loves the natural grassland landscape said,

> I spent all my childhood living on a farm high in the Alps. The colourful field reminds me of my early years when I used to play outside in the fields. I do not feel nostalgic but I do really like this view of yellow and pink flowers from the penthouse apartment and, at the same time, be able to be in the city centre in less than 15 minutes.[11]

However, a few tenants from an older generation (Second World War) identify more with a traditional English garden layout where grass and flowers require high and intensive maintenance.

> At the beginning, the future meadow looked like a 'moon-land' and some neighbours began to be impatient. There was also a shortage of shade because the trees were too young. However, now the variety of plant colours from yellow to lilac makes this landscape as one of the nicest interventions we have ever done.[12]

Places for children: Hegianwandweg is an ideal place for children and that is one of the reasons why families with children are in the majority. Children can play in almost all of the outdoor spaces and be observed by their parents through the windows or from the balconies. The vegetable garden brings an additional educational advantage where children, by helping their families, can learn about plant cultivation and compost practices.

Rules: Users do not need to place any personal objects in the outdoor spaces to fulfil their needs. The large balconies allow every inhabitant the room to fulfil their own private activities outside. Verbal and visual communication between neighbours across balconies is a frequent practice.

OWNER ASSESSMENT

This project was realised with the support of the Zurich municipal government. They sold land which had formerly been used as gardens and a small-animal reserve to the FGZ. Consequently, the project had to be realised through an architectural competition that, from the very beginning, invited the participation of architects, landscape architects, and artists. The owners very clearly stated, from the very beginning, that they wanted an innovative project that contributes to increasing the quality of the garden city of Uetilberg.

The project is located in an area with a strong tradition of small gardens. The cooperative was providing terraced houses with small gardens from 1924 until 1997. Then, they started to work with new typologies. FGZ is a cooperative concerned about green spaces and therefore they include a 'green concept' in all their projects.

In 1999, the owners organised an architectural competition. The young architect team EM2N won their first big project. Despite the project's success, some planning difficulties were encountered. Architects and clients had to compromise between their needs and aesthetic features like porch roofs, staircases, and final paving for the terraces. At completion, the project was a little more expensive (3 per cent) than planned, but the owners said they would do it again. The landscape architects and the Rapperswill Hochschule collaborated on testing plant species in a new way. At first nothing grew in the fields because of the special local substrata. The neighbourhood had to wait patiently until the first flowers appeared. The clients were also interested in restoring old habitats for flora and fauna. Thus the concept of the natural meadow fitted perfectly. The cooperative is quite engaged with ecological topics and is the largest producer of compost in Switzerland.

Neighbourhood participation was organised according to a green-concept commission. People's wishes and needs were heard and implementation was attempted. Despite their general satisfaction with the initial plans, they asked for another 'playground island' for children from 10 to 15 years old. This resulted in two different playgrounds.

The semi-private outdoor spaces have a strong social concept: an open character where everybody can meet. For this reason, the ground-floor apartments have a terrace elevated one metre above the ground. In each apartment, everybody has his/her own private outdoor space but, at the ground level, the space belongs to all. The second feature of the open space was to provide a place for children to play: playgrounds with swings and sandboxes. The complex is particularly suitable for children, who can play on the asphalt surface, in the grass fields, and in the playground islands. The space is used in different ways. People from different cultural backgrounds meet, often to chat and spend their leisure time simply relaxing and reading. The cooperative's regulations require that big apartments, for example with 5.5 rooms, must be inhabited by families with children. Thus, when the children grow up and leave the 'parents' nest', the parents must also leave their apartment. Usually the cooperative offers them a variety of new housing that better fits their new requirements. In Hegianwandweg, approximately one third of the apartments (small ones) are used by people without children. Around 12 per cent of the budget was invested in greenery and outdoor spaces. The owners are very satisfied with this. The main reason is that the inhabitants' identification with the spaces gives an extra value to the complex. This makes it very attractive for families who want to interact with other families; this is the most popular of all the cooperative's projects. Possible improvements could include paying more attention to the insulation between the apartments. Big apartments need better acoustic insulation to limit noise from the neighbours. However, the outdoor spaces need no improvements. They are considered perfect.

The FGZ has its own gardening service. Nine people are fully employed and throughout the year maintain the complex's green spaces and those of the cooperative's other housing developments. A control commission makes annual checks on the quality of the work. In addition, every neighbour must take care of his or her garden. In cases where residents do not maintain their own gardens, the right to the land is given to another resident.

Conclusions

The Pflegi Areal demonstrates how different qualities of outdoor spaces bring extra value to the housing development. This project's first success is completely fulfilling the requirements of the owners. The spaces were created with a strong and powerful artificial-design concept, which combined very well with the buildings. The Diakonises Stiftung found this to be a very good investment due to the quality of the project. They are able to rent the apartments easily and charge very high rents (between 4,000 CHF and 7,600 CHF). This outstanding design adapts very well to the inhabitant's needs. The target user group for these spaces includes professionals, workers, couples, and a few families with children. They find that the project satisfies their urban lifestyles. Consequently, the outdoor spaces were not made with the intention of promoting contact between the neighbours (probably most residents prefer to have a degree of anonymity, meeting their friends or colleagues somewhere else in the city), but rather to convey a special atmosphere. Architects and landscape architects worked together to find a solution that makes the project an outstanding one. Outside and inside spaces are in harmony and the whole housing development has unity. This project demonstrates how collaboration between architects and landscape architects is very desirable; it should be a common practice creating extra value for housing developments.

The needs of the inhabitants in Hegianwandweg are different from the ones from Pflegi Areal, but their needs were also fulfilled. Families with children or families who had lived previously in the neighbourhood (Friesenberg) had a strong desire for natural green spaces. The vegetable gardens and the natural meadow are the perfect answer for these residents. People use the outdoor spaces as planned, for example to meet, to talk, to walk, and to play. The vegetable gardens are noteworthy and require additional comment because the inhabitants really appreciate and love them. People who have moved to another housing complex still remain attached to their small garden and return to take care of it. This example shows how it is possible to combine, in a smart way, users' wishes and ecological objectives. Some new projects which also use these concepts can be seen in Siedlung Vista Verde in Zürich and in Siedlung Hardegg in Bern (Gadient, 2009). Native fauna and flora were restored allowing different species to grow again. Composting techniques have been used here, and they contribute to one of the biggest Swiss compost associations (FGZ). The cooperation between architects, landscape architects and, in this case, some artists from the very beginning of the competition phase, produced very fruitful results. The outdoor spaces are configured following a strong idea that fits with the architecture composition: different functions which bring different qualities of space.

Considering that the main urban fabric consists of housing complexes, each of these types of buildings carries with it an important contribution to increasing and restoring biodiversity in an urban context.

A critical mass now demands a new architecture focusing on sustainable construction and environmental practices. For sensitive and environmentally concerned people, ecological issues are a decisive factor when buying or renting an apartment. They want to have full identification with the place where they live. Having a green space goes beyond the pragmatic and objective natural benefits to a more subjective and personal field, where inhabitants want to make their own contribution to 'sustainability' by living in 'green' dwellings which, in turn, contribute to a sense of belonging with values that are associated with quality of life and well-being.

The social contribution from green spaces is more about offering possibilities of use, comfort, and well-being than to impose social behaviour. These semi-private, outdoor spaces are framed in a dense, urban context where issues like access to nature, free space for children to play (Hübscher and Kohler, 2007), car-free areas and open-air places for informal meetings constitute a palette of elements to achieve a better quality of life.

Although this work does not closely examine the economic aspects of greenery, some lessons can be learned concerning this important third pillar of sustainability (economic, environmental, and social). Greenery can also be a good economic investment that can bring extra value to the architecture. The price for rental or purchase can reflect this extra value. Good quality usually has a high price; however, some examples have revealed that the best green places do not need a huge investment.

Quality outdoor spaces with greenery can be achieved with interdisciplinary professional teams that work together from the beginning of the design process and integrate and fulfil owners' needs and wishes by implementing solutions within the budget frame. Greenery maintenance costs play an important role and must fit the owners' budgets and needs. Again, professional advice and recommendations are relevant and reveal the importance of communication between planners and owners.

Notes

1 Heat from the Earth is trapped in the atmosphere due to high levels of carbon dioxide (CO_2) and other heat trapping gases that limit release of heat into space – creating a phenomenon known as the 'green-house effect'. Plants remove (sequester) CO_2 from the atmosphere during photosynthesis to form carbohydrates used in plant structure/function and return oxygen back to the atmosphere as a by-product.
2 The SIA (Schweizerischer Architekten und Ingenieur-Verein) recommendation SIA 112/1 'Sustainable construction – building construction' is a tool for communication between commissioning and planners in the order and the provision of special planning services for sustainable building in the areas of society, economy, and environment.
3 Gigon & Guyer Architects, email to the author, 26 April 2010.
4 Conversation with inhabitant of the Pflegi Areal, 10 December 2009.
5 Dr Hans Thöni (Business Director of Stiftung Diakoniewerk Neumünster-Schweizerische Pflegerinnenschule), email message to author, 7 May 2010.
6 FGZ: Familienheim-Genossenschaft Zürich
7 MINERGIE, a Swiss concept and registered trade mark, is an advanced building standard and a quality label for new and modernised buildings. It is building standard which stands for lower energy consumption at a higher level of comfort. A MINERGIE building consumes around 60 per cent less energy than a conventional building. The most important arguments in favour of MINERGIE buildings are comfort and good long-term maintenance of value. Thanks to good and consistent thermal insulation and a fan-assisted, balanced ventilation system MINERGIE guarantees a higher quality of life and increases the value of the building to a considerable degree. Building clients, architects, and planners are completely free in the design and choice of materials and in the internal and external structure of their building. MINERGIE is designed to be economically competitive and therefore one of its rules is that the construction costs of new MINERGIE buildings should not be more than 10 per cent higher than the average conventional building.
8 Die Gärten am Friesenberg-Bedeutung der Grünraumen für das Quartier, Zürich: Familienheim-Genossenschaft Zürich, 12–13
9 BiodiverCity: http://www.biodivercity.ch (accessed 20 May 2013).
10 Annelies Adam (architect and expert in housing), interviewed 26 June 2010.
11 Conversation with resident of Hegianwandweg, 17 May 2010.
12 Heinz Aeberli (Director of Construction and Planning Department FGZ), interviewed 26 April 2010.

References

A+U N°11 (2006). *Die Gärten am Friesenberg-Bedeutung der Grünraumen für das Quartier*, Zürich: Familienheim Genossenschaft Zürich, 103.

Elser, O. and Rieper, M. (2009). *Wohnmodelle: Experiment und Alltag* [im Rahmen der Ausstellung Wohnmodelle – Experiment und Alltag, 16. Dezember 2008 bis 22. Februar 2009 im Künstlerhaus Wien], Wien: Folio Verl., 177–8.

Gadient, H. (2009). *Für Kinder und Käfer:* Wohnen: Wohnbaugenossenschaften Schweiz, Verband der gemeinnützigen Wohnbauträger, 6. Zürich: Wohnbaugenossenschaften Schweiz, Verband der gemeinnützigen Wohnbauträger, 24–7.

Hübscher, S. and Kohler, E. (2007). Beurteilung öffentlicher und privater Spielplätze in der Stadt Zürich, Zurich: Internal Study from Grün Stadt Zürich.

Hürlimann, L. and Frey, S. (2006). Die Aussenräume: Pflegi-Areal, Gigon/Guyer: Regina Kägi-Hof, Theo Hotz, Zürich: ETH Zürich, Departement Architektur.

Moll, C. (2006). *Zürich: Ein Begleiter zu neuer Landschaftsarchitektur*, München: Callwey, 22–3.

Rigutto, S. (2004). 'Kaserne der Schönheit'. *Weltwoche*. Die Weltwoche Ausgabe, http://www.weltwoche.ch/ausgaben/2004-12/artikel-2004-12-kaserne-der-schoenheit.html (accessed 26 May 2010).

Schmid, P. and Karn, S. (2008). 'Freiraum und Landschaftsarchitektur im gemeinnützigen Wohnungsbau in Zürich – Wohnen morgen: Standortbestimmung und Perspektiven des gemeinnützigen Wohnungsbaus', Zürich: Neue Zürcher Zeitung, 99–109.

7

THIRD PLACES FOR THE THIRD AGE

The contribution of playable space to the well-being of older people

Benedict Spencer, Katie Williams, Lamine Mahdjoubi and Rachel Sara

Introduction

The urban public realm offers the potential opportunity for people of all ages to experience and benefit from the joy, excitement, creativity and fun associated with play. Public open spaces have huge potential to improve the well-being of older people and the aspiration of providing enjoyable public places has been included in many manifestos and principles for urban design (Jacobs and Appleyard, 1987; Project for Public Spaces, 2010). However, the opportunity for joyfulness, let alone playfulness, is lacking in much of England's public realm, which still has the potential to be transformed from the barely functional to the playful and delightful.

The lack of playfulness in the public realm particularly affects older people as they have the potential time and opportunity to undertake a variety of activities there but do not have the outdoor spaces that respond to their needs. This is important as the demography of the UK is changing, with both greater numbers and a larger proportion of older people in the population; it is predicted that by 2035, 23 per cent of the population will be aged 65 or over (Office for National Statistics, 2011). The third age (Laslett, 1996) has been characterised as 'a period which can be dedicated to self, self-realisation and intrinsic satisfaction' (Blane, 2005). This suggests that the third age could be an ideal time for playfulness.

The importance for older people of 'third places' 'that host the regular, voluntary, informal and happily anticipated gatherings of individuals beyond the realms of home and work' (Oldenburg, 1999) has been acknowledged. Some have argued for the provision of 'neighbourhoods with more enriching resources' for older people (Lawton, 1986). However, the possibility of third places as spaces in which older people can play has, to date, only been explored in terms of fast food restaurants (Cheang, 2002). At a time when the number of appropriate indoor third places in England (such as restaurants, cafés and pubs) is thought to be reducing, particularly in deprived neighbourhoods (Hickman, 2010), it is important to consider the potential role of the broader public realm – including outdoor space.

The concept of 'playable space', which has been incorporated within planning guidance in the UK (Greater London Authority, 2012), is important in this context. The playable space strategy seeks to integrate opportunities for play into the wider built environment, and to make these play opportunities more accessible to a wider range of people. Current design principles for playable space (Shackell et al., 2008) focus on use by children; however, there is real potential to extend the concept of playable space to include older people. Indeed, the think tank Demos, in a piece of research examining contemporary issues relating to the use of public space, concluded that 'play should be possible across the entire public realm and involve all generations (not just children)' (Beunderman et al., 2007).

Literature relating to play by adults in the public realm concentrates mainly on physical activities such as skateboarding (for example Borden (2001) and Németh (2006)). Even in literature which takes a broader view of play, such as Stevens' *The Ludic City* (2007), the focus is largely on physically challenging activities, undertaken mainly by younger men. Nonetheless, Stevens' definitions of the characteristics of urban spaces that are used to prompt adults' playful experiences are useful. He identifies five kinds of 'spatial elements': paths, intersections, boundaries, props and thresholds. These are rather broadly defined elements and do not relate specifically to older people although Peace et al. (2006) also suggest thresholds between older people's private and public spheres as places where play can happen. Despite this emerging aspiration for playable outdoor space, very little research has been done on older people and play in the public realm.

There is, however, better understanding of how public open space can be designed to facilitate general use by older people, for example through the Inclusive Design for Getting Outdoors (IDGO) project (2007c). This has tended to concentrate on the more functional aspects of access to outdoor spaces, although there is acknowledgement of the importance of such spaces for older people's social engagement and physical exercise. Indeed, manufacturers of play equipment are producing products which have been installed in parts of the UK that are suitable for use by older people in 'pensioner playgrounds' (Mitchell et al., 2007).

It is accepted that the public realm has the potential for play; it is also accepted that there is a need for better outdoor third spaces for a growing number of people in the third age. This chapter examines the relationship between play and quality of life for older people before describing older people's understanding of play and the playful characteristics of the public realm that can support and enhance older people's well-being. This builds on the very limited literature on older people's play through the findings of a series of focus groups carried out in Bristol, UK.

Older people and quality of life

There has been a move towards a positive view of old age as a time of freedom and possibility, rather than dependence (Blane, 2005). As people reach retirement they have increased leisure time, and the length of time that they are independent and healthy is predicted to increase (Howse and Harper, 2009). This makes older people a key group to consider when thinking about the design and use of public space.

There is an extensive literature on the nature and the measurement of older people's quality of life. While there is no consensus over the definition of quality of life, there has been a move to include social and psychological aspects along with the physical, and also a shift from perceptions of quality of life by physicians and carers to the individual's subjective feelings (Bowling, 1997). Measures have been developed to assess health status, functional ability, social networks and social support, psychological well-being, life satisfaction and morale.

The needs-satisfaction model of quality of life (Higgs et al., 2003) is based on a series of non-hierarchical human needs, originally identified by Maslow (1970), where quality of life is provided by a combination of satisfying the needs for control and autonomy amongst other more basic needs that are taken as given in a post-materialist culture. 'Autonomy is defined as the right of an individual to be free from the unwanted interference of others... Control is understood as the ability to actively intervene in one's environment' (Higgs et al., 2003). This measure tries to separate quality of life from influences on quality of life, such as health and income. Higgs et al. (ibid.) challenged such factors as focusing on the relative lack of something and ignoring the agency of older people. They call instead for the recognition of the positive dimensions of old age, reflecting their relatively good health and the greater amount of enjoyable activity that older people can consequently take part in at the end of their lives. In addition, they stressed that when conditions are right for the realisation of autonomy and control then older people can 'pursue the reflexive process of self-realisation through activities that make them happy' (ibid). This approach was developed into the CASP-19 measure of quality of life which has subsequently been tested and adopted by researchers into older people's access to outdoor space, such as within the Inclusive Design for Getting Outdoors research programme (2007b).

Studies of older people's overall quality of life have identified, amongst other factors, the importance of social relationships, social and solo activities and the quality and facilities provided by the local neighbourhood (Bowling and Stafford, 2007). This has also been supported by the Marmot review of strategies for reducing health inequalities in England which noted that 'older people in particular often feel excluded from public spaces' (Marmot, 2010). This, again, suggests that neighbourhood public open spaces have a potentially important role in contributing to older people's well-being.

Play by adults

There is a large and well-established literature on play, the majority of which focuses on play by children. The literature on play by adults is much more limited, and suffers from definitional problems in that play is often characterised as being something that children do. In addition, given the association of play with children, other terminology is more commonly used when considering playful behaviour by adults, such as leisure, recreation, entertainment, happiness and enjoyment.

Despite the acknowledgement that 'Defining play and its role is one of the greatest challenges facing... the social sciences generally' (Burghardt, 2005), it is a challenge that has not yet been met. Sutton-Smith's work *The Ambiguity of Play* (1997) is often quoted, where he warns of the difficulty of defining play: 'we all know what playing feels like. But when it comes to making theoretical statements about what play is we fall into silliness, there is little agreement among us and much ambiguity'.

This difficulty was re-emphasised recently in a comprehensive review of research into children's play, *Play for a Change* (Lester and Russell, 2008), which notes that there is great variety in the types of play that have been researched and in the variety of disciplines, paradigms and methods used. This leads to appreciation of the 'implausibility of one single truth to explain a phenomenon as complex, multilayered and diverse as playing' (Lester and Russell, 2008).

Play for a Change notes that it is difficult to define play in terms that apply always and only to play, but summarises children's play as consisting of:

- freedom of personal choice and control (though this is sometimes compromised within groups in order to make play workable)
- feelings of personal power and control
- non-literal 'as-if' behaviour (pretending)
- intrinsic motivation
- positive affect (pleasure and enjoyment)
- flexible and adaptive use of objects and rules.

The report notes that play can also at times be: repetitive, unpredictable, spontaneous, innovative, creative and seeking out physical and emotional uncertainty.

So, children's play can be seen as complex, varied and hard to define, but described in ways that could also apply to adult play. However, the current dominant paradigm for understanding play is rooted in child development theory, which sees children's play as preparation for adulthood. This implies that adults have no need to play or that it is not important. Nonetheless, writers and researchers have argued that adults *do* play in many ways and that this is important for adults too. The *Play for a Change* report concludes that 'development is a lifelong process' (Lester and Russell, 2008), with the benefits of play not restricted to childhood and adolescence.

There are a small number of key works about the importance of play for humankind as a whole, implying relevance for adults as well as children. Pre-eminent amongst these is the work of Huizinga who wrote *Homo Ludens: A Study of the Play-Element in Culture* (1955). He argues that the whole of human 'civilization arises and unfolds in and as play', analysing the important role of play in art, politics, philosophy and religion and concluding that mankind had evolved beyond being 'Homo Sapiens to Homo Ludens'.

Caillois acknowledges the originality and influence of this thinking but argues that Huizinga's definition is 'at the same time too broad and too narrow' (Caillois, 1961) and should include a wider variety of activities, including games of chance. Caillois goes on to explore why people play, concluding that 'people choose to play for hedonistic reasons' and that they receive psychological benefit from the activity as an end in itself. He identifies a continuum of playful behaviour, from what he termed 'Paidia', which includes the spontaneous and the destructive, to 'Ludus' consisting of rule-based games. This is a useful terminology for understanding the range of types of play and was used to frame a study of play by adults in *The Ludic City* by Stevens (2007).

In *The Ambiguity of Play* Sutton-Smith (1997) takes a postmodern approach to understanding play, using the idea of rhetorics. A rhetoric is 'a persuasive discourse, or an implicit narrative... adopted... to persuade others of the veracity and worthwhileness of their beliefs' (ibid.). He warns that these often include values and ways of thought that are part of political, religious, social and educational systems 'which are assumed by the theorists of play rather than studied directly by them' (ibid.).

Sutton-Smith (1997) describes the first three of these rhetorics, progress, imagination and selfhood, as being accepted modern constructs of play, contrasting them with the ancient discourses of fate, power and communal identity. The final category, play as frivolity, is seen by Kane (2004) as a rhetoric that has devalued the worth of play. Using Sutton-Smith's rhetorics it appears that adults play according to every rhetoric except the rhetoric of progress. Consequently, this understanding of play has been linked to children, but it is increasingly being challenged and extended to include adults (Kane, 2004; Brown, 2009).

A recurring theme in the literature on play is the concept of play being predicated on a 'playful' state of mind. Piaget, the highly influential child psychologist, identified play as a state of mind which allows children to become engrossed in what they are doing. Parallels can be drawn with the work of Csikszentmihalyi (1990), which can be placed within the rhetoric of selfhood. Csikszentmihalyi theorises that people have optimal experience when they are in a state of 'flow'. This is a state in which a person is fully immersed in what he or she is doing, characterised by a feeling of great freedom, enjoyment and fulfillment, and during which temporal concerns (time, food, ego-self) are typically ignored. Csikszentmihalyi's concept of flow can arise in a work situation (e.g. a designer wrestling with a problem) or leisure (e.g. a game of chess).

Another well-regarded developmental psychologist, Bruner, stated that 'The main characteristic of play – child or adult – is not its content, but its mode. Play is an approach to action, not a form of activity' (Bruner, quoted in National Playing Fields Association (NPFA, 2000)). This was reiterated by Kane who emphasised that 'play is an attitude before it is anything else' (2004). So play can be seen not as a particular set of activities, but as a characteristic state of mind, that of playfulness, which is present to varying degrees in many different types of human behaviour. For example, a business meeting could be conducted in a formal manner with an agenda, minutes and comments addressed to the chair or in a more playful way with participants writing their thoughts and reactions onto large communal sheets of paper – or each other (see Brown, 2009).

This playful state of mind is different to that which is commonly found in functional everyday life, but can still be present in instrumental activities. The playful state of mind may be expressed in playful physical activity and outward expression of emotion, such as laughter, but may be purely internal, happening in the mind.

Play, therefore, has a range of characteristics, but how can play be distinguished from the perhaps broader notion of leisure which tends to be used more commonly in connection with adults?

Play or leisure?

The term leisure has been defined in a number of ways, for example as 'discretionary time left free from obligations... the pursuit of freely chosen recreational activities... or time spent in activities that provide intrinsically rewarding experiences' (Csikszentmihalyi and LeFevre, 1989).

Understanding leisure as discretionary or free time, without obligations, is straightforward; this suggests time during which play can take place (although play may also take place in work time). More difficult to differentiate from play is leisure defined as an intrinsically rewarding experience. Neulinger describes leisure as a 'state of mind' (Neulinger, 1974, 1981) that required perceived freedom, intrinsic motivation and internal locus of control (quoted in Patterson (2006)). Kelly and Kelly (1994) see difficulties in defining leisure simply in terms of perceived freedom and identify a number of potential constraints. They point out that Neulinger's definition of leisure can apply to many human activities and go on to describe a number of 'life domains' including work, family/community and leisure. However, Kelly and Kelly warn that these are not distinct but 'fuzzy' and include a number of dimensions such as productivity, bonding, expression and learning which are present to different extents and at different times in the domains. Interestingly, Csikszentmihalyi found that flow, associated with play, was attained more often in work than leisure situations.

Stebbins identified the importance of 'serious leisure' in terms of long-term commitment to hobbies and volunteering (quoted in Patterson (2006)). This could be seen to contrast with the spontaneity and often short-lived nature of playful behaviour. Kelly and Kelly describe how such serious leisure can contribute to learning, skill development and creating identity.

So, definitions of leisure are imprecise, depend on the individual, and change over time. There are many similarities between active, engaged leisure activity and play. The definition of leisure used here is a life domain that contains discretionary time, free of obligations, during which individuals can undertake activities, which they perceive to be freely chosen, in the pursuit of pleasure. Play can therefore be freely chosen as a part of leisure but is qualitatively different.

Play by older people

In stark contrast to the extensive literature on children's play, the literature on play by older adults is very limited. A study attempting to identify the difference in understanding between 'work' and 'play' for older people concluded that 'the meaning of play for elderly persons may be orientated around activities customarily regarded as discretionary, non-remunerative, and enjoyable' (Mobily and Bedford, 2003).

A study of women involved in the Red Hat Society (a social organisation for older women), claimed that there had not been any previous studies of older women and play (Yarnal et al., 2008). It clearly shows that there is a desire for, and expression of, playful thinking and behaviour by women over 50, and that the women attach importance to such playfulness. The Red Hat Society has grown quickly in the USA and UK and is based on the sentiments of Jenny Jones's (1973) well known poem, 'Warning', with the lines: 'When I am an old woman I shall wear purple, With a red hat which doesn't go, and doesn't suit me.'

The society's aims are to promote and support 'fun, friendship, freedom, fulfilment and fitness' (The Red Hat Society, 2013) and Yarnal et al. explore the members' understanding of the concept of play and what they benefit from it. Activities undertaken by the women included a group 'spitting contest, eating dessert first at a restaurant, riding in a stretch limousine, a pajama breakfast in a local park, and "scooting" around in a parade in a scooter decorated with purple feathers' (Yarnal et al., 2008).

Similar findings were evident in the Look at me! photographic project (Warren and Richards, 2011). This gave older women the opportunity to explore how they portrayed themselves, and playful images were often created. Although the evidence is limited, it indicates that Sennett may be correct in saying that: 'The loss of a sense of play in reality… is the loss, or more exactly the *repression* of a childhood power' (Sennett, 1976, emphasis added) and that many older people have a playful instinct that they want to express given the right circumstances (Figure 7.1).

Much of the research with older people is framed in terms of leisure. Kelly et al. use a 'core and balance' model in which there is a balancing set of activities that change through the life course due to changing roles, self-definitions, aims and opportunities. Older people have 'a reduction of physical exertion and a constriction of the range of the social world' (Kelly et al., 1986) which is manifested in reduced participation in sport, exercise and outdoor activity and more emphasis on social and travel activities.

In terms of leisure activities with characteristics of play, seeking novelty has been reported to decrease with age, whereas the tendency for continuity of experience increased (Stebbins, 1997). Kelly et al. (1986) found that older people's leisure time tended not to be spent in organised recreation 'in the special environments of public recreation venues or programs' but in more informal settings such as parks or their homes.

So, for older people, leisure can be seen as a life domain where individuals can undertake activities, which they perceive to be freely chosen, in the pursuit of pleasure. These tend to reduce in terms of range of type and location and in terms of novelty. Play can be part of leisure but is qualitatively different in that it relates to a playful state of mind rather than a life domain or particular activities and is often spontaneous and short-lived.

FIGURE 7.1 Play in public space

Potential benefits of play

The benefits of play are contested. There is a spectrum of claims, from those who dismiss play as potentially having no function but to prepare for more play (Sutton-Smith, 1997), through to those who believe it is essential for the survival of the human race (Kane, 2004; Brown, 2009). A distinction can be made between immediate benefits (such as the development, practice and maintenance of physical and cognitive ability and social relationships) and deferred benefits which are useful in later life (Pellegrini, 2009). Even in the case of immediate benefits of play to children there is debate about whether play has a unique role or whether benefits can be gained in other ways (Smith, 1988). In contrast, from the perspective of sociobiology, it has been suggested that play at all stages of life can bring an evolutionary advantage in terms of the survival of genes. Thus, play with children by parents and grandparents will give an advantage to those children (Yarnal et al., 2008).

Some types of play may also be seen as a dis-benefit to the individual or to society. *Play for a Change* (Lester and Russell, 2008) notes that types of play including play-fighting, war play, teasing, bullying and in open spaces 'thrill-seeking play such as parkour and skateboarding, adolescent experiments with drugs and sex as well as behaviour in the public realm that is increasingly understood as dangerous or antisocial' do not appear to be beneficial in a directly causal way. In contrast to this view, Stevens (2007) advocates the importance of such play in critiquing and challenging established uses of public space and those who control it.

In their study of older women Yarnal et al. (2008) conclude that play is a 'context for fun, laughter, and feeling good', and that older women appreciate the opportunity to 'be silly and goofy' around each other in an unstructured context that offers both freedom from the grind of everyday life and freedom to think and behave in different ways to usual. Cheang (2002) also reported that the main benefit of the play he observed was enjoyment, rather than social support.

Psychologists argue that happiness, the experience of frequent short-term positive affect including joy and interest (and infrequent negative emotions), leads to long-term success in life as a whole (Lyubomirsky et al., 2005). Positive affect has also been linked to resilience (Fredrickson, 2004), with positive emotions playing an important role in reinforcing the resources that help people to cope with negative events, such as humour, optimistic thinking and an openness to new experiences (Tugade et al., 2004). In this way, play may help older people to deal with difficulties in their lives.

Frederickson (2004) argues that 'positive emotions prompt individuals to engage with their environments and partake in activities' and that 'Joy … creates the urge to play, push the limits and be creative; urges not only in social and physical behaviour, but also intellectual and artistic behavior.' She goes on to state that this playful activity has a longer-term social impact, with shared amusement and smiles creating social bonds. So play may also be an expression of well-being.

Pursuing a variety of enjoyable intentional activities is also seen by Sheldon and Lyubomirsky (2009) as contributing to a sustained improvement in well-being that outweighs the effects of people's genetic predispositions. More specifically, the humour and laughter which are often involved in play have been examined in terms of their benefits, including the initiation and regulation of social interaction, giving the signal that play is happening, and improving resistance to health risks (Pressman and Cohen, 2005).

So, this approach to understanding the benefits of play suggests that, rather than only signaling well-being, positive emotions can produce well-being. This implies that through providing opportunities for joyful play, public open spaces could encourage positive emotions that build long-term well-being for the individual.

The relationship between quality of life and play

Quality of life (QOL) and well-being are broad, contested and interwoven concepts. There is an extensive literature on the nature and the measurement of older people's QOL and well-being in the context of how to help people to age well. While some researchers such as Smith et al. (2004) see QOL as an overarching term others use well-being as a multidimensional construct including aspects such as good QOL, high satisfaction with life and lower incidences of negative feelings of depression and loneliness (Demakakos et al., 2010).

Highlighting one instructive approach Table 7.1 summarises the similarities between the CASP-19 model of QOL (Higgs et al., 2003) and the fundamental qualities of play defined earlier.

It is notable that both are dependent on an individual's feeling of autonomy and control. In order to experience a good QOL, older people need to feel that they have both freedom from unwanted interference and freedom to pursue their own personal projects. Likewise, play requires the perception that activities are freely chosen and are controlled by the individual. When those factors are in place, pleasure and enjoyment can be pursued, driven by a need for

TABLE 7.1 Quality of life and play compared

Quality of life	*Play*
Autonomy	Freely chosen
Control	Personally directed
Pleasure	Enjoyment
Self-realisation	Intrinsic motivation
	Non-instrumental
	State of mind

Source: Higgs et al., 2003.

self-realisation in the case of the QOL model, and intrinsic motivation in the case of play. This suggests that play may have a contribution to make to QOL. In a context which provides feelings of autonomy and control the intrinsic motivation to achieve self-realisation through pleasure can be expressed in play, providing QOL.

Benefits of, and access to, public open space for older people

The literature on older people's use of public open space suggests that there are a number of potential benefits. Most important of these are physical activity, improvements to mental health through contact with nature and positive social contacts (Ward Thompson, 2011). In addition, access to public open space has been linked to a sense of freedom, escape from routine places, feelings of independence, reduced need for care, enjoyment and longevity (Takano et al., 2002; Burton and Mitchell, 2006; IDGO, 2007b; Sugiyama and Ward Thompson, 2007a, 2007b; Alves et al., 2008; Newton et al., 2010).

There is also evidence about which aspects of the environment enable and encourage older people's access to public open space in the UK. These are summarised in Table 7.2.

Play in public open space

If play is defined as a state of mind then, potentially, play can take place in any part of the public realm; for example, someone can play the saxophone under the Los Angeles freeway next to the rush hour traffic (Flusty, 2000). What is of interest is the degree to which public space can enable or encourage play, through providing spaces in which people can experience freedom and a sense of personal control over their experiences.

The public realm has been critiqued and categorised in many ways (Carmona, 2010a, 2010b) but can be defined as including all the spaces that are accessible to, and that can be used by, the public. This includes: public open space such as squares, streets and parks in urban areas; internal public spaces which can be found in libraries, museums, town halls and public transport facilities such as bus stations; and quasi-public or privatised public spaces (both internal and external) which are legally private and where the owners and operators can control access and behaviour, including shopping centres, restaurants, university campuses and sports grounds (Carmona et al., 2003). Ideally, the public realm functions as a political forum, a neutral common ground for social interaction and communication and a place for personal development and social learning (Loukaitou-Sideris and Bannerjee, 1998) but, given the varied nature of the functions, perceptions and ownerships of the public realm, there is a spectrum of potential public access and of possible activities (Carmona, 2010b).

Although a recent concept, playable space appears to be increasingly accepted and encouraged in urban design practice. For example, the Greater London

TABLE 7.2 Aspects of the environment which enable and encourage access by older people

	Theme	Features	References
Factors supporting autonomy and control	Security	Feeling safe from attack/assault/robbery Street lighting Visible police/staff presence	IDGO (2007b); Biggs and Tinker (2007); Sugiyama et al. (2009)
	Lack of nuisance	Lack of unattended dogs Lack of dog fouling Lack of young people hanging around	IDGO (2007b); Alves et al. (2008); Sugiyama and Ward Thompson (2008); Sugiyama et al. (2009)
	Safety and comfort	Good paths (smooth, flat, well-maintained) Safety from traffic (separation, good crossings) Benches/seating Nearby toilets (open, clean) Shelter Café/food vending Little air pollution	Hilder (2001); IDGO (2007b); WHO (2007); Biggs and Tinker (2007); Shackell et al. (2008); Alves et al. (2008); Day (2008); Buffel et al. (2012)
	Mobility	Ease of access to facilities/amenities and open space (including with assistive technology); way finding ability Proximity to home Existence and quality of footpaths Walkable	IDGO (2007b); WHO (2007); Alves et al (2008); Shackell et al. (2008); Day (2008); Sugiyama et al. (2009)
	Weather	Warm/dry/calm Lack of ice and snow	Burton and Mitchell (2006); Wennberg et al. (2009)

Authority (2008) stressed that such places for play 'should be designed and managed so as to make engaging offers to a wide range of potential users'. The playability of an urban space for adults can be considered as depending on interrelating components of people's experience and the physical nature of the space. The complexity of the interaction between older people and the environment has been acknowledged, with physical (natural and built), social (occupation, organisation and interaction) and psychological (meaning, emotions and attachment) facets 'that may be examined separately but are intimately connected' (Peace et al., 2006). The authors also report how the use of space is influenced by cultural, social and individual practices.

An interesting question is the extent to which public space enables play rather than more passive forms of leisure. Hannigan (2002) describes how theme parks and shopping malls, with their many rules and regulations, provide safety and predictability at the expense of freedom of imagination. On a similar theme,

	Theme	Features	References
Factors encouraging engagement and stimulation	Attractive environment	Cleanliness Pleasantness – welcoming and relaxing Lack of noise/graffiti Well maintained Aesthetic quality Green space Trees /plants Positive sensory experience	Hilder (2001); Bowling et al. (2006); IDGO (2007b); WHO (2007); Alves et al. (2008); Day (2008); Sugiyama and Ward Thompson (2008); Sugiyama et al. (2009)
	Opportunities for socialising	Benches/ seating Food/drink Paths intersecting Thresholds of buildings and spaces Events and activities Suitable for adults to chat Suitable for children to play Neighbourliness	Hilder (2001); Stevens (2006); Peace et al. (2006); Bowling et al. (2006); IDGO (2007b); WHO (2007); Day (2008); Sugiyama et al. (2009)
	Involvement in design	Community consultation in the development of spaces	IDGO (2007b); Shackell et al. (2008)
	Things to watch	Wildlife View Water/water features Other people	Burton and Mitchell (2006); Alves et al. (2008); Sugiyama and Ward Thompson (2008)
	Activities	Things to do Shops	Burton and Mitchell (2006); Bowling et al. (2006); Sugiyama and Ward Thompson (2007a); Sugiyama et al. (2009)

Sorkin (2002) sees Disneyland as fun but 'anti-carnivalesque', in that it celebrates the existing order of things; it is hygienic, ordered and controlled in a way that suggests it does not allow play at the carnivalesque/paidia end of the play spectrum.

There are an increasing number of 'playgrounds' developed specifically for older people in the UK, inspired by provision in China and mainland Europe. 'Pensioner playgrounds' have been installed in Manchester, Eastbourne, London and a growing list of other locations. The Hyde Park Senior Playground (The Royal Parks, 2010) is one example where the aim was to encourage physical exercise but also, as described by the Knightsbridge Association, '… [to] encourage users to socialise and have fun together. People need to stay active, maintain independence and are never too old to play' (Elsdon quoted in *The Daily Telegraph*, 2010).

Whilst there has been no formal evaluation of these playgrounds in the UK to date, one manufacturer, Lappset in Finland, claims that older people using their equipment reported improved balance, agility, mood and confidence in going out on their own (Lappset, 2011). Other small-scale research has shown an interest by older people in using such equipment in the UK (Moore, 2006) but this very much depends on the physical and social context (Mitchell et al., 2007). These playgrounds are limited in the ways in which they can be used, which perhaps suggests that they should be viewed as providing opportunities for exercise rather than play.

Design guidance has been produced which promotes older people's physical activity, for example through enabling access by older people to parks and streets (IDGO, 2007a, 2007c). This does not look directly at design for playful activity by older people. It does, however, include underlying elements that encourage any use of the outdoors, such as maintenance, safety and security, along with aspects such as the design of seating, footpaths and street art to encourage social interaction (see Table 7.2). The authors highlight the fact that the role of social interaction in public open space and the environmental factors that promote such interaction are not well understood in the case of older people (Sugiyama and Ward Thompson, 2007a).

In some places, and for some individuals, public open space appears to be able to provide the right combination of physical and social features to enable older people's play and contribute to their QOL. The next section examines the experience of play in public open space through the thoughts of older people themselves.

Older people's reflections on play in public open space

In the light of the lack of understanding of older people's definition of play (Sutton-Smith, 1997), and the possible contribution of public open space towards play for older people, focus groups were carried out to explore these issues with people from Bristol, UK, who were over 65 and from a range of backgrounds.

Analysis revealed a number of themes relating to the literature. The older people tended to relate their experience of play to interacting with children – 'you have to join in with the fun, you have to play with the granddaughter'; or with pets – 'I used to play about with the dog'; or to sports – 'I played badminton with my son'.

Their definitions centred on enjoyment – 'Enjoyable, amusing, fun'; being sociable – 'I think with playing you need other people'; being frivolous – 'not serious'; and taking risks – 'A bit daring …let yourself go'. Overall, the response was that older people did not generally identify with the word 'play' as describing something that they did – 'No, you don't really say "are you coming out to play?"'.

However, the older people enthusiastically reported doing a variety of activities that could be categorised as playful in that they were unconstrained, freely chosen, pleasurable, unpredictable, spontaneous, sociable and creative. Such activities included recapturing a friend's dog that had escaped, dancing to live music in a park, following squirrels and woodpeckers through parks and interacting with sculpture trails. The older people also often reported finding pleasure in watching other people acting playfully, particularly their own offspring, but also strangers engaged in dancing, raft races and fun runs, amongst other activities.

The older people identified the following benefits of the playful and enjoyable use of public open space: the promotion of well-being; feeling and keeping young; preventing introspection; staying in contact and preventing loneliness; variety and mental refreshment; something to talk about; exercise; and experiencing positive emotions.

However, a major preoccupation was the basic accessibility and suitability of public spaces, particularly parks, for older people. Above all, participants wanted toilets that were nearby, clean and staffed, and they also frequently talked about the importance of sufficient benches in suitable locations. Participants wanted spaces free of litter and dog mess, where dogs were under control, where there was no crime and antisocial behaviour (especially from young people), and where cyclists rode respectfully. Many felt that park wardens would help with this issue. These opinions come as no surprise, having already been identified in the literature, but also confirm a common conclusion of much research into play, that a basic level of safety and comfort is required before play can happen (Pellegrini, 2009).

Looking beyond a basic level of provision, there was a demand for enjoyable things to do. Older people felt that often there was very little on offer apart from sitting on a bench, if one was available, and looking at the view. However, while there was recognition of the potential benefits of enjoyable activities and an enthusiasm for taking part, the participants' suggestions of what might be provided were limited. Suggestions included the availability of refreshments, particularly picnics and barbecues, and the provision of free events involving music for listening and dancing along to.

Opportunities to exercise were also requested, with the example given of t'ai chi and also pensioner-specific outdoor gym equipment – 'you wouldn't feel embarrassed about using something like that, where you might feel more embarrassed about something like running round the park'.

This comment also reflects another significant theme, which was the need for an excuse or 'permission' to behave in a playful way without embarrassment. 'Excuses' included the presence of grandchildren, music, celebrations and other events, and 'trails' with suggested activities.

Participants raised the fact that they were of a generation which had lived through the 1960s and wanted different things from public open space than previous 'rose sniffing' generations of older people. One participant stated that the problem with many public spaces was that there was too much undesirable behaviour and not enough fun for her generation – 'just drinking, drugs and sex ... but no rock 'n' roll'.

In summary, participants were clear that basic amenities, particularly toilets and benches, had to be in place before play could occur. The older people needed to feel safe, secure and free from intimidation by other users of the outdoor space (including dogs, teenagers and cyclists) in order to feel free enough to be able to play. Finally, they highlighted the need for 'permission' to act in a playful way, such as being with a young member of the family, through the presence of a pensioner playground that was expressly for them, a labelled trail or playful 'events'.

Conclusion

There are an increasing number of older people in the UK, who are living for longer, are in better physical health and have more leisure time than ever before. However, this 'third age' of life can also be a time of loneliness and increasing isolation.

Simultaneously, there is an increasing interest in the development of the public realm, and open space in particular, as a playable 'third space'. An analysis of the nature of play which identifies the outcomes of pleasure and self-development implies that play could contribute to older people's QOL. Indeed, there is much congruence between definitions of play and the underlying nature of QOL for older people.

Whilst people in the third age find the term 'play' problematic (in that they do not perceive 'play' to be something that they do), they express a desire for a range of experiences that emphasise the value of enjoyable and playful activities in public open space. This suggests that designing for playfulness might contribute to older people's QOL, even if the term itself is not something they would associate themselves with.

In order for there to be more enjoyable and beneficial use of public open space by older people certain elements are required, including toilets and benches and a feeling of safety and security. This supports the suggestion, from the literature relating to play, that safety and comfort are required before participants can relax and playful activity can take place. Sadly, in many of the places described by participants these basic facilities were lacking.

However, there was a keen appetite for playful activities in public open space and participants felt that the needs of older people were not being recognised across the public realm as a whole; for example, those in authority were criticised for not giving sufficient consideration to the fact that as 'you got older you still need to go into an open space and have some enjoyment'. In particular, older people highlighted the need for cues designed into outdoor spaces which give 'permission' for them to play.

Public open spaces have huge potential to improve the well-being of older people. They can provide spaces for people to meet and socialise, to engage with the world by observing, to be out in the fresh air and to escape from routine places. Where there is a basic provision of amenities and security, they have the potential to be spaces of freedom, where older people can be sociable, spontaneous, creative and have fun. Conceptualising outdoor spaces as playable spaces suggests that, through the addition of environmental and social cues which give 'permission' for playful activities, these 'third places' can become places of pleasure and self-development, with psychological and physical benefit to the well-being of people in the third age.

References

Alves, S., Aspinall, P., Ward Thompson, C., Sugiyama, T., Brice, R. and Vickers, A. (2008) Preferences of older people for environmental attributes of local parks: The use of choice-based conjoint analysis. *Facilities*. 26 (11/12), 433.

Beunderman, J., Hannon, C. and Bradwell, P. (2007) *Seen and Heard: Reclaiming the Public Realm with Children and Young People*. London: Demos.

Biggs, S. and Tinker, A. (2007) *What Makes a City Age-Friendly? London's Contribution to the World Health Organization's Age-Friendly Cities Project*. London: Help the Aged.

Blane, D. (2005) *Influences on Quality of Life in Early Old Age*. Swindon: Economic and Social Research Council (ESRC).

Borden, I. (2001) *Skateboarding, Space and the City*. Oxford: Berg.

Bowling, A. (1997) *Measuring Health: A Review of Quality of Life Measurement Scales*. Buckingham: Open University Press.

Bowling, A. and Stafford, M. (2007) How do objective and subjective assessments of neighbourhood influence social and physical functioning in older age? Findings from a British survey of ageing. *Social Science & Medicine*. 64 (12), 2533–2549.

Bowling, A., Barber, J., Morris, R. and Ebrahim, S. (2006) Do perceptions of neighbourhood environment influence health? Baseline findings from a British survey of aging. *Journal of Epidemiology and Community Health*. 60 (6), 476–483.

Brown, S. (2009) *Play: How it Shapes the Brain, Opens the Imagination, and Invigorates the Soul*. New York: Avery.

Buffel, T., Phillipson, C. and Scharf, T. (2012) Ageing in urban environments: Developing 'age-friendly' cities. *Critical Social Policy*. 32 (4), 597–617.

Burghardt, G. (2005) *The Genesis of Animal Play: Testing the Limits*. Boston MA: MIT Press.

Burton, E. and Mitchell, L. (2006) *Inclusive Urban Design: Streets for Life*. Oxford: Architectural Press.

Caillois, R. (1961) *Man, Play and Games*. Chicago, IL: University of Illinois Press.

Carmona, M. (2010a) Contemporary public space: Critique and classification, part one: Critique. *Journal of Urban Design*. 15 (1), 1357.

Carmona, M. (2010b) Contemporary public space: Critique and classification, part two: Classification. *Journal of Urban Design*. 15 (2), 157.

Carmona, M., Heath, T., Oc, T. and Tiesdell, S. (2003) *Public Places, Urban Spaces: The Dimensions of Urban Design*. Oxford: Architectural Press.

Cheang, M. (2002) Older adults' frequent visits to a fast-food restaurant: Nonobligatory social interaction and the significance of play in a 'third place'. *Journal of Aging Studies*. 16, 303.

Csikszentmihalyi, M. (1990) *Optimal Experience*. New York: Harper Row.

Csikszentmihalyi, M. and LeFevre, J. (1989) Optimal experience in work and leisure. *Journal of Personality and Social Psychology*. 56 (5), 815.

Day, R. (2008) *Local Urban Environments and the Wellbeing of Older People*. Glasgow: Scotish Centre for Research on Social Justice.

Demakakos, P., McMunn, A. and Steptoe, A. (2010) Well-being in older age: A multidimensional perspective. In Banks, J., Lessof, C., Nazroo, J., Rogers, N.,

Stafford, M. and Steptoe, A., eds. (2010) *Financial Circumstances, Health and Well-being of the Older Population in England*. London: The Institute for Fiscal Studies, p. 115.

Flusty, S. (2000) Thrashing downtown: Play as resistance to the spatial and representational regulation of Los Angeles. *Cities*. 17 (2), 149.

Fredrickson, B. (2004) The broaden-and-build theory of positive emotions. *Philosophical Transactions Royal Society London B*. 359, 1367.

Greater London Authority. (2008) *Supplementary Planning Guidance: Providing for Children and Young people's Play and Informal Recreation*. London: Greater London Authority.

Greater London Authority. (2012) *Shaping Neighbourhoods: Play and Informal Recreation Supplementary Planning Guidance*. London: Greater London Authority.

Hannigan, J. (2002) Fantasy city: Pleasure and profit in the postmodern metropolis. In Fainstein, S., ed. (2002) *Readings in Urban Theory*. Oxford: Blackwell.

Hickman, P., ed. (2010) *Housing in an Era of Change*. University of York, 14–16 April 2010. Housing Studies Association.

Higgs, P., Hyde, M., Wiggins, R.D. and Blane, D. (2003) A measure of quality of life in early old age: The theory, development, and properties of a needs satisfaction model (CASP-19). *Ageing & Mental Health*. 7 (3), 186.

Hilder, B. (2001) At risk of enjoyment. *Landscape Design*. 299 (April), 17–18.

Howse, K. and Harper, S. (2009) Review of longevity trends in the United Kingdom to 2025 and beyond. *Journal of Population Ageing*. 1, 225–240.

Huizinga, J. (1955) *Homo Ludens: A Study of the Play-Element in Culture*. Boston, MA: Beacon Press.

IDGO (Inclusive Design for Getting Outdoors) (2007a) *The Design of Streets with Older People in Mind*. Available from: http://www.idgo.ac.uk/design_guidance/streets.htm (accessed 31 January 2013).

IDGO (Inclusive Design for Getting Outdoors) (2007b) *How does the Outdoor Environment Affect Older People's Quality of Life?* Available from: http://www.idgo.ac.uk/older_people_outdoors/outdoor_environment_qol.htm#aspectstable (accessed 31 January 2013).

IDGO (Inclusive Design for Getting Outdoors) (2007c) *Lifelong Access to Parks and Public Open Spaces*. Available from: http://www.idgo.ac.uk/design_guidance/open_spaces.htm (accessed 31 January 2013).

Jacobs, A. and Appleyard, D. (1987) Towards an urban design manifesto. *Journal of the American Planning Association*. 53, 112.

Jones, J. (1973) Warning. In Larkin, P., ed., *The Oxford Book of Twentieth Century English Verse*. Oxford: Oxford University Press.

Kane, P. (2004) *The Play Ethic: A Manifesto for a Different Way of Living*. London: Macmillan.

Kelly, J.R. and Kelly, J.R. (1994) Multiple dimensions of meaning in the domains of work, family and leisure. *Journal of Leisure Research*. 26 (3), 250.

Kelly, J.R., Steinkamp, M.W. and Kelly, J.R. (1986) Later life leisure: How they play in Peoria. *The Gerontologist*. 26 (5), 531–537.

Lappset (2011) *Aging and Play – More Excitement, Less Isolation, Courage*. Available from: http://www.lappset.co.uk/Pro_Play/The_Elderly_.iw3 (accessed 31 January 2013).

Laslett, P. (1996) *A Fresh Map of Life*. 2nd ed. London: Macmillan.

Lawton, M.P. (1986) *Environment and Aging*. Albany, NY: Centre for the Study of Aging.

Lester, S. and Russell, W. (2008) *Play for a Change: Play, Policy and Practice, a Review of Contemporary Perspectives*. London: Play England/National Children's Bureau.

Loukaitou-Sideris, A. and Bannerjee, T. (1998) *Urban Design Downtown: Poetics and Politics of Form*. Berkeley, CA: University of California Press.

Lyubomirsky, S., Deiner, E. and King, L. (2005) The benefits of frequent positive affect: Does happiness lead to success? *Psychological Bulletin*. 131 (6), 803.

Marmot, M. (2010) *Fair Society, Healthy Lives: the Marmot Review: Strategic Review of Health Inequalities in England Post-2010*. London: The Marmot Review. http://www.marmotreview.org

Maslow, A.H. (1970) *Motivation and Personality*. New York: Harper and Row.

Mitchell, V., Elton, E., Clift, L. and Moore, H., (2007) *Do Older Adults Want Playgrounds?*. Loughborough: Loughborough University.

Mobily, K.E. and Bedford, R.L. (2003) Language, play and work among elderly persons. *Leisure Studies*. 12 (3), 203.

Moore, H. (2006) *Investigating Requirements for True Inclusivity in Playgrounds*. MA Ergonomics, Loughborough University.

Németh, J. (2006) Conflict, exclusion, relocation: Skateboarding and public space. *Journal of Urban Design*. 11 (3), 297.

Neulinger, J. (1974) *The Psychology of Leisure*. Springfield, IL: Charles C Thomas.

Neulinger, J. (1981) *To Leisure: An Introduction*. Boston, MA: Allyn & Bacon.

Newton, R., Ormerod, M., Burton, E., Mitchell, L. and Ward Thompson, C. (2010) Increasing independence for older people through good street design. *Journal of Integrated Care*. 18 (3), 24.

NPFA (2000) *Best Play: What Play Provision should do for Children*. London: National Playing Fields Association (NPFA).

Office for National Statistics. (2011) *Statistical Bulletin: Older People's Day 2011*. London: Office for National Statistics.

Oldenburg, R. (1999) *The Great Good Place: Cafes, Coffee Shops, Bookstores, Bars, Hair Salons, and Other Hangouts at the Heart of a Community*. New York: Marlowe and Co.

Patterson, I. (2006) *Growing Older: Tourism and Leisure Behaviour of Older Adults*. Wallingford, Oxfordshire: CABI.

Peace, S., Holland, C. and Kellaher, L. (2006) *Environment and Identity in Later Life*. Maidenhead, UK: Open University Press.

Pellegrini, A. (2009) *The Role of Play in Human Development*. New York: Oxford University Press.

Pressman, S. and Cohen, S. (2005) Does positive affect influence health? *Psychological Bulletin*. 131 (6), 925–971.

Project for Public Spaces (2010) *What is Placemaking?* Available from: http://www.pps.org/what_is_placemaking/ (accessed 20 May 2013).

Sennett, R. (1976) *The Fall of Public Man*. London: Penguin.

Shackell, A., Butler, N., Doyle, P. and Ball, D. (2008) *Design for Play: A Guide to Creating Successful Play Spaces*. London: DCSF (Department for Children, Schools and Families), DCMS and Play England.

Sheldon, K.M. and Lyubomirsky, S. (2009) Change your actions, not your circumstances: An experimental test of the Sustainable Happiness Model. In Dutt, A.K. and Radcliff, B., eds. (2009) *Happiness, Economics, and Politics: Toward a Multi-Disciplinary Approach*. Cheltenham: Edward Elgar, 324–342.

Smith, A., Sim, J., Scharf, T. and Phillipson, C. (2004) Determinants of quality of life amongst older people in deprived neighbourhoods. *Ageing and Society*. 24 (5), 793–814.

Smith, P.K. (1988) Children's play and its role in early development: A re-evaluation of the 'play ethos'. In Pellegrini, A., ed., *Psychological Bases for Early Education*. Chichester, UK: Wiley, 207.

Sorkin, M. (2002) See You in Disneyland. In Fainstein, S., ed., *Readings in Urban Theory*. Oxford: Blackwell.

Stebbins, R.A. (1997) Casual leisure: A conceptual statement. *Leisure Studies.* 16 (1), 17.

Stevens, Q. (2006) The shape of urban experience: A re-evaluation of Lynch's five elements. *Environment and Planning B: Planning and Design.* 33, 803–823.

Stevens, Q. (2007) *The Ludic City – Exploring the Potential of Public Spaces.* Oxford: Routledge.

Sugiyama, T. and Ward Thompson, C. (2007a) Older people's health, outdoor activity and supportiveness of neighbourhood environments. *Landscape and Urban Planning.* 83, 168.

Sugiyama, T. and Ward Thompson, C. (2007b) Outdoor environments, activity and the well-being of older people: Conceptualising environmental support. *Environment and Planning A.* 39, 1943.

Sugiyama, T. and Ward Thompson, C. (2008) Associations between characteristics of neighbourhood open space and older people's walking. *Urban Forestry & Urban Greening.* 7 (1), 41.

Sugiyama, T., Ward Thompson, C. and Alves, S. (2009) Associations between neighborhood open space attributes and quality of life for older people in Britain. *Environment and Behavior.* 41 (1), 3.

Sutton-Smith, B. (1997) *The Ambiguity of Play.* Cambridge, MA: Harvard University Press.

Takano, T., Nakamura, K. and Watanabe, M. (2002) Urban residential environments and senior citizens' longevity in megacity areas: The importance of walkable green spaces. *Journal of Epidemiology and Community Health.* 56, 913.

The Daily Telegraph (2010) *Pensioners' Playground to be Built in Hyde Park.* Available from: http://www.telegraph.co.uk/news/newstopics/howaboutthat/7201045/Pensioners-playground-to-be-built-in-Hyde-Park.html (accessed 20 May 2013).

The Red Hat Society (2013) *The Red Hat Society.* Available from: http://www.redhatsociety.com/join (accessed 16 June 2013).

The Royal Parks (2010) *Hyde Park Senior Playground.* Available from: http://www.royalparks.org.uk/about/hyde_park_senior_playground.cfm (accessed 20 May 2013).

Tugade, M.M., Fredrickson, B.L. and Feldman-Barrett, L. (2004) Psychological resilience and positive emotional granularity: Examining the benefits of positive emotions on coping and health. *Journal of Personality.* 72 (6), 1161–1190.

Ward Thompson, C. (2011) Linking landscape and health: the recurring theme. *Landscape and Urban Planning,* 99 (3), 187–195.

Warren, L. and Richards, N. (2011) *Look at Me!.* Unpublished.

Wennberg, H., Ståhl, A. and Hydén, C. (2009) Older pedestrians' perceptions of the outdoor environment in a year-round perspective. *European Journal of Ageing.* 6 (4), 277–290.

WHO (World Health Organization) (2007) *Global Age Friendly Cities: A Guide.* Geneva, Switzerland: World Health Organization.

Yarnal, C.M., Chick, G. and Kerstetter, D.L. (2008) 'I did not have time to play growing up… so this is my play time. It's the best thing I have ever done for myself': What is play to older women? *Leisure Sciences.* 30, 235.

8
KIDS IN THE CITY

Differing perceptions of one neighbourhood in Aotearoa/New Zealand

Penelope Carroll, Lanuola Asiasiga, Nicola Tava'e and Karen Witten

Introduction

This chapter reports on findings from our Kids in the City research conducted in Auckland, Aotearoa/New Zealand, investigating the impacts of neighbourhood attributes and residents' perceptions on children's independent mobility (unsupervised outdoor play and travel) and activity levels – and thus their well-being. It is set in the context of decreasing levels of physical activity and rising child obesity rates amongst children in Aotearoa/New Zealand, coupled with an urban intensification which is changing neighbourhood environments. Physical activity and independent mobility are essential for children's development and well-being (Christensen and O'Brien, 2003; Valentine, 2004); yet a combination of safety-conscious parenting, car reliance and auto-centric urban design, sees children living ever more sedentary lives (Ministry of Transport, 2009). The United Nations Convention on the Rights of the Child, to which New Zealand is a signatory, sees children's well-being and quality of life as the ultimate indicators of sustainable development (Malone, 2001). How can we best ensure that the well-being of children is to the fore in urban planning?

With Auckland's present population of 1.5 million expected to top two million in the next 30 years, a strategy of residential intensification is in place to contain urban sprawl (Auckland Council, 2012). There has already been erosion in play and independent mobility opportunities for children, with increasing traffic volumes fuelling parents' fears for their children's safety (Kearns and Collins, 2006). How can residential intensification be achieved without further diminishing children's opportunities for play and independent mobility, and compromising their development and well-being? Here well-being is taken to include physical, psychological and social well-being (Carr, 2004).

Planning practice in Aotearoa/New Zealand has largely confined children's use of public spaces to specific places such as swimming pools, libraries and playgrounds (Freeman, 2006). It has also largely excluded children from the planning process. Internationally and here there are calls for greater participation by young people in urban planning (Carroll et al., 2011; Freeman & Aitken-Rose, 2005; UNICEF, 2010) along with appeals for a prioritisation of children's needs in service and infrastructure provision. An emphasis on the well-being of the city's 300,000 children in the 2012 Auckland Plan (Auckland Council, 2012) is encouraging.

To be socially sustainable cities must provide for the well-being of children (Carroll et al., 2011; Karsten, 2009). This includes their cognitive, physical and social development. Gleeson and Sipe (2006) write of 'toxic cities' which fail to nurture children. Kids in the City seeks to provide an evidence base to help ensure children's well-being is to the fore in policy and planning decisions in Auckland and elsewhere. It attempts to understand how different neighbourhood environments are experienced by children and their parents; to investigate relationships between neighbourhood urban design attributes, perceptions of neighbourhood and children's independent mobility and physical activity levels; and to contribute children's experience and voice to urban planning. The chapter draws on qualitative data gathered in March and April 2011 from 30 children through 'go-along' neighbourhood walking interviews and travel diaries, and from computer-assisted telephone interviews (CATIs) and focus group interviews with their parents. The authors, as 'participant researchers' have provided 'outsider' observations (Angrosino et al., 2000; Cannuscio et al., 2009).

Firstly we consider background issues relating to physical activity/independent mobility and well-being and place the neighbourhood study area within the context of Auckland, Aotearoa/New Zealand. Next, we briefly outline data collection methods. We then offer accounts of child, parent and researcher neighbourhood perceptions and experiences. Lastly we consider some implications of these for children's levels of physical activity and independent mobility – and well-being – within their neighbourhood.

Background

Neighbourhood characteristics, physical activity, independent mobility and well-being

Neighbourhood characteristics influence the routines and opportunities of everyday life in ways that impact on health and well-being (Ellaway et al., 2001; Witten et al., 2009). Children are particularly vulnerable, as their lived environment has a strong influence on their cognitive, social and physical development (Cooper, 1992; Lali, 1992; Tranter and Pawson, 2001). Young children learn from their surroundings (Moore, 1986; Morrow, 2003; Wilson, 1997), with experiences of place contributing to self-identity (Proshansky &

Gottleib, 1989) and independent mobility fostering social connections (Carroll et al., 2011).

Research shows children are consistently more physically active outdoors than indoors (Burdette & Whitaker, 2005; Clements, 2004), with access to outdoor recreational opportunities linked to increased physical activity levels (Dagkas & Stathi, 2007). Thus neighbourhood attributes which facilitate children's physical activity and independent mobility contribute to their well-being, both as children and as adults. Physical activity in childhood is essential for optimal physical and psychological health later in life (Strong et al., 2005; Wang & Beydoun, 2007). Yet today's children are less physically active than previous generations in Aotearoa/New Zealand and elsewhere (Janz et al., 2009; Strong et al., 2005). For instance, there has been a considerable decline in the percentage of children walking to and from school, and time spent walking overall (Ministry of Transport, 2009; Wang & Beydoun, 2007).

Independent mobility, an integral part of children's physical activity levels, has also declined (Karsten, 2005; Valentine, 2004; Whitsman & Mizrachi, 2009). Children are increasingly chauffeured between activities and supervised while outdoors (Gleeson & Sipe, 2006) at least in part because of higher traffic volumes (Carver et al., 2008) and fears of neighbourhood crime (Flynn et al., 2006). As physical activity and independent mobility rates have fallen, childhood obesity rates have risen, with 21 per cent of New Zealand children aged 2–14 years overweight and 8 per cent obese in 2006/2007 (Ministry of Health, 2008). The effects of obesity in childhood are pervasive, affecting physical and psychological well-being and increasing the likelihood of obesity in adulthood (Flynn et al., 2006; Reilly, 2005). Thus, restricted outdoor play and independent mobility impacts on many aspects of children's social, emotional, cognitive and physical development and well-being.

Parents' fears for their children's safety, particularly relating to traffic and 'stranger danger', have been identified as a major contributor to the decline in children's independent mobility (Carver et al., 2008; Malone, 2007). The media's role in influencing the way residents perceive the safety of their neighbourhood is also well recognised (Heath, 1984; Romer et al., 2003; Tyler & Cook, 1984). Yet to be established is the impact of urban intensification on children's physical activity and independent mobility. While studies in New Zealand and elsewhere consistently show higher levels of walking amongst adults in higher density neighbourhoods (Ewing, 2009; Witten et al., 2012), it is not known whether the same relationship holds for children.

Auckland context

Auckland City (Figure 8.1), the largest urban area in Aotearoa/New Zealand, spans a narrow isthmus between two extensive harbours (the Manukau Harbour to the west and the Waitemata Harbour to the east), and sprawls north and south of this isthmus. Population density is low, with detached houses and gardens the

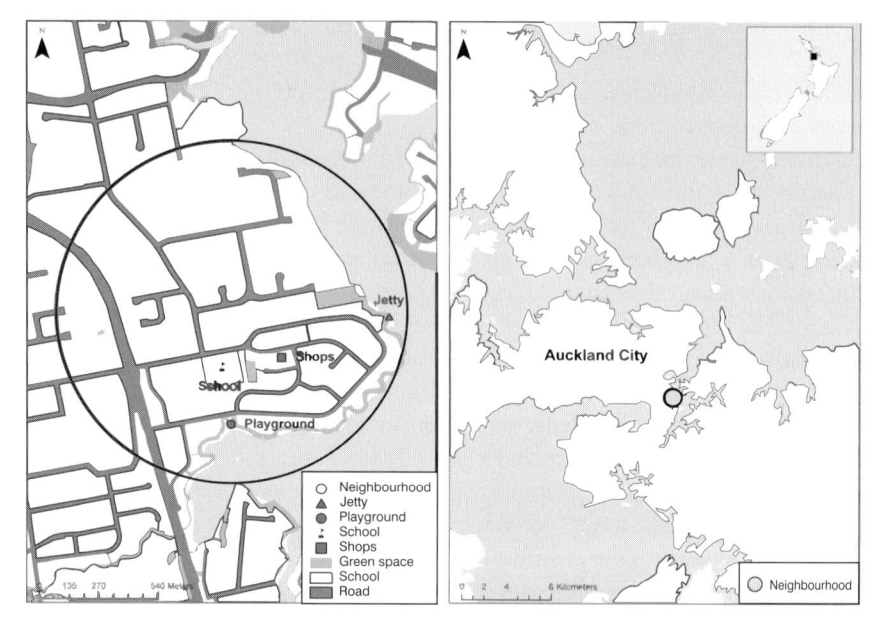

FIGURE 8.1 Auckland City and case study neighbourhood

most common dwelling type (around two thirds owner-occupied and one third rented). It is an ethnically diverse city; 56.5 per cent Pakeha/European, 18.9 per cent Asian, 14.1 per cent Pacific, 11.1 per cent Maori and 2 per cent other, according to 2006 Census figures (some people identify with more than one ethnicity). Children aged 0–14 make up 22 per cent of the population (Statistics New Zealand, 2009).

The city is changing in ways that are likely to affect many children's well-being. Nearly half the dwellings built since 2000 have been multi-unit developments, in line with the goal of 30 per cent of Aucklanders living in multi-unit housing by 2050 (Auckland Regional Growth Forum, 1999). For many children this means private outdoor play spaces are declining– and there has been little investment in accompanying supportive infrastructure to create walkable and playable urban neighbourhoods.

Case study neighbourhood

The case study neighbourhood is bounded by an estuary to the east and a major motorway to the west on the Auckland isthmus. It is a small, ethnically diverse community (52.6 per cent Pacific, 22.8 per cent Pakeha/European, 19.7 per cent Maori, 12.7 per cent Asian and 1.6 per cent other) of around 5,500 people, with a third of the population aged under 15 years. This neighbourhood is one of the more socio-economically deprived areas of Aotearoa/New Zealand (Auckland City Council, 2009), with less than a third of residents owning their own homes.

Many of the remaining two thirds of residents live in social housing. Kids in the City has focused on children in lower-socio-economic neighbourhoods as these are the children most likely to be disadvantaged by intensification strategies across Auckland (Carroll et al., 2011).

An audit of play spaces conducted as part of Kids in the City showed five playable public open spaces (three of these bordering the estuary) within a one kilometre radius of the school which the child participants attended.

Participants

Thirty children aged 9–11 (23 Pacific and 7 Maori) were recruited through the local school as collaborating 'young researchers' following classroom presentations introducing the research; these children in turn recruited their parents/caregivers.

The children participated in go-along interviews. To encourage ease of dialogue and the sharing of local knowledge by children, the interviews were conducted by young local interviewers (one Pacific, one Maori) who were employed and trained in interviewing techniques. The four authors (all New Zealand-born, two Pakeha/European and two Pacific) assisted as 'participant researchers'.

Methods

Kids in the City used mixed methods and an insider–outsider design (Cannuscio et al., 2009) to measure children's levels of physical activity and independent mobility; to gather child, parent and researcher perceptions of neighbourhood attributes across six neighbourhoods; and to explore how these might influence children's independent mobility and physical activity levels. Objective measures (including geographical positioning systems (GPS), accelerometers and travel diaries) used to ascertain independent mobility and physical activity levels have been reported on elsewhere (Oliver et al., 2011). In this chapter we focus on a subset of the data on neighbourhood experiences and perceptions collected in one neighbourhood. 'Insider' neighbourhood perceptions were gathered from children, parents/caregivers and key informants resident in the neighbourhood and 'outsider' perspectives were provided by the participant researchers.

Children were active agents in the research process (Kellett, 2010), keeping travel diaries (Mackett et al., 2007), taking participant researchers and young local interviewers on go-along neighbourhood walking interviews (Carpiano, 2009; Jones et al., 2008) and reporting on and photographing aspects of interest to them. Parents/caregivers participated in a CATI (computer assisted telephone interviewing) and a follow-up focus group. The authors, as participant researchers, made observations and took photographs of neighbourhood attributes which they considered were likely to influence children's independent mobility and physical activity levels.

The travel diaries were completed by children daily for seven consecutive days, detailing destinations and activities, time and mode of travel and with whom trips were made. Diary details were checked by researchers in informal interviews with every child each school day. The child-directed 'go-alongs' started from their home and lasted between 25 minutes and one hour. Children talked to the young local interviewers about places they often went to, neighbourhood attributes they liked and disliked, family rules and restrictions, play opportunities and safety perceptions. Photographs children took of neighbourhood attributes which interested them as they walked are yet to be analysed.

All 30 parents/caregivers participated in the CATIs, which included questions on trips to and from school, perceptions of physical and social neighbourhood environments, neighbourhood safety concerns, independent mobility considerations and lasted around 20 minutes. Twelve parents also took part in a follow-up focus group facilitated by two researchers.

The four authors, as 'participant researchers', took photographs of neighbourhood attributes as they assisted on go-along interviews and noted neighbourhood features which might facilitate or discourage children's physical activity and independent mobility. Key informant interviews with one of the young local interviewers and a school staff member provided contextual understanding of social and structural neighbourhood attributes. All interviews were audio-recorded, transcribed and thematically analysed.

Child, parent, key informant and participant researcher data were analysed independently before being examined for convergent and divergent understandings of neighbourhood perceptions and their impact on children's levels of physical activity and independent mobility. Multiple readings and discussion of interview transcripts by two or more of the research team preceded developing a preliminary coding frame for data analysis, with text excerpts sorted into theme files within NVivo and thematic descriptions developed (Braun & Clarke, 2006; Patton, 1990). Children's trip diaries and CATIs were examined to explore children's levels of physical activity and independent mobility.

Findings

Children's physical activity and independent mobility

Travel diaries showed that in the week in March 2011 when they were completed, few children made trips or took part in activities not linked to home or school, aside from shopping, visiting family, and, for a third of the children, going to church (and these trips were made accompanied by an adult). Their diaries suggest children seldom went anywhere unsupervised by a parent/caregiver or older sibling. Twelve of the 30 children (nine girls and three boys) reported going nowhere independently during that week – including trips to school.

Only 15 of the 30 children walked to school (and 22 walked home). The rest of the trips to and from school were by car (sometimes for reasons of convenience and sometimes because of safety concerns), even though all children lived within a 10 minute walk of the school. Many children, when asked, said they liked walking to school and would like to walk more; but they were restricted in where they could go in the neighbourhood.

> I'm not allowed to go anywhere that's far from my house…only can go near.

However, their limited independent mobility and reported physical activity outside the home may not mean they were physically inactive. Pene, for instance, spoke of an after-school routine of getting something to eat when she got home, and then going outside to play with her cousins. Others talked of backyard games of basketball and 'touch' with friends; and several of the children also played formally for sports teams, which involved weekly practices and games.

The extent to which children were physically active in their neighbourhood (including the amount of walking they did) appeared to depend largely on parental (or older sibling) involvement in outdoor activities. For instance some children talked of going for walks in the street and to the playground with their parents; and some parents spoke of family outings on the reserve or to the jetty. Other family outings were further afield: Tom played volleyball and 'touch' with his family most fine evenings at a sports ground in a neighbouring suburb.

Most children spoke of not wanting to go anywhere on their own (except to friends' houses), and many were fearful of public spaces which, to us as outside observers, appeared to provide good opportunities for play and exploration.

For most parents this seemed fine – when their children were home they were safe; but a few spoke of trying to encourage their children to go out and play and of their children's reluctance to do so:

> She doesn't want to go out. Sometimes I have to beg her, please, please… she can go to the shops by herself but she doesn't want to.

> I think these days they just want to sit in front of the TV and computer… they don't want to go outside.

'Outsider–insider' perceptions

Perceptions of the neighbourhood as safe or unsafe, and of neighbourhood attributes which were more, or less, desirable, varied considerably among parents, children and participant researchers. In addition, while we as 'outsider' participant researchers, lacking the insights of local experience, tended to focus on structural and visual neighbourhood attributes, children and parents, as 'insiders', were more concerned with social attributes. Largely dependent on parental perceptions, some children felt safe and confident as they moved from the confines of their homes and school, while others felt unsafe and fearful. 'Insider' child and parent perceptions are presented below against a backdrop of 'outsider' participant researcher observations.

'Outsider' perceptions

Participant researchers' neighbourhood perceptions

As outsiders walking around the neighbourhood on several weekday afternoons, we noted quiet suburban streets with few cars, apart from two main thoroughfares, and fewer pedestrians. Children were presumably playing out of sight in houses and backyards. While there was some multi-unit housing, most homes were detached with gardens. A motorway was a noisy, dominating feature to the west of the study area, along with towering electricity pylons.

There appeared to be a range of suitable green spaces for children to play in and explore, including an extensive reserve bordering the estuary, a large playground with play equipment, sports fields and a community centre outdoor play area. But, like the streets, these public spaces were almost deserted, apart from some men fishing and boys swimming off a jetty, and rowing teams on the estuary. In contrast, a local dairy – the only remaining shop in a now mostly boarded-up block – was well frequented. Liquor advertising dominated, along with the mural of superheroes painted by local school children as part of a community-building project. Further afield was a still-functioning shopping centre.

The school appeared to be the focal point of the community, at least during school hours. Outside these hours the gates were locked and a tall surrounding spiked fence kept people out ('to limit vandalism', according to our key informant).

'Insider perceptions'

Children's neighbourhood perceptions

Children generally defined their 'neighbourhood' in terms of where their friends lived. While a few ranged widely and confidently, others were fearful. Sam felt unsafe because of 'scary dogs' and 'scary people'. He did not want to go anywhere by himself 'cause there's strangers around' and 'heaps of drunk people'. Lyn, too, talked of only ever going out with her mother and younger sister because otherwise it would be 'scary':

> I think it's kind of scary…because there's lots of people, they might come and, you know, bash you up.

She never wanted to go anywhere alone, because her mother had told her 'somebody might take her':

> My mum doesn't want me to walk with my sister by ourselves, she comes and picks us up…somebody might take my little sister or me, that's why.

Lyn and Sam almost never ventured out alone. In contrast, Kelly talked of going to many friends' houses, to the shop and to the park with friends. She enjoyed walking and exploring around the neighbourhood and found 'nothing scary' in the area. Tom similarly said he was allowed to go 'anywhere' by himself, and he did: 'I pretty much just go anywhere.'

Go-along interviewer perceptions

Kim, who had lived in the area for all of her 20 years and had attended the same school as the children she interviewed, said as a child of 10 she had roamed the neighbourhood freely on her bike, her older cousins keeping an eye on her. She felt safe. Now, she said, there is a feeling of wariness and fear, and an increase in bullying (by boys from outside the area): 'You can feel the tension.'

The area had changed a lot in the past decade and she no longer thought it safe for children to roam freely as she had.

> I used to always go down to the park and meet my friends, but then as I got older I stopped going to the park because the park wasn't cool. And then the park was dangerous…

Such perceptions of danger, particularly 'stranger danger', and changes over time, surfaced in parent and focus group interviews.

Parents' perceptions

Many parents did not consider anywhere outside of their own home or the school safe for their children. When asked if there were specific places of concern, seven parents said 'everywhere'. Violence from strangers and teenagers, thugs, drunkenness and speeding cars were given as reasons for this, and especially fear of strangers. Traffic was less of a concern than 'stranger danger'.

> I get nervous. About people. There's some freaky looking people roaming our streets.

> You know we read the newspaper and there are not nice people out there who will take advantage of your children…and that's every parent's fear.

Sam and Lyn's mothers were two of the parents who felt nowhere was safe. Sam's fears (above) mirrored those of his mother, who said she would not let him go 'past the second hump in the driveway' without adult supervision.

> I don't trust people. [There's] too much violence, drug and alcohol abuse.

Other parents, however, contradicted this and saw their neighbourhood as a good place for kids to grow up. They spoke of good neighbours and allowing their children to go and play at nearby houses of friends and family (in one street five brothers and their families lived in separate households at Numbers 5, 7, 10, 11 and 16).

> The neighbours are very good…Yeah, the kids they go out to play. It's really good, they [the neighbours] watch out for the kids as well.

Fears their children could drown in the estuary were commonly expressed. Many parents emphasised the dangers of water and had stories about people who had drowned.

> There have been two or three kids who have drowned.

This was countered by one parent:

> Like we never heard anybody drowned and all of that…I've been living here for 20 years plus, I've never heard anybody drowned.

The three parents who had grown up in the area had, like the young local interviewer, Kim, freely explored this neighbourhood as children. One of these was Kelly's mother. While she, along with the other two, afforded their children more licence than many other parents, all commented on changes over time making the neighbourhood less safe.

> When I was a kid I could go running all around, out of sight. But over the years a lot of things have happened…

Contrasting perceptions of specific local places

The neighbourhood places (Figure 8.2), which researchers saw as likely to encourage children's play and exploration, were viewed differently by parents and children.

Researchers saw the jetty as a wonderful neighbourhood attribute: a place for playing and exploring; a place for fishing, swimming, boating and other physical activities.

Children and parents saw a dangerous place, unsuitable for children and strictly off limits unless accompanied by an adult (or very occasionally an older sibling). While one or two children talked of going fishing or swimming, throwing stones in the water or simply looking on, most never went to the jetty, and did not want to.

> I don't like going to the wharf. I might fall in the water. I might drown.

> I never, never, never come. I'm not allowed...cause I might drown.

They echoed parents' spoken fears of drowning and danger.

Some parents also talked of concerns about teenagers getting drunk and broken glass around the jetty.

FIGURE 8.2 Participant researcher photographs of neighbourhood places

> Some of the local thugs hang out down there sometimes and it is not really a place to be because there is nothing for kids.

Researchers saw the reserve bordering the estuary as a valuable neighbourhood attribute: a place of great natural beauty in which to play and explore and to learn about the natural environment.

Again, most children and parents saw a place of danger which was largely off limits to children unless accompanied by adults or older siblings/cousins.

A few children talked of liking going to the reserve, but taking care not to go near the water or the mud and worrying about dogs from houses backing onto the reserve.

> I go with my sister but I don't actually go down there [near the water] – I just go not far because I'm too scared.

> There's lots of scary dogs.

Parents also voiced concerns about dogs, the water, other people who might be on the reserve – and the mud.

> The nature of the mud...and anything can happen if [children are] unsupervised.

However, two parents living near the reserve stressed its natural beauty.

> It's not too bad being close to the water, you can walk there. And it can be pretty. It can be nice.

Researchers saw a playground with equipment children could enjoy and a good open space for them to run around and play games.

Children liked playing there, but the playground was generally off limits unless they went there with a parent or older sibling/cousin. Some worried about being bullied and others about the proximity of the water.

> I'm not allowed to go to the park [without my older brother] cause its dangerous...cause there's bigger people than us...um they might, they'll be bad for me.

> The water [beside the park] is scary 'cause you could slip and fall in.

Parents feared their children might be bullied, and also worried about their children being near the water (a walkway led to the water's edge).

Sometimes we take the children to the park. But they can't go by themselves because sometimes the children fight there. They make arguments and things like that.

Researchers saw signs of urban decay in the boarded-up shopfronts. Only the dairy was still open for business – and alcohol rather than milk, bread or ice-creams was what was most prominently advertised.

But the shop was a magnet for many of the children and some were allowed to go there alone.

[I like] buying stuff...[I] buy some lollies and drinks and stuff.

I go to the shop for my mum to buy milk.

Other children are fearful of going alone to the dairy, because of adjacent gang-affiliated houses.

There is mostly gangs around here.

We always need to go with an adult because usually the [gang] is there, so yeah.

Many parents talked of the proximity of the gangs to the dairy and this making it unsafe for their children.

Homes leading to the dairy are gang-affiliated and trouble.

Others were less specific about why the shop was off limits to their children.

It's too far away...all sorts of people hang around there.

In all of the examples above, children's fears mirrored those of their parents; and the combination of children's fears and parental restrictions because of fears for their children's safety, limited levels of physical activity and independent mobility.

Discussion

The focus of our Kids in the City research is the well-being of children in urban areas. The aim is to explore the influence of the neighbourhood environment and parents' and children's neighbourhood perceptions on children's levels of physical activity and independent mobility, both important for child development and well-being. We want to ensure that the well-being of children is to the fore in urban planning. This is not presently the case in Aotearoa/New

Zealand, although Auckland Council's concern that that the needs of the city's 300,000 children must be better met (Auckland Council, 2012) is encouraging.

It is clear from the data that the children's independent mobility was extremely limited, and for some children non-existent. Children's out-of-school activities tended to centre around the home, in large part because of parental fears – real or imagined – of dangers in the neighbourhood.

Parents' perceptions of danger and risk were high – some fuelled by media reports ('we read the newspaper and there are not nice people out there who will take advantage of your children'). This supports findings in the literature that the media influences the way residents perceive the safety of their neighbourhood (Heath, 1984; Romer et al., 2003). Some perceptions of danger, particularly concerning the estuary, were fuelled by residents' stories of incidences of drowning (one, two or three, depending on the teller) and near-drownings. Several parents repeated these stories during CATIs and the focus group, although their veracity was challenged by the focus group participant who said she'd 'lived in the neighbourhood for 20 years and had never heard of anybody drowning'. Children, too, spoke of drownings, and their own fears that they might drown. These fears restricted children's access to what seemed to us, as outside observers, a wonderful natural resource for children's play and exploration. Many parents would not let their children play near the water because they feared they would drown – and so did their children. New Zealand has a high rate of death by drowning, with ongoing campaigns in the media focusing on children learning to swim and keep themselves safe in and around water to reduce drownings. Of the 123 people who drowned in 2011, none drowned in estuaries (Water Safety New Zealand, 2012).

Where parents' perceptions of risk were high, their children's tended to be also. Sam's mother would not let him venture unsupervised from home because of 'stranger danger' and drunkenness, and Sam in turn was scared to go out 'cause there's strangers around' and 'heaps of drunk people'; similarly Lyn worried she would be 'taken', just as her mother worried. Most of the children, like Sam and Lyn, did not question their parents' perceptions and, convinced that their neighbourhood was dangerous, did not want to go anywhere by themselves. However, a few challenged parental perceptions and/or restrictions. Kelly would have liked to go unaccompanied to her best friend's house – even though her mother wouldn't let her, because 'she thinks that there's lots of people around here that are bad'; and Tom rode his bike down to the jetty, despite his mother telling him it was out of bounds 'because it is too dangerous'. This unquestioning acceptance of parental restrictions is likely to change as children leave primary school (up to Year six – 5–10/11year olds) and move on to intermediate school (Years seven and eight – 11–13 year olds). Other research we are involved in with children living in the inner city shows greater levels of independent mobility – and fewer parental restrictions – once children move onto intermediate school.

There is a paradox at play here: parents, in their acute concern for their children's well-being and fears that they are unsafe walking and playing in their neighbourhood without adult supervision, are limiting their independent mobility and physical activity levels, thereby potentially affecting their children's long term well-being.

The literature shows children are more physically active outdoors than indoors, and when they have access to a range of outdoor recreational opportunities. This neighbourhood appeared to us as 'outsider' researchers to be well endowed with public spaces and amenities for play and exploration; but parental perceptions of danger and risk, echoed by their children, limited many children's recreational opportunities. Travel diaries showed many children made few excursions into their neighbourhood apart from trips between home and school in the seven days of data collection (and for some children even these were in a car). We do not yet know the effects of this on overall physical activity levels: whether time spent at home was time engaged in essentially sedentary activities; or whether children were involved in a lot of physical activity at home playing with siblings, cousins and friends – and whether their physical activity levels are high despite their lack of independent mobility and limited opportunities for walking, playing and engaging in outside recreational opportunities.

International research also shows that social engagement is fostered by children's independent mobility. Children in this neighbourhood had very little independent mobility; however, they nevertheless appeared to have high levels of social engagement as many had family members – aunties, uncles, cousins and grandparents – living close by, and interacted frequently with them. Travel diaries revealed children were often in the company of cousins, whether walking to school, visiting the mall or engaging in a variety of activities, including playing.

It is too soon to consider the extent of the influence of different urban forms on children's activity and independent mobility levels or explore similarities and differences across the six study neighbourhoods; this must await further data analysis. The literature suggests urban form influences physical activity levels in adults, and once the analysis of children's GPS and accelerometer data is complete it will provide insights into possible influences on children's activity levels also.

As outside observers we focused, like urban planners, on the visible attributes of the neighbourhood – streets, housing, gardens, parks and community facilities – and aspects of those attributes identified in the literature as promoting health and well-being (including physical activity and independent mobility). We were largely unaware of the social aspects known to insiders (resident children, parents and key informants) which affect these. Thus where we saw wonderful green spaces for children to explore around the estuary, most children saw a place off limits because of risks of drowning and feared they might drown or be attacked by dogs; and most parents saw a dangerous place close to the water where children could drown and young people drank alcohol (leaving broken glass to be trodden on) – and too far from home if anything went wrong. Similarly, where we saw a park well-endowed with playground equipment, children were not allowed to play there unsupervised because parents again saw somewhere close to water (they could drown) and where other children 'hung out' (children might get into fights). This combination of outsider–insider perspectives has generated 'a more layered portrait of the physical and social environments' (Cannuscio et al., 2009) that acknowledges the interplay between people and the places they inhabit and provides a more nuanced understanding of structural and social impacts on children's physical activity and independent mobility. Already these findings raise concerns about the well-being of urban children, likely to be further compromised as urban intensification continues.

It is instructive to note the differing perceptions of researchers, parents and children of this neighbourhood and specific features of it. The differences underline not only the influences of past experience, family, culture and media representations on perceptions, but also the importance of real consultation with people who live in an area, before decisions are made which affect their lives.

The United Nations Convention on the Rights of the Child, to which New Zealand is a signatory, sees children's well-being and quality of life as the ultimate indicators of sustainable development (Malone, 2001). How can we best ensure that the well-being of children is to the fore in urban planning? A good starting point is to contribute their experience and voice to the urban planning process.

References

Angrosino, M. V. and Mays de Perez, K. A. (2000) 'Rethinking observation: from method to context', in Denzin, N. K. and Lincoln. Y. S. (Eds), *Handbook of Qualitative Research*, 2nd edn, 673–702, Thousand Oaks, CA: Sage Publications.

Auckland City Council (2009) *Strong and Healthy Communities Strategy*, Draft, Auckland: Auckland City Council. Available at http://www.aucklandcity.govt.nz/council/documents/10yearplan/docs/TYPFULLfinal.pdf (April 2011).

Auckland Council (2012) *The Auckland Plan,* Auckland: Auckland Council.

Auckland Regional Growth Forum (1999) *A Vision for Managing Growth in the Auckland Region. Auckland Regional Growth Strategy: 2050*, Auckland: Auckland Regional Growth Forum.

Braun, V. and Clarke, V. (2006) 'Using thematic analysis in psychology', *Qualitative Research in Psychology*, 3, 77–101.

Burdette, H. L. and Whitaker, R. C. (2005) 'A national study of neighbourhood safety, outdoor play, television viewing, and obesity in preschool children', *Pediatrics*, 116, 657–662.

Cannuscio, C., Weiss, E. E., Fruchtman, H., Schroeder, J., Weiner, J. and Asch, D. A. (2009) 'Visual epidemiology: Photographs as tools for probing street-level etiologies', *Social Science and Medicine*, 69, 553–564.

Carpiano, R. (2009) 'Come take a walk with me: The "go-along" interview as a novel method of studying the implications of place for health and well-being', *Health & Place*, 15, 263–272.

Carr, A. (2004) *Positive Psychology*, Hove: Brunner-Routledge.

Carroll P., Witten K. and Kearns, R. (2011) 'Housing intensification in Auckland, New Zealand: Implications for children and families', *Housing Studies*, 26(3), 353–367.

Carver, A., Timperio, A. and Crawford, D. (2008) 'Playing it safe: The influence of neighbourhood safety on children's physical activity: A review', *Health & Place*, 14, 217–227.

Christensen, P. and O'Brien, M. (2003) 'Children in the city: Introducing new perspectives', in Christensen, P. and O'Brien, M. (Eds) *Children in the City, Home, Neighbourhood and Community,* 1–12, London: Routledge Falmer.
Clements, R. (2004) 'An investigation of the status of outdoor play', *Contemporary Issues in Early Childhood,* 5, 68–79.
Cooper, M. (1992) 'Environmental memories', in Altman, I. and Low, S. (Eds), *Place Attachment,* 87–112, New York: Plenum Press.
Dagkas, S. and Stathi, A. (2007) 'Exploring social and environmental factors affecting adolescents' participation in physical activity', *European Physical Education Review,* 13, 369.
Ellaway, A., MacIntyre, S. and Kearns, A. (2001) 'Perceptions of place and health in socially contrasting neighbourhoods', *Urban Studies,* 38, 2299–2316.
Ewing, R. (2009) *Travel and the Built Environment – A Meta-Analysis,* Washington, DC: U.S. Environmental Protection Agency.
Flynn, M., McNeil, D., Maloff, B., Mutasingwa, D., Wu, M. and Ford, C. et al. (2006) 'Reducing obesity and related chronic disease risk in children and youth: A synthesis of evidence with "best practice" recommendations', *Obesity Reviews,* 7, 7–66.
Freeman, C. (2006) 'Colliding worlds: Planning with children and young people for better cities', in Gleeson, B. and Sipe, N. (Eds) *Creating Child Friendly Cities: Reinstating Kids in the City,* London: Routledge.
Freeman C. and Aitken-Rose, E. (2005) 'Voices of youth: Planning projects with children and young people in New Zealand local government', *Town Planning Review,* 76, 375–400.
Gleeson, B. and Sipe, N. (Eds) (2006) *Creating Child Friendly Cities: Reinstating Kids in the City,* London: Routledge.
Heath, L. (1984) 'Impact of newspaper crime reports on fear of crime – Multimethodological investigation', *Journal of Personality and Social Psychology,* 47(2), 263–276.
Janz, K., Kwon, S., Letuchy, E., Gilmore, J., Burns, T. and Toner, J. et al. (2009) 'Sustained effect of early physical activity on body fat mass in older children', *American Journal of Preventative Medicine,* 37, 35–40.
Jones, P., Bunce, G., Evans, J., Gibbs, H. and Ricketts Hein, J. (2008) 'Exploring space and place with walking interviews', *Journal of Research Practice,* 4(2), http://jrp.icaap.org/index.php/jrp/article/view/150/161.
Karsten, L. (2005) 'It all used to be better?', *Children's Geographies,* 3, 275–290.
Karsten, L. (2009) 'From a top-down to a bottom-up urban discourse: (Re) constructing the city in a family-inclusive way', *Journal of Housing and the Built Environment,* 24(3), 317–329.
Kearns, R. and Collins, D. (2006) 'Children in the intensifying city: Lessons from Auckland's walking school buses', in Gleeson, B. and Sipe, N. (Eds), *Creating Child Friendly Cities: Reinstating Kids in the City,* 105–120, London: Routledge.
Kellett, M. (2010) *Rethinking Children and Research.* London: Continuum.
Lali, M. (1992) 'Urban-related identity: Theory, measurement and empirical findings', *Journal of Environmental Psychology,* 12, 285–303.
Mackett, R., Brown B., Gong Y., Kitazawa, K. and Paskins, J. (2007) 'Children's independent movement in the local environment', *Built Environment,* 33, 454–468.
Malone, K. (2001) 'Children, youth and sustainable cities', *Local Environment,* 6, 5–12.
Malone, K. (2007) 'The bubble-wrap generation: Children growing up in walled gardens', *Environmental Education Research,* 13, 513–527.
Ministry of Health (2008) *A Portrait of Health: Key results of the 2006/07 New Zealand Health Survey.* Available at: http://www.moh.govt.nz/moh.nsf/pagesmh/7601/$File/portrait-of-health-june08.pdf (May 2011).

Ministry of Transport (2009) *How New Zealanders Travel: Trends in the NZ Household Travel Survey 1989-2008*. Wellington: Ministry of Transport.

Moore, R. (1986) *Childhood's Domain,* London: Croom Helm.

Morrow, V. (2003) 'Improving the neighbourhood for children', in Christensen, P. and O'Brien, M. (Eds) *Children in the City, Home, Neighbourhood and Community*, 162–183, London: Routledge Falmer.

Oliver, M., Witten, K., Kearns, R., Mavoa, S., Badland, H. and Carroll, P. et al. (2011) 'Kids in the City Study (KITC): Research design and methodology', *BMC Public Health*, 11, 587.

Patton, M. Q. (1990) *Qualitative Evaluation and Research Methods* (2nd edn.), Beverly Hills, CA: Sage.

Proshansky, H. and Gottlieb, N. (1989) 'The development of place identity in the child', *Zero to Three* (December), 18–25.

Reilly, J. (2005) 'Descriptive epidemiology and health consequences of childhood obesity', *Best Practice & Research Clinical Endocrinology & Metabolism*, 14, 327–341.

Romer, D., Jamieson, K. and Aday, S. (2003) 'Television news and the cultivation of fear of crime', *Journal of Communication*, 53, 1, 88–104.

Statistics New Zealand (2009) *Quick Stats about Auckland Region*. Available at http://www.stats.govt.nz/Census/2006CensusHomePage/QuickStats/AboutAPlace/SnapShot.aspx?tab=Work&id=1000002 (May, 2011).

Strong, W. B., Malina, R. M., Blimkie, C. J., Daniels, S. R., Dishman, R. K. and Gutin, B. et al. (2005) 'Evidence-based physical activity for school-age youth', *Journal of Pediatrics*, 146, 732–737.

Tranter, P. and Pawson, E. (2001) 'Children's access to local environments: A case-study of Christchurch, New Zealand', *Local Environment*, 6, 27–48.

Tyler, T. R. and Cook, F. L. (1984) 'The mass media and judgments of risk: Distinguishing impact on personal and societal level judgments', *Journal of Personality and Social Psychology*, 47(4), 693–708.

UNICEF (2010) *Child Friendly Cities*. Available from: http://www.childfriendlycities.org/, (January 2010).

Valentine, G. (2004) *Public Space and the Culture of Childhood,* Aldershot: Ashgate.

Wang, Y. and Beydoun, M. (2007) 'The obesity epidemic in the United States – gender, age, socioeconomic, racial/ethnic and geographic characteristics: A systematic review and meta-regression analysis', *Epidemiologic Reviews*, 29, 6–28.

Water Safety New Zealand (2012) http://www.watersafety.org.nz/news/latest-news/drowning-toll-at-eight-year-high; http://www.watersafety.org.nz/assets/PDFs/Drowning/2011-Fact-Sheets/Environment-Tidal-Waters.pdf (January 2013)

Whitsman, C. and Mizrachi, D. (2009) *Vertical Living Kids: Creating Supportive High Rise Environments for Children in Melbourne, Australia*. A report to the Health Promotion Foundation, Melbourne: Faculty of Architecture, Building and Planning, University of Melbourne.

Wilson, R. (1997) 'A sense of place', *Early Childhood Education Journal*, 24, 191–195.

Witten, K., Blakely, T., Bagheri, N., Badland, H., Ivory, V. and Pearce, J. et al (2012) 'Neighbourhood built environment is associated with transport and leisure physical activity: New Zealand findings using objective exposure and outcome measures', *Environmental Health Perspectives*, 120(7), 971–977.

Witten, K., Kearns, R., McCreanor, T., Penney, L. and Faalau, F. (2009) 'Connecting place and the everyday practices of parenting: Insights from Auckland, New Zealand', *Environment and Planning*, 41, 2893–2910.

9

CULTURE'S PLACE IN WELL-BEING

Measuring museum well-being interventions

Erica Ander, Linda Thomson and Helen Chatterjee

Introduction

The museum sector is beginning to see their work in terms of the well-being benefits it can bring. Well-being is an ambiguous term which is individualised and personally constructed and this chapter explores questions surrounding the work of the museum sector including: Can museums' subtle work on well-being be measured? Can museums' experience in evaluation and articulating bring value to the measurement of well-being? It examines well-being in five health care contexts via a cultural well-being intervention adapted to the capabilities of patients and the health care environment, using mixed qualitative and quantitative methods, psychological scales and grounded theory, to consider ways of working and the well-being benefits accrued.

Culture has historically been treated as an 'added-extra' by many local and central governments although its instrumental value to other government priorities has begun to be recognised in the past few decades. However, with the introduction of 'well-being' as a priority, the means of achieving it in the population has been seen as much more diverse, including a role for culture. For museums, heritage and arts organisations that have been struggling to show their worth in the funding maelstrom for decades and losing out to 'harder' imperatives such as education, health and the economy, the amorphousness and enveloping nature of the new priority 'well-being' is a boon. Those who work in museums and culture have known that the outcomes of their work contribute in subtle and idiosyncratic ways to individual and community health and well-being, 'Rather than the cherry on the policy cake to which they are so often compared, the arts should be seen as the yeast without which nothing will rise' (Matarasso,1997). Now with well-being at the top of most governments' agendas, the time has come to attempt to capture, measure and advocate this effect. Museums have a history of showing impact in instrumental outcomes such as regeneration, social inclusion and, in particular, education. Can this experience be put to use in understanding and measuring cultural well-being outcomes? This chapter looks at museums' previous evaluation experience, mainly in learning, and reports on a museum-based project to measure well-being in several health care settings, called 'Heritage in Hospitals'.

Learning from museum 'learning'

Museums have always been designated educational institutions from the foundation of the first public museums. As Britain came through the Thatcher and then the Blair years, cultural organisations, along with other publicly funded institutions were asked to justify their subsidies. Education or 'learning' as it became known, including 'lifelong learning', was brought to the fore as a large contribution many museums were making to government priorities. Anderson's 1997 report, revised in 1999, 'A Common Wealth' (Anderson, 1999) set up museums as education providers but also recommended they improve these services to become more consistent and better quality. Since then, many museums have upgraded their provision and 'learning in the museum' has become mainstream.

Museum learning is idiosyncratic, free choice, non-prescriptive and different for everyone. It is influenced by personal experience and background, by motivation, by the social circumstance of the museum visit and even by the impact of the physical surroundings and environment. Falk and Dierking described this with their concept of the Interactive Learning Experience (Falk & Dierking, 1992). The educational theory of Constructivist Learning chimed well with the type of learning that happened in museums; it saw visitors constructing their own experience and taking what they wanted from a museum visit according to their interest and levels of previous learning. This theory presumed that testing visitors on the content of an exhibition on exit would not capture all the learning that had happened. Museum learning was in danger of being underestimated because it was so different from the traditional concept of how learning happened and what it was. In order to acknowledge the type of learning that was happening in museums, a new practice of evaluation of outcomes developed. Museum learning evaluation employs observational methods such as tracking and timing visitors and qualitative methods such as interviews, focus groups and accompanied visits to try to understand how people learn from a museum encounter.

In 2004, the Museums, Libraries and Archives Council (MLA) launched Inspiring Learning for All (MLA, 2011), a set of learning standards and principles that museums, archives and libraries could aim to organise their learning programmes around, as well as an evaluation template that was based upon constructivist theory. Museums could now use a loose set of evaluation techniques including qualitative and quantitative methods to assess programme achievements in areas of: 1) Knowledge and Understanding; 2) Skills; 3)

Enjoyment, Inspiration and Creativity; 4) Attitudes and Values; and 5) Actions, Behaviour and Progress, collectively known as the Generic Learning Outcomes (GLOs). Research showed that many museums, archives and libraries developed this conceptual framework as 'a means of understanding, analysing and talking about learning' (Research Centre for Museums and Galleries, 2003). At the same time, a central government funding stream for regional museums, 'Renaissance in the Regions' was being implemented with education as a major priority (and a major promise on the part of the museums). *What did you Learn in the Museum Today?* (Research Centre for Museums and Galleries, 2004) was an evaluation of the educational outcomes of the museum hubs receiving Renaissance money utilising the GLO scheme of evaluation.

During the last couple of decades museums have also been more involved in their communities, partly driven by government imperatives mainly from the Department of Culture, Media and Sport (DCMS) and partly from an internal realisation among the sector that development of new audiences required innovative approaches to different types of people. Expecting people to visit from traditionally non-visiting groups was futile; museums needed to reach out into the community and show people what they could gain from involvement in their heritage. The impacts of these gradual changes in approaches were felt in terms of regeneration of areas, community cohesion, social inclusion and other social improvements. The instrumental benefits of museum work became a mainstream expectation finding its way into DCMS and Heritage Lottery Funding conditions (DCMS, 2012).

In a similar way to 'learning theory' that started to broaden its definition of how learning could and did happen a few years ago, the health care sector and local governments are now at the stage where they are re-examining what is meant by good health and healthy communities, and looking to preventative medicine, multi-agency approaches and promotion of well-being in line with ongoing changes to the National Health Service (NHS) and the development of clinical commissioning groups in place of primary care trusts. The UK Medical Collections group recently commissioned research, funded by Arts Council England, into how medical museums could successfully engage with diverse audiences and contribute to people's health and well-being (Bodley, 2012). Drawing together existing work in this area the research highlights the UK's changing health agendas and offers insights into how museums might align their work in light of these changes. Perhaps this is a critical time for museums to promote their own contribution to this newly broadened agenda, as they did with learning before; however, a new approach to evaluation may be necessary as with museum learning. In common with museum learning, well-being has an individual and constructivist nature. Individual well-being resources (e.g. health and education) and experiences are different and constructed from a person's own starting point. Measuring an increase or improvement in well-being will need to be as flexible and versatile as measuring museum learning but, nevertheless, employ baseline measures with which to compare subsequent improvement.

Museums and well-being

Before measuring the well-being resulting from a museum intervention or programme, it is important to understand how museums can contribute to this area. Why would museums be a legitimate part of a well-being programme? Understanding the nature of museum objects and what is already known about how people respond to them is key to their contribution; it might, for example, be surmised that some intrinsic power of objects as well as the activities that the museums arrange for participants (exhibitions, outreach, debates, art classes, volunteer schemes, etc.) will have specific well-being outcomes. The neutral and inviting museum environment might also play a part in increasing well-being; 'The spatial importance of museums, libraries and archives should not be underestimated...They are notable, safe, open, public accessible spaces in the community which exist to help or enlighten people rather than oppress them or cost them money' (SWMLAC, 2004).

Museum sector bodies have been exploring health and well-being as a result of museum activity for several years. The appearance of the term 'well-being' in UK museum policy and strategy can be traced back through the MLA commissioned research into Generic Social Outcomes (GSOs) (Burns Owen Partnership, 2005), and the New Directions in Social Policy documents (MLA, 2004). The GSOs, a framework for museums to evaluate their programmes, were developed within a major strand called 'health and well-being' with an aspiration to fill gaps found as a result of the Burns Owen Partnership (2005) research. GSO sub-outcomes within this research included 'encouraging healthy lifestyles and contributing to mental and physical well-being', 'supporting care and recovery', 'supporting older people to live independent lives' and 'helping children and young people to enjoy life and make a positive contribution' (MLA, 2010).

In the last few years museums' role in well-being is beginning to be recognised by both the health care and the museum sectors. There are now numerous examples of 'museums in health' projects and programmes across the UK museum sector and beyond. Broadly this can be broken down into a number of different areas of provision:

- public health education
- mental health services and service/users
- older adults and reminiscence services
- children and hospital schools
- health professionals' and carers' training
- other (including health literacy, rehabilitation, intergenerational health projects).

A number of flagship projects have helped to raise the profile of the sector's work in relation to health and well-being. The 'Who Cares?' programme was a collaboration between six major museums and art galleries in the North West of England, health professionals and researchers from the University of Central Lancashire (Renaissance North West, 2011). The projects worked with a range of different audiences including homeless people, young people from a hospital psychiatric unit and audiences from residential and day care centres. National Museums Liverpool's 'House of Memories' programme showed how a museum can provide the social care sector with practical skills and knowledge to facilitate access to previously untapped cultural resources. The project targeted those people living with dementia and their carers, including health and social care staff from across Merseyside and North Cheshire (National Museums Liverpool, 2012). The programme was recently cited in *The Prime Minister's Challenge on Dementia* report, published by the Department of Health (Department of Health, 2012), exemplifying the growing profile that museums in health work is enjoying, beyond the museums sector. Museums as well as libraries have been involved in health literacy; examples include the Health Matters exhibition at the Science Museum, London; the Wellcome Collection's exhibition programme; and several exhibitions exploring and displaying issues around mental illness (e.g. Museum of Croydon; Manchester Art Gallery; Great North Museum; The Lightbox, Woking). Beyond health literacy, museums' contribution to well-being could be very important in terms of building personal resources, prevention of mental problems and de-medicalising health and well-being. This view is increasing among the highest levels of the medical establishment, as this quote from the editor of the *British Medical Journal* shows:

> Indeed the physical aspects of health may be the least important. We will all be sick, suffer loss and hurt, and die. Health is not to do with avoiding these givens but with accepting them, even making sense of them. If health is about adaptation, understanding and acceptance then the arts may be more potent than anything medicine has to offer.
>
> (Culture Unlimited, 2008)

An advocacy report presenting evidence of museums' role in underwriting mental health and emotional well-being, *Museums of the Mind* (Culture Unlimited, 2008) lists the special characteristics of museums in terms of their emotional well-being as: pedigree in philosophy, poetry and art seen as happiness-promoting phenomena; collections of stories and artefacts that are the meaning of life; strength in perspectives both of time and of various visitors; seeing the person not the illness; having artefacts which communicate in 3D and spark emotions and imagination; not selling anything; acting as calm sanctuaries, collective memory banks and anchors for mental health; being not medicalised or compulsory (Culture Unlimited, 2008). This description resonates with much of what museum workers know when they witness people exploring their museums, that they offer free choice (and are therefore accessible) learning environments dealing in identity, memory, the senses and insight; all of value for mental health including dementia. Engagement with objects is an asset to well-being yet to be fully explored although University College London (UCL) Museums & Public Engagement held a series of workshops in 2008 and published a book (Chatterjee, 2008) examining the health and well-being benefits of touching objects.

The idea of community well-being in museum practice is much wider and includes what policymakers variously name as community cohesion, neighbourhood renewal, civic engagement, local participation, safe spaces and environmental sustainability. Nearly all of the work that museums currently undertake with local communities, hard-to-reach and excluded audiences could be included in the 'social well-being' remit of local governments. The museums' role in regeneration, built heritage, tourism and retail relates successfully to 'economic' and 'environmental' well-being. Community issues in turn are seen more and more to influence preventative mental health and individual well-being. The potential contributions to community well-being are too numerous to list and originate from nearly every museum but they have mostly not been seen or evaluated as such. The synergy between well-being and museums, culture, communities and health care is conceptualised in Figure 9.1 and is explored in detail in Chatterjee and Noble's (2013) *Museums, Health and Well-being*.

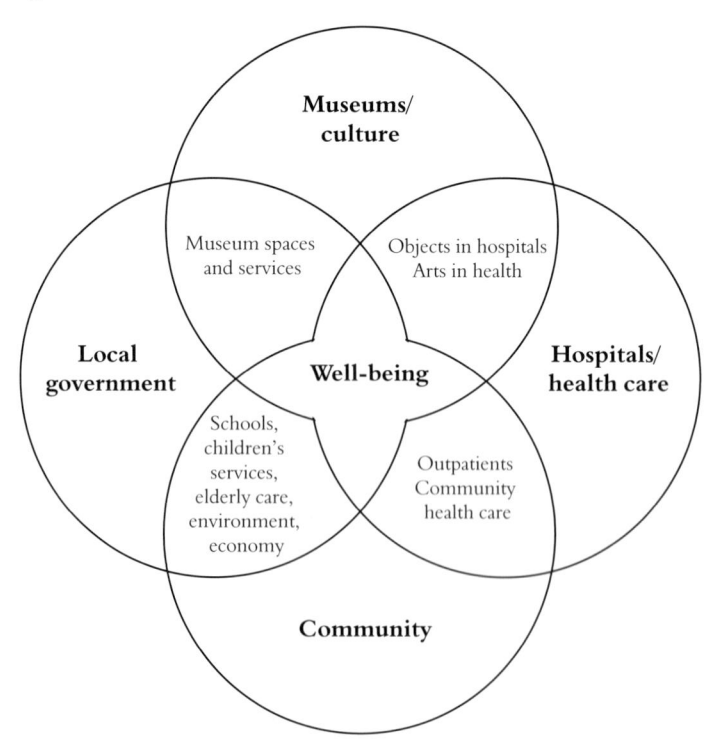

FIGURE 9.1 Well-being in museum practice (Adapted from Ander et al., 2011)

The New Economics Foundation (NEF, 2009) developed 'Five Ways to Well-being' as a simple way to conceptualise well-being along the same lines as healthy eating strategies (five portions of fruit or vegetable per day); they comprise:

- Connect – with the people around you
- Be Active
- Take Notice – Be curious, catch sight of the beautiful, remark on the unusual
- Keep Learning – Try something new, rediscover an old interest
- Give – Do something nice for a friend or a stranger (including volunteering)

(NEF, 2009)

Museums can address these ways to well-being in providing opportunities and encouragement for people to connect with others around them, take notice and keep learning, mainly through exhibitions and community and education programming. Museums' long pedigree in learning may in fact be contributing to well-being since, according to NEF, they appear highly correlated. Perhaps less obviously, museums touch on being active and giving through their volunteer programmes (e.g. conserving parts of a building or garden, providing a dance or music workshop connected with an exhibition, giving a guided walk) or having friends' programmes where people can meet and give their time and resources.

Approaches to measuring well-being

Since there is no single accepted way of measuring well-being, museums need to find a way of evaluating their contribution to well-being, as well as using their findings as an advocacy tool. Different disciplines have taken routes to measure well-being in line with their theoretical frameworks and research paradigms. Some examples of approaches are outlined here to explore their 'fit' with culture and museum evaluation.

Economists most often define well-being as happiness or life satisfaction, either generally or satisfaction with a number of life domains (Galloway & Bell, 2006a). They tend to look at it in terms of population rather than individuals and connect it with wealth (utilitarianism). Can a score on someone's level of life satisfaction actually explain someone's experience of life? The fact that 'happiness' levels have stayed flat while the gross domestic product (GDP) has risen in the last century in western democracies (Bacon et al., 2010; Lane, 2000; NEF, 2009) suggests the wealth/happiness correlation is no longer valid. Economists are now looking at population-scale indexes other than GDP.

The NEF, a think tank directed at policymakers, is part of a new cohort of researchers who define well-being along two or more dimensions, not just life satisfaction or emotion. In particular there is another essential component of well-being, something that NEF (2004) call 'personal development' in their evaluation of well-being. According to NEF research into young people's well-being in the city of Nottingham (NEF, 2004), at least two of these dimensions – life satisfaction and personal development – can operate independently of each other, with some people when measured scoring much higher or lower on one dimension than the other. The 'meaningfulness' element has been identified and developed by others, such as Seligman who sees 'the good life' or working towards 'gratifications' with some element of skill and challenge as essential to well-being alongside 'the pleasant life' (Seligman, 2002, cited in NEF, 2004). Lane (2000) includes life satisfaction, human development and justice as elements of well-being, a 'Trinity of Good'. Ryff (1989) validated a theory and scale of six dimensions of well-being including autonomy, purpose in life and personal growth, which all relate to the personal development dimension of well-being, rather than just 'feeling good' or pleasure.

Experimental psychologists and health care researchers have developed scales to quantify individual well-being specifically for use in clinical settings. (For a review see Thomson et al., 2011). A typical example of a well-being measure is the Psychological General Well-being Scale (Dupuy, 1984) that consists of eighteen items within six dimensions (anxiety, depression, positive well-being, self-control, vitality, general health). Respondents are required to rate statement items (e.g. has your daily life been full of things that were interesting to you?) on a scale of one to six. Although well-being scales can indicate anomalies in wellness or illness, from which action or treatment could be instituted, in standardising psychological well-being there appears to be little room for the voice of the individual which may have a very different perspective on what makes them happy or well. The scales also do not indicate why the individual has a certain well-being level; however, it is not always necessary to know this if baseline measured from the start of a museum-related activity is compared with those further down the line, either at the end of a session or a course of several sessions.

Some cultural evaluations have used qualitative research as a way to capture the subtle nature of both well-being changes and culture on an individual. Arts-in-health, a related field, of interest to museums, has often used this approach. Often evaluation is undertaken with a few individuals taking part in a programme, and the changes within them as a result of an arts intervention can sometimes only be explained in words not numbers. These words are then interpreted to show well-being, for example work by the North West Culture Observatory (2006); Manchester Metropolitan University (2007); and Stickley et al. (2011) at University of Nottingham. These approaches, although producing more valid descriptions of what is happening within individuals, have problems with the causality and generalisability needed for policy change. Although health care trusts are beginning to accept these 'soft' approaches, 'hard' data is often better understood by a sector that works on cost–benefit systems. Staricoff's (2004) review of arts-in-health research covers many evaluations which use numerical, statistical and physiological data to support well-being benefits. These assessments could be a learning point for museums wishing to evaluate their work.

Challenges to measuring well-being in museum work

Measuring the effect of culture and, in particular, museums on well-being is afflicted by several difficulties, including a lack of consistency in the definition of well-being, the subtle and unique nature of museum experiences that make it difficult to apply an empirical research method, and a lack of theory that relates culture to well-being. Although the word 'well-being' appears to be ubiquitous there are few comprehensive definitions in academic literature, policy documents or everyday use, producing difficulties when compiling evidence. Well-being is often conflated with 'health', 'quality of life' and 'happiness'. A literature review compiled for the Scottish Government on cultural indicators of quality of life (QoL) and well-being admits that 'QoL is a vague and difficult concept to define, widely used but with little consistency... "well-being" is even more ambiguous, abstract and nebulous a term... Put simply, an accepted, uniform definition of either term does not exist' (Galloway & Bell, 2006c).

The NEF (2009) defines well-being as 'most usefully thought of as the dynamic process that gives people a sense of how their lives are going, through the interaction between their circumstances, activities and psychological resources or "mental capital"'. NEF suggests that in order to achieve well-being, people need a broader and more subjective definition that involves: 'a sense of individual vitality', 'to undertake activities which are meaningful, engaging, and which make them feel competent and autonomous' and 'a stock of inner resources to help them cope when things go wrong and be resilient to changes beyond their immediate control'. NEF expressed that

> It is also crucial that people feel a sense of relatedness to other people, so that in addition to the personal, internally focused elements, people's social experiences – the degree to which they have supportive relationships and a sense of connection with others – form a vital aspect of well-being.
> (NEF, 2009)

Beyond definition problems, the subtle, individual and focused approach needed in the measurement of culture outcomes sits in conflict with the needs of policy and health care service evaluation.

> Public policymakers world-wide require research that demonstrates causal relationships between cultural participation and desired policy outcomes, and for these to be single-causal relationships... Another key issue for public policymakers is the need for research whose results can be extrapolated or *generalised* to the population as a whole... the majority of individual level studies of culture and sport and QoL do not allow this.
> (Galloway & Bell, 2006c, emphasis original)

Data that evidence cultural transformation or experience or indeed changes in individual feelings of well-being tend to be subtle, fugitive and qualitative; they have to be teased out of conversation and behaviour, rather than asked point-blank. Cultural programmes work with small numbers so sample sizes tend to be small and it is difficult to make predictions or generalise. People engage with culture in myriad different ways, sitting alongside all other aspects of their life such as family, health, education, job, holidays etc. The difficulty of isolating the effect of culture in one's life means attributing the cause of change or transformation to culture (causality) is also difficult. In gathering evidence for culture's effect on well-being a clash between validity and policy needs exists. Policy dictates what needs to be measured and yet:

> When researchers impose the domains of life to be measured, they risk omitting important aspects that may have greater relevance to that person or imposing aspects that have little or no relevance. The results therefore may have little validity.
> (Day & Jankey, 1996, cited in Galloway & Bell, 2006d)

The risk of underestimating culture and arts' influence on well-being may occur as happened when using orthodox methods of measuring learning. Galloway and Bell in concluding their literature review suggest that QoL (and well-being within it) may be:

> Just not a fruitful subject for research: useful as an 'organizing concept' but just too complex to be 'do-able'. Alternatively, these points might lead to the view that the natural science research model, of which notions of 'causality' and 'generalizability' are part, may not be the most useful for this type of research subject'.
> (Galloway & Bell, 2006b)

At a practical level it can be debated how museums might progress in terms of measuring well-being impacts in order to persuade a health care or local authority that museum participation will increase well-being. Another issue is whether museums use the language and paradigms of medical and/or policy-based methods while staying 'true' to the subtle and subjective well-being benefits which museums deliver. Perhaps once again museums can benefit from 'learning' since this concept once seemed so diverse, free choice and individual that a 'one-size-fits-all' standard for people's achievements in museums could not be attained:

> it would be inappropriate for museums, archives and libraries to set specific learning outcomes for learners to achieve. They do not know the prior knowledge of their users and so would be unable to make judgments about how much users had learnt. Users themselves, however, are capable of making such judgments about their own learning.
> (RCMG, 2003)

The museum evaluators need to look at relative improvement in people's well-being under their own standards and in the dimensions they feel are important to them, while attempting to isolate the specific role of culture or museums within this.

'Heritage in Hospitals' project

'Heritage in Hospitals' is a successful example of how museums can measure their impact in terms of well-being. This Arts and Humanities Research Council (AHRC) funded project was carried out by UCL Museums & Public Engagement in conjunction with University College London Hospitals (UCLH) Arts (MREC No: 06/Q0505/78). Researchers on the project took boxes of museum objects into hospitals and other health care settings and carried out one-to-one sessions at participants' bedsides in order to examine benefits to well-being. Sessions lasting 30–40 minutes consisted of discussing and handling a selection of different objects sourced from UCL's art, archaeology, Egyptology, geology and zoology collections (see Figure 9.2). Quantitative measures comprising the Positive Affect Negative Affect Scale (PANAS) (Watson et al., 1988) for psychological well-being and Visual Analogue Scales (VAS) (EuroQol Group, 1990) for subjective well-being and happiness, were taken before and after the session and audio was recorded for subsequent qualitative analysis. Prior to the selection of PANAS and VAS, several hundred measurement scales for psychological well-being, QoL and health status were reviewed for their suitability to evaluate well-being occurring from an object handling session at patients' bedsides (Thomson et al., 2011). Measures were shortlisted using selection criteria of internal and external validity, practicality and sensitivity. Focus on the extent of usage in health care, breadth of application, ease of administration and degree of responsiveness informed the recommendation of optimum measures for the research. Measures indirectly related to well-being (e.g. physical disability and social support) or unlikely to reflect change after a short intervention (e.g. symptoms worsening with age) were omitted from the review.

The PANAS (Watson et al., 1988) consists of a self-report mood adjective list where 10 positive emotions (e.g. enthusiastic, attentive) and 10 negative emotions (e.g. irritated, distressed) are assessed on a one to five Likert scale to the strength of their mood at that moment in time. The VAS asks respondents to indicate their level of 'well-being' and 'happiness' on a vertical scale running from 0 to 100. Positive and Negative PANAS scores were analysed separately since the scale's authors had found little correlation between positive and negative mood implying the two dimensions were orthogonal, representing independent aspects of emotion. Furthermore the PANAS was successfully tested on factors concerned with reliability (e.g. test–retest reliability) and validity (e.g. construct validity). A possible disadvantage of the PANAS, however, was that some mood adjectives such as 'afraid' and 'scared' or 'guilty' and 'ashamed' could be

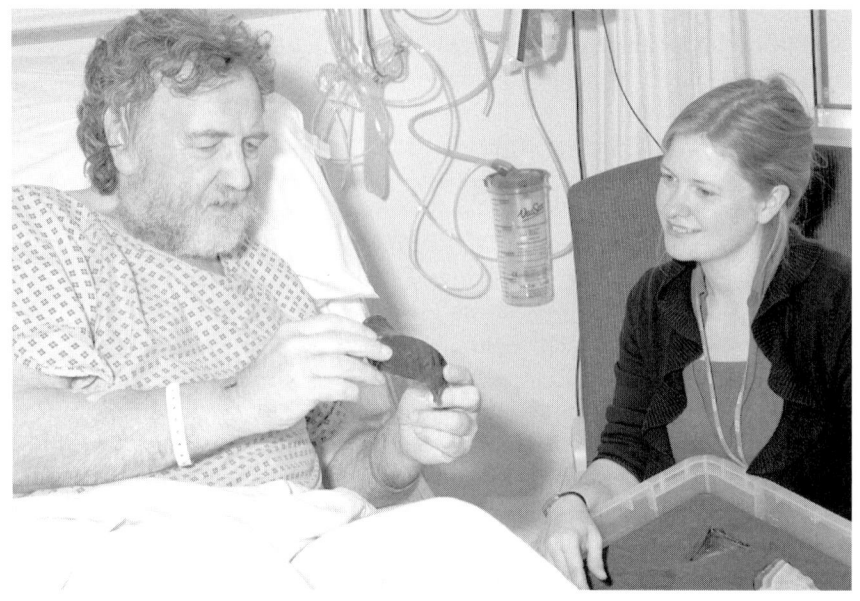

FIGURE 9.2 Bedside museum object handling session

interpreted as the same emotion particularly within a hospital environment. Findings revealed positive benefits for object handling when compared with a control group only able to discuss photographs of museum objects, and implicated the tactile component as beneficial in optimising well-being and happiness (Thomson et al., 2012a; 2012b).

In addition to UCLH, the 'Heritage in Hospitals' project collaborated with partners from the British Museum, Oxford University Museums (OUM), Reading Museum and a North London care home to research well-being outcomes of a museum object handling session with a variety of participants receiving health care. The project focused on adults and older adults in a number of health care settings within a general hospital (acute and elderly care, oncology and surgical admissions), a psychiatric hospital (older adult inpatients), two neurological rehabilitation hospitals (inpatient and outpatient) and a residential care home (older adults and those with dementia). A mixed methodology of quantitative and qualitative analysis was used to both quantify positive emotion, happiness and well-being and capture outcomes responsible for these changes, in this newly studied area (Thomson et al., 2012a; 2012b; Ander et al., 2012).

The session protocol comprised recruitment of volunteer patients and care home residents; explanation and questions regarding the patient information leaflet (PIL) and consent form; washing hands with soap and water or alcohol gel; taking baseline pre-session well-being measures; conducting a facilitated, one-to-one handling session; taking a post-session set of well-being measures and re-washing hands. On some occasions, further conversation or interviews were undertaken by the facilitator to collect additional qualitative data. Session protocols employed a semi-structured interview format which offered ways of interacting with the patients about the objects (e.g. What does it feel like? How does it make you feel?) with a recommended order of questions so that most sessions were sufficiently similar to compare. Within the residential care home and the psychiatric hospital, the protocol was adapted slightly, in consultation with staff, as group sessions rather than one-to-one sessions.

Although it was important to produce numerical results, particularly for the health care partners, the nature of the research area was also ideal for qualitative research as there was little existing theory about museums and well-being to support a hypothetical approach, the intervention was subtle, individual and cultural and the outcomes were unknown. A qualitative research approach could aim to understand (rather than quantify) phenomena and inductively generate new theory. Grounded theory method (Charmaz, 2006; Corbin & Strauss, 2008) was identified as the best analysis approach to generate new theories in this unexplored research area. Qualitative data comprised audio recordings of the handling sessions and interviews with participants, health care staff and museum professionals, and field notes written by facilitators. Staff gave insights into well-being outcomes among participants, particularly where qualitative measures were difficult to gather because of depressive symptoms or cognitive/attentional deficits (Ander et al., 2012). Transcripts of the qualitative data were entered into NVivo (qualitative analysis software) and firstly open coded, focusing to core theme coding; memos were used to generate relationships between themes, particularly session processes, outcomes and well-being.

The core themes that emerged were evidence of participant 'engagement' in the sessions, observed 'well-being' outcomes and participant 'background'. The range and nature of these phenomena were coded and descriptions and relationships emerged. In many ways the handling sessions appeared similar to those evaluated for 'learning' in that through conversation and sensory perception, participant 'engagement' with museum objects was noted. The research, however, was looking for engagement that led to 'well-being' rather than 'learning', even though learning may be an aspect of well-being. Participant well-being was inextricably linked to their health care context and quite conceivably altered by their hospital or medical experience, so any well-being benefits of handling objects should show improvement in this altered state.

It was not always possible to use theoretical sampling (Charmaz, 2006; Corbin & Strauss, 2008) as is ideal with grounded theory due to the constraints of the quantitative data collection, but because of the amount of sessions completed (over 200) theoretical sampling happened to a certain extent, meaning that core themes could be explored from within the collected sample when needed. The qualitative analysis revealed the following key outcomes for participants who took part in museum object handling sessions (originally listed by Ander et al., 2012):

- new perspectives
- positive feelings (excitement, enjoyment, wonder, privilege, luck, surprise)

- learning (including skills and confidence)
- energy, alertness
- positive mood (e.g. cheered up)
- sense of identity
- something different, inspiring
- calming, relieves anxiety
- passing time
- social experience
- tactile experience.

Review of methodology

The 'Heritage in Hospitals' project took a multi-centred approach, working with a number of health care settings each with their own characteristics, consequently research methodologies between different environments, staff systems and dominant medical conditions could be contrasted. The differences had significant effects on participant background, engagement and well-being leading to adaptions of the research protocol for different circumstances. Health care settings and participants varied in terms of:

- length of stay
- cognitive impairment
- physical impairment
- sensory impairment
- beginning, middle or end of illness/accident trajectory
- amount of professional medical attention/monitoring
- schedule of treatment or therapies
- low mental or physical health
- provision of 'living' quarters or communal areas
- size of institution
- staff support level
- critical or long term condition
- patient familiarity with hospital
- existence of treatment/therapy goals – criteria for discharge.

These characteristics affected aspects such as when the research could be conducted and respondents' ability to take part in it. The main challenges encountered were connected to patient impairment, particularly cognitive and attentional deficits in the care home residents and neurological rehabilitation patients. These participants found it difficult to understand the quantitative scales and at the same time were not always capable of showing 'engagement' in the activity, even though well-being might have occurred. With these participants the researcher needed to be aware of more subtle behavioural signs, helped by the medical staff and background knowledge of the participant's symptoms and conditions, and memos from the field became more important in data collection. The research team also concluded that simpler and quicker well-being scales were needed with these groups as the PANAS and VAS scales were difficult to use with groups since they were time-consuming and required individual explanation. Shorter and more readily understandable well-being scales are currently being trialled for use in these types of environments.

Although data could be gathered at the time of the handling sessions it was difficult to carry out follow-up interviews days or weeks afterwards to understand the longer term impacts, particularly in the general hospital wards due to high turnover and surgical timetables. At the general hospital rostering of staff on shift work made it difficult to interview staff who had been present while the sessions were taking place. Compared with other health care contexts, hospital staff got to know patients on a much shorter term basis and therefore provided less insightful comments. This had implications for the success of the sessions as well as for data collection. However, at other health care contexts, the team worked more closely with medical and pastoral staff able to give a good insight in the impact they felt the sessions were having. The health care context, and in particular staff availability, had a large influence on the quality of data collection.

Another challenge within the data collection framework was finding a way to record how people touched the objects. As a major part of the handling session, it was felt that the tactile interaction would have a special impact on well-being. Qualitative data derived from observation and session recordings revealed the touch experiences to some extent but were dependent upon the facilitator's memory and observation skills. Since little research has been conducted in this area there was no checklist of tactile behaviours to look for. In some instances permission was given for photography and video recording, and this provided a valuable source of information about the handling behaviours, that could be used more extensively in the future. The NHS guidelines on patient consent, however, made it onerous to obtain 'media' consent from patients on a large scale. The bulk of consent, scales and other paperwork were already an issue with many patients and, in some cases, proved to be a barrier to engagement.

The facilitator's role and prior experience proved critical to the success of the object handling sessions, particularly with regard to administering the scales. Participants were eager to answer according to their personalities or traits, but they needed to answer according to their mood at that point in time, i.e. state rather than trait emotion. It was found that although the VAS scales are in the form of a 100-increment scale, most people fill them in as if they were a 10-increment scale, only looking at the round numbers. People may well be not able to conceptualise their wellness or happiness in such subtle intervals of 100ths, or they may just find it quicker and easier to point to a multiple of 10. The staff at the psychiatric hospital confirmed that their patients found it difficult to conceptualise their own well-being, even on a simple scale.

Furthermore, several participants had difficulty in assessing their well-being directly, being unable to dissociate their psychological perception from their physical state. A shortened mood adjective list would be possible in the future and aid quick administration of the scales. However, different health care contexts produced different mood changes, so different versions may need to be produced.

Reliability and validity

Reliability and validity have different meanings in terms of quantitative and qualitative research. Quantitative reliability is achieved by ensuring the independent variable (object handling) is free of – controlling for or randomising extraneous and potentially confounding variables, necessary to ensure cause and effect on the dependent variable (well-being measures). Validity is achieved by ensuring that scales measure what they purport to measure. Qualitative reliability means minimising facilitator bias and, consequently, recording all analysis and data collection decisions to make them accountable and understandable to others (although not necessarily repeatable) is important. Validity is achieved by making sure that participants are given voice in the research.

The quantitative research was carried out as a field experiment rather than a laboratory experiment, still following the scientific method but in a real world environment so was able to examine causality. In addition to participants providing their own baseline measures of well-being and happiness, a control condition was instigated where, rather than handling and discussing museum objects, participants instead looked at and discussed photographs of these objects. The control condition removed the tactile element from the object sessions; however, all sessions still provided social and heritage interaction, consequently it was difficult to separate out these factors further without establishing a series of control groups to control for social aspects (e.g. a participant could handle objects and respond to a questionnaire in the absence of a facilitator) and cultural aspects (e.g. a participant could handle and discuss non-heritage objects). Although significant differences were found between sessions where objects were handled compared with sessions where objects were viewed as photographs that implied a role for tactile interaction in enhancing well-being, it is possible that the social and cultural aspects were partly responsible for the benefits to psychological and subjective well-being and happiness experienced. The qualitative data suggested that tactile, social and cultural aspects were all needed to produce effective and dynamic interaction with a well-being outcome greater than the sum of its parts.

Summary and conclusions

There is huge potential for museums to work within health care institutions and to create increased well-being among participants. Moving on from their experience in evaluating museum learning, museums can begin to evaluate their work in terms of well-being. 'Heritage in Hospitals' was a project that examined effects of museum object handling on well-being in hospital and health care settings and the methodologies it used have been reviewed here, providing a conceptual and practice-based framework for continuing much needed research regarding the impact of museums interventions in health care environments. The psychometric scales employed in 'Heritage in Hospitals' were useful in most contexts and quantified increases in well-being and happiness but needed adaptation for certain types of patients experiencing cognitive or attentional deficits. It was found, however, that qualitative data were needed to explain why these improvements occurred as the higher level of extraneous variables engendered through a field rather than a laboratory experiment made it more difficult to separate out tactile, social and cultural aspects.

Using a mixed methods framework for museum research works towards decreasing the paucity of theory about culture and well-being within the heritage sector and provides a much needed evidence base. Novel findings emerging from 'Heritage in Hospitals' exemplify the advantages of outreach sessions within the health care sector. Museums need to continue to be confident of their worth, utilising new ideas about well-being and multi-agency health approaches to develop offers to health care institutions and their service users. Given the ongoing changes in the UK's health care system, enacted as part of the Health and Social Care Act (2012) (see http://www.legislation.gov.uk/ukpga/2012/7/contents/enacted), third sector agencies and the role of the environment are playing an increasingly important role, helping to keeping people living independently in the community for longer. The notion of a 'Big Society', which seeks to create an environment that empowers local communities and people to take collective responsibility for their environment, communities and public health, will see a shift towards 'prevention is better than cure', within a model which will require a multi-agency approach, with an increased reliance on third sector organisations, including the museums and cultural heritage sector. The current body of evidence and good practice in the area of 'museums in health' described here and elsewhere (Chatterjee & Noble, 2013), sets the scene for a new era of museum programming which is more closely aligned with the health and well-being needs of individuals and communities.

References

Ander, E.E., Thomson, L.J., Lanceley, A., Menon, U., Noble, G. and Chatterjee, H.J. (2011). Generic well-being outcomes: Towards a conceptual framework for well-being outcomes in museums. *Museum Management and Curatorship, 26(3),* 237–259, http://dx.doi.org/10.1080/09647775.2011.585798.

Ander, E.E., Thomson, L.J., Lanceley, A., Menon, U., Noble, G. and Chatterjee H.J. (2012). Heritage, health and well-being: Assessing the impact of a heritage focused intervention on health and well-being. *International Journal of Heritage Studies*, http://dx.doi.org/10.1080/13527258.2011.651740.

Anderson, D. (1999). *A Common Wealth: Museums in the learning age*, 2nd edition. London: DCMS.
Bacon, N., Brophy, M., Mguni, N., Mulgan, G. and Shandro, A. (2010). *The State of Happiness: Can public policy shape people's well-being and resilience?* London: The Young Foundation.
Bodley, A. (2012). *History to Health: Research into changing health agendas for the UK Medical Collections Group*. Leeds: UKMCG. Available at: http://www.thackraymedicalmuseum.co.uk/.
Burns Owen Partnership (BOP). (2005). *New Directions in Social Policy: Developing the evidence base for museums, libraries and archives in England*. London: Museums, Libraries Archives Council.
Charmaz, K. (2006). *Constructing Grounded Theory*. London: Sage.
Chatterjee, H.J. (Ed.) (2008). *Touch in Museums: Policy and practice in object handling*. Oxford: Berg.
Chatterjee, H.J. and Noble, G. (2013). *Museums, Health and Well-being*. Farnham, Surrey: Ashgate Publishing Ltd.
Corbin, J. and Strauss, A. (2008). *Basics of Qualitative Research* (3rd edition). London: Sage.
Culture Unlimited. (2008). *Museums of the Mind: Mental health, emotional well-being and museums*. Available at: http://www.cultureunlimited.org/museums-of-the-mind.php.
Day, H. and Jankey, S.G. (1996). Lessons from the literature: Towards a holistic model of quality of life. In R. Renwick, I. Brown and M. Nagler (Eds.) *Quality of Life in Health Promotion and Rehabilitation. Conceptual approaches, issues and applications*, Thousand Oaks, CA: Sage
DCMS (2012) Sponsored Museums Annual Performance Indicators. Available at: www.gov.uk/government/organisations/department-for-culture-media-sport/series/sponsored-museums-annual-performance-indicators
Department of Health. (2012). *The Prime Minister's Challenge on Dementia. Delivering major improvements in dementia care and research by 2015: A report on progress*. Available at: https://www.wp.dh.gov.uk/dementiachallenge/files/2012/11/The-Prime-Ministers-Challenge-on-Dementia-Delivering-major-improvements-in-dementia-care-and-research-by-2015-A-report-of-progress.pdf.
Dupuy, H.J. (1984). The psychological general well-being index. In M.E. Matsson, C.D. Furberg and I. Elinson (Eds.). *Assessment of Quality of Life in Clinical Trials of Cardiovascular Therapy*. New York: Le Jacq Publications.
EuroQol Group. (1990). EuroQol: A new facility for the measurement of health-related quality of life. *Health Policy*, 16: 199–208.
Falk, J. and L. Dierking. (1992). *The Museum Experience*. Ann Arbor, MI: Whalesback Books.
Galloway, S. and D. Bell. (2006a). *Quality of Life and Well-being: Measuring the benefits of culture and sport: Literature review*. Scottish Government. section 6.57. Available at: http://www.scotland.gov.uk/Publications/2006/01/13110743/0.
Galloway, S. and D. Bell. (2006b). *Quality of Life and Well-being: Measuring the benefits of culture and sport: Literature review*. Scottish Government. section 8.54. Available at: http://www.scotland.gov.uk/Publications/2006/01/13110743/0.
Galloway, S. and D. Bell. (2006c). *Quality of Life and Well-being: Measuring the benefits of culture and sport: Literature review*. Scottish Government. section 2.6-7. Available at: http://www.scotland.gov.uk/Publications/2006/01/13110743/0.
Galloway, S and Bell, D. (2006d). *Quality of Life and Well-being: Measuring the benefits of culture and sport: Literature Review*. Scottish Government section 5.4 http://www.scotland.gov.uk/Publications/2006/01/13110743/0.

Heritage Lottery Fund (HLF). (2011). *Strategy and Planning*. Available at: http://www.hlf.org.uk/aboutus/howwework/strategy/Pages/Strategy.aspx.

Lane, R. (2000). *The Loss of Happiness in Market Democracies*. London: Yale University Press.

Manchester Metropolitan University. (2007). *Invest to Save: Arts in health evaluation*. Available at: http://www.miriad.mmu.ac.uk/investtosave/reports/.

Matarasso, F. (1997). *Use or Ornament? The social impact of participation in the Arts*. Stroud: Comedia. Available at: http://www.institutumeni.cz/res/data/004/000571.pdf.

Museums, Libraries and Archives Council (MLA). (2004). *New Directions in Social Policy: Health policy for museums, libraries and archives*. London: MLA. Available at: http://www.mla.gov.uk/what/publications/~/media/Files/pdf/2004/ndsp_health.ashx.

Museums, Libraries and Archives Council (MLA). (2010). *Generic Social Outcomes*. London: MLA. Available at: http://www.inspiringlearningforall.gov.uk/toolstemplates/genericsocial/.

Museums, Libraries and Archives Council (MLA). (2011). *Inspiring Learning*. London: MLA. Available at: http://www.inspiringlearningforall.gov.uk/.

National Museums Liverpool. (2012). *House of Memories. National museums Liverpool. Evaluation report*. Available at: http://www.liverpoolmuseums.org.uk/learning/documents/House-of-Memories-evaluation-report.pdf.

New Economics Foundation (NEF). (2004). *The Power and Potential of Well-being: Measuring young people's well-being in Nottingham*. London: NEF. Available at: http://www.neweconomics.org/publications/power-and-potential-well-being-indicators.

New Economics Foundation (NEF). (2009). *National Accounts of Well-being: What is well-being?* London: NEF. Available at: http://www.nationalaccountsofwell-being.org/learn/what-is-well-being.html.

North West Culture Observatory. (2006). *Culture and Health Building the Evidence*. Available at: http://www.northwestcultureobservatory.co.uk/well-being.asp.

Renaissance North West. (2011). *Who Cares? Museums, health and well-being*. MLA Renaissance North West.

Research Centre for Museums and Galleries (RCMG). (2003). *Measuring the Outcomes and Impact of Learning in Museums, Archives and Libraries: The Learning Impact Research Project end of project paper*. Leicester: RCMG. Available at: http://www.le.ac.uk/ms/research/pub1110.html pg 7.

Research Centre for Museums and Galleries (RCMG). (2004). *What did you Learn at the Museum Today?* Leicester: RCMG. Available at: http://www.mla.gov.uk/what/programmes/renaissance/~/media/Files/pdf/2004/what_did_you_learn_study1_v2.

Ryff, C. (1989). Happiness is everything, or is it? Explorations on the meaning of psychological well-being. *Journal of Personality and Social Psychology*, 57: 1069–1081.

Seligman, M. (2002). *Authentic Happiness*. New York: Free Press.

Staricoff, R. (2004). *Arts in Health: A review of the medical literature*. London: Arts Council England.

Stickley, T., Hui, A. and Duncan, K. (2011). *Arts on Prescription*. Nottingham: City Arts. Available at: http://www.lahf.org.uk/sites/default/files/Final%20AOP%20report%202011.pdf.

South West Museums & Libraries Association Champion (SWMLAC). (2004). *Regeneration and Renewal in the South West*. Taunton: SWMLAC, p. 4.

Thomson, L.J., Ander, E.E., Menon, U., Lanceley, A. and Chatterjee, H.J. (2011). Evaluating the therapeutic effects of museum object handling with hospital patients: A review and initial trial of well-being measures. *Journal of Applied Arts and Health*, 2(1), 37–56, http://dx.doi.org/10.1386/jaah.2.1.37_1.

Thomson, L.J., Ander, E.E., Lanceley, A., Menon, U. and Chatterjee, H.J. (2012a). Evidence for enhanced well-being in cancer patients from a non-pharmacological intervention. *Journal of Pain and Symptom Management*, 44(5), 731–740, http://dx.doi.org/10.1016/j.jpainsymman.2011.10.026.

Thomson, L.J., Ander, E.E., Menon, U., Lanceley, A. and Chatterjee, H.J. (2012b). Quantitative evidence for well-being benefits from a heritage-in-health intervention with hospital patients. *International Journal of Art Therapy*, 17(2), 63–79, http://dx.doi.org/10.1080/17454832.2012.687750.

Watson, D., Clark, L. and Tellegen, A. (1988). Development and validation of brief measures of positive and negative affect: The PANAS scales. *Journal of Personality and Social Psychology*, 54: 1063–1070.

10
USING WOODLANDS TO IMPROVE INDIVIDUAL AND COMMUNITY WELL-BEING

Liz O'Brien and Jake Morris

Introduction

There is a strong policy and research focus on the well-being of the British population; how this is identified, measured, and how it changes over time. A key question is how well-being is affected by various types of natural environment and in this chapter we draw on research carried out by (UK) Forest Research over the past decade to explore how woodlands and forests contribute to individual and community well-being.

The interest in well-being spans a wide range of policy arenas such as health, community cohesion, education, social justice and environment. In academia there is much research concerning well-being, primarily amongst psychologists and economists, but also more recently neuroscientists (exploring whether happiness is 'hardwired' in the brain), and also planners, geographers, philosophers, sociologists, and health promotion specialists (Layard, 2005; SDRN, no date). The present government in the UK initiated a consultation through the Office for National Statistics to develop a new suite of national indicators that capture well-being and extend the focus beyond measures such as gross domestic product (GDP) (Office for National Statistics, 2010). There is no single definition of well-being; however, a cross government well-being working group developed the following:

> Well-being is a positive physical, social and mental state; it is not just the absence of pain, discomfort and incapacity. It arises not only from the action of individuals, but from a host of collective goods and relationships with other people. It requires that basic needs are met, that individuals have a sense of purpose and that they feel able to achieve important personal goals and participate in society. It is enhanced by conditions that include

supportive personal relationships, security, rewarding employment and a healthy and attractive environment.

(Steuer and Marks, no date)

The above definition highlights the complexity of well-being and its key dimensions, of which the environment is one aspect. There is much debate about how well-being is measured. Dolan et al. (2006) identifies objective lists collected through administrative sources focusing on attributes of well-being, such as education, health status, housing and income. Identifying preference satisfaction (e.g. fulfilling desires) is a focus for economists. Flourishing accounts include ideas of personal growth and people realising their potential, while subjective well-being includes dimensions of how people feel (hedonic) and how they assess their well-being (e.g. life satisfaction) (Newton, 2007)

The natural environment figures within some of these typologies and in assessments of well-being. For example, in the sustainable development suite of well-being indicators (Defra, 2008), the value and use of green space is one of a number of indicators of well-being. The Millennium Ecosystem Assessment developed a model of how ecosystem services (supporting, provisioning, regulating and cultural) contribute to human well-being (security, health, good life, social relations, freedom) (Millennium Ecosystem Assessment, 2005). The UK National Ecosystem Assessment (2011) outlined the importance of nature and biodiversity to people's well-being and economic prosperity, but suggested that this is consistently undervalued in economic analysis and decision making.

In this chapter we are primarily concerned with woodlands and forests and how these contribute to people's personal well-being. We also explore how they contribute to people's sense of place and attachment to their local community. A range of research has highlighted that trees and woodlands hold many meanings for different people; with trees representing nature, the cycle of life, and holding symbolic and longevity value (Henwood and Pidgeon, 2001; Bishop et al., 2002). Access to woodlands is highly valued by the British population. For example, 358 million visits were made to woodlands in England in 2011 (Natural England, 2011). The cancellation of a public consultation on the future of the public forest estate in England in 2011, managed by Forestry Commission England (FCE), highlights the importance of public access to woodlands, feelings of ownership of public spaces and the well-being that can be gained from this access. The cancelled consultation was followed by the formation of an Independent Panel on Forestry (IPF) set up to explore the future of forestry in England (Defra, 2012). The IPF asked for comments from the public and 42,000 responses were received. A final report by the IPF called for a new woodland culture where woodlands are valued for the wide range of environmental, social and economic benefits they provide (Defra, 2012).

Over the past decade the Social and Economic Research Group (SERG) at Forest Research (the research agency of the Forestry Commission in Great Britain) has carried out a range of social science studies exploring the benefits that individuals and groups can gain from contact with woodlands. In this chapter we draw on the body of evidence built up by SERG to explore the role of woodlands in improving individual and community well-being, particularly in relation to the subjective and flourishing aspects of well-being. We also present a dynamic conceptual framework outlining the factors that can enable or restrict the realisation of well-being benefits from woodlands.

Type of research undertaken

SERG's research on well-being can be grouped into two broad themes: 1) research focused primarily on health and well-being, and 2) research focused on broader social and cultural values and well-being. The studies have been undertaken in England, Scotland and Wales and the majority are either qualitative or use mixed methods. The qualitative studies have included focus groups, interviews and participant observation, with some studies also using accompanied visits. This involves participating with respondents in an activity at a woodland site (e.g. cycling, volunteering, walking) and conducting interviews or focus group discussions either during or after the activity. The studies primarily include users of woodlands, but a number of representative surveys include those who do not visit woodlands but who may still consider woods important as part of their local community or as part of the landscape.

In this chapter we explore the relationship between woodlands and individual and community well-being under five main headings. The chapter begins by outlining issues of governance, in particular some of the programmes and infrastructure changes that are used to engage people in using woods to improve well-being. We then focus on some of the types of engagement and activities that people get involved in, before outlining the well-being benefits they gain from them. Barriers to accessing woodlands are identified to show that some people experience difficulties in visiting woodlands and gaining well-being benefits. Finally, a framework is presented that can be used to explore how woodlands contribute to well-being in future research and in the design of woodland-based interventions.

Governance processes

Forest governance research focuses on the decision making processes that underpin sustainable forest management, such as the integration of trees and woodlands into wider planning frameworks and the creation of sustainable partnerships for delivery of benefits from woodlands. Forestry in Britain is devolved and there are forestry strategies and policies for Scotland, Wales and England. In Wales a strategic forestry theme is 'woodlands for people' focusing on local needs for health, education and jobs (Welsh Assembly Government, 2009). In Scotland the forestry strategy has a key theme of 'access and health' (Scottish Government, 2006) and current policy in England highlights the importance of trees and woods for recreation and leisure (Defra, 2011a). There are a range of ways in which well-being might be delivered via woodland use and engagement and can involve a diverse range of individuals and organisations, from government bodies such as the Forestry Commission, to social enterprises, non-governmental organisations, community woodland groups, local authorities and private woodland owners. The Forestry Commission in England, Scotland and Wales manages approximately a million hectares of woodland called the 'public forest estate' that is managed for public benefit (Forestry Commission, 2012). It also administers a grants scheme in each country to which private owners, charitable organisations and other woodland owners can apply for funding to manage their woodlands for specific outcomes such as biodiversity protection, public access, woodland creation and wood fuel. Some grants are targeted at specific issues. For example, in 2003 a health woodland improvement grant was set up in the West Midlands in England to encourage woodland owners to link with health professionals and encourage people to access woodlands to improve their physical health and mental well-being (Interface NRM Ltd, 2004; O'Brien et al., 2006). Another grant in East Anglia was used to encourage the creation of Forest Schools which offer opportunities for children to undertake some of their education in woodlands (Glynn, 2007).

Research shows that people are often not aware of who owns the woodlands they visit. Indeed, ownership is often not a consideration for woodland users unless access to the woodland is changed, reduced or threatened (Carter et al., 2009). However, whether people have knowledge of ownership or not, they do have strong views about how public money should be spent on public woodlands. Research has also shown that more people associate benefits with public woodlands (70 per cent) than with private woodlands (55 per cent) (Carter et al., 2009). This may be due to the range of facilities and activities provided in some large public woodlands, particularly by organisations such as the Forestry Commission. It may also be due to people feeling more welcome at publically owned sites. The type of woodlands people visit will vary in size, location, ownership, tree type (coniferous, broadleaved, mixed), distance from where they live and the available infrastructure and facilities, such as car parks. In terms of improving well-being through accessing woodlands a distinction can be made between: 1) the provision of woodlands through new planting or opening up existing woods to public access, 2) physical improvements to woodlands such as providing facilities and infrastructure to encourage and enable access, and 3) addressing the needs of individuals and groups through different types of interventions to encourage access and enjoyment (Molteno et al., 2012). Various types of infrastructure can be introduced to sites to broaden appeal and encourage use, such as children's play areas, all ability trails for the able and disabled, cycle routes and specific walking trails. An evaluation of the woodland-based Active England projects in England highlighted significant increases in activities such as cycling, use of play areas and mountain biking at three woodland sites (Haldon Forest Park, Devon; Bedgebury Forest, Kent;

Rosliton, Derbyshire) that invested in infrastructure and equipment (O'Brien and Morris, 2009; Morris and O'Brien, 2011). Because of the increased 'recreation offer' at these sites, the average visit duration also increased.

Interventions to encourage physical activity in woodlands have become widespread. For example, the Chopwell Wood Health Project in north-east England was created in partnership with two primary care trusts to work with schoolchildren to help them use the woodland as a healthy resource. The Chopwell project also worked with local general practitioners (GPs) to help patients on referrals by providing a destination for healthy activity and exercise as an alternative to gyms and leisure centres (O'Brien and Snowdon, 2007). There are also a number of long term programmes. For example, Forest School (Figure 10.1) enables schoolchildren to spend part of their time learning in a woodland over a period of months and has become increasingly popular across Britain (O'Brien and Murray, 2007). 'Walking to Health' in England and Wales and 'Paths to Health' in Scotland run programmes, many of which are in woodlands, to encourage people to exercise and socialise to improve health and well-being (Natural England, 2011; Physical Activity and Health Alliance, 2011). There are also volunteering programmes that provide practical conservation activity opportunities in various woodlands run by a number of organisations. A range of events in woodlands are also organised to encourage engagement with the woodland environment.

FIGURE 10.1 Children and parents at Forest School

Engagement with and activities in woodlands

There are a number of possible modes of engagement with woodlands, from virtual engagement via webcams and Internet links; to looking at a woodland view; or passing by trees and woods en route to work or shopping; using and being in woodlands; active hands on engagement through volunteering; through to participation in decision making and potentially ownership or management of woodlands. People may engage at a number of these levels and an individual's or group's mode of engagement may change over time, depending on changing motivations and circumstances. The experiences and benefits gained may vary dramatically for different individuals, groups and sections of society. For example, viewing trees from an office window will yield a very different experience from engaging in environmental volunteering activities. The majority of the research presented in this chapter involves either being in and using woodlands (e.g. engaging in activities such as cycling, walking, relaxing) or active 'hands on' activities such as volunteering, or gathering non-timber forest products (NTFPs), or being involved in organised activities such as a Forest School.

Results from population surveys reveal the range and type of activities people undertake in woodlands. In two national surveys run in consecutive years in Scotland, dog walking and walking were the most popular activities (Edwards et al., 2008), followed by nature watching and taking children to play. Numbers involved in volunteering in woodlands are difficult to capture; however, a study in Scotland found that there were approximately 7,500 volunteers (in the 12 months mid-2006 to mid-2007) undertaking 47,500 volunteer days (Edwards et al., 2008). The most recent Public Opinion of Forestry (POF) survey in the UK (Forestry Commission, 2011) found that 66 per cent of people were exercising (walking, running, mountain biking) in woods, 36 per cent relaxing, 35 per cent watching nature, and 35 per cent playing with children. In 2011, 84 per cent of those who had visited woods in the past few years visited woodlands in the countryside, 62 per cent visited woodlands in and around towns and 47 per cent stated visiting both (Forestry Commission, 2011).

Well-being benefits gained from woodlands

The well-being benefits emerging from our body of research can be grouped into six high level themes, the majority of which relate to primarily subjective and flourishing accounts of well-being (O'Brien and Morris, in press). Although people talk about the well-being they gain themselves, they often also comment on the value of woodlands for others, i.e. their importance to children, wider society, the local community, and for nature, i.e. their importance as a habitat for wildlife and biodiversity.

Health

Physical well-being

Those involved in active contact with woodlands through activities such as mountain biking, walking, cycling, volunteering and those gathering NTFPs talk about gaining physical benefits that include improving stamina, feeling fitter, losing weight or toning muscles (O'Brien, 2005; Emery et al., 2006; O'Brien and Morris, 2009). Women mountain bikers talk about feelings of exhilaration, and increased adrenaline from riding routes together (O'Brien and Morris, 2009). Unstructured play opportunities are important for children. Led health walks, and other led activities such as cycling and t'ai chi provide opportunities for regular, scheduled exercise that becomes part of the weekly routine (O'Brien and Snowdon, 2007; O'Brien and Morris, 2009). Participants talk about the importance of this from a confidence and motivational perspective, explaining that even if they are not familiar with a particular site, they can turn up at the appointed time and not worry about where to go or getting lost.

> This is a commitment which actually gets you to do a specific walk.
> (over 50s health walk group) (O'Brien and Morris, 2009)

Mental restoration

People often describe woodlands as peaceful places, somewhere to go to relax, to release tension and be calm. This points to the restorative benefits people gain from contact with woodlands (O'Brien, 2005; O'Brien and Morris, 2009; O'Brien et al., 2012). Also, undertaking more vigorous activities such as mountain biking has been described as fun and enjoyable, and also a source of mental restoration. For those in urban areas, woodlands are often described as an 'escape' from the built environment, the busy roads, noise and the crowdedness of urban places (O'Brien, 2005).

> It's just nice and quiet, getting away from the general stresses of city life…
> (Urban woodland user, male) (Carter et al., 2009)

Escape and restoration can also be related to getting away from other people, or getting away from a problem or source of anxiety. This resonates with the Kaplans' category of 'being away' in their theory of attention restoration (Kaplan, 1995). The results of the 2011 UK POF survey show that of those who visited woodlands in the last few years, 95 per cent strongly agree or agree that woods are places to relax and de-stress (Forestry Commission, 2011).

Nature and landscape connections

Having contact with nature and the natural environment is a motivation for accessing woodlands that is commonly cited by research participants (O'Brien, 2005; 2006; O'Brien and Snowdon, 2007). In a national survey in Scotland, 95 per cent of respondents strongly agreed or agreed with the statement that Scottish woodlands are an important part of the country's natural and cultural heritage (Edwards et al., 2008). In the UK POF 2011 survey, 71 per cent strongly agreed or agreed that woods and forests are places where people can learn about local culture or history. Of respondents to surveys of resident populations local to three woodland sites in England, 91 per cent thought their local woods made the area a nicer place to live (Morris and Doick, 2010).

> Well they're a very essential part of the landscape for me..., our lives would be poorer without them shall we say. They enrich the landscape, they enrich the whole experience of walking and they're just very special places...
>
> (Gay outdoor club group, male) (Carter et al., 2009)

Volunteers enjoy making changes and improvements to woodland spaces, knowing they are caring for local places that communities can then use and enjoy (O'Brien et al., 2010). Contact with wooded spaces and trees can also lead people to reflect about their place in the world. For example, tasked with taking photographs of anything that had a positive or negative impact on their well-being during a woodland walk, one respondent took a photograph of a tree canopy and wrote the following text to go with the picture:

> It makes me feel peaceful – insignificant not important – small – but makes your earthly worries less fierce.
>
> (Female, health study) (O'Brien et al., 2012)

Sensory stimulation

Being outdoors in the fresh air is a benefit of woodlands commonly cited by respondents (O'Brien, 2005; O'Brien and Snowdon, 2007). For those with disabilities, being in woodlands stimulates the senses. Deaf respondents highlight the importance of the vistas provided by woodlands, while the blind enjoy other sensory experiences such as feeling the wind, sun and the tactile experiences of a woodland visit (Burns et al., 2008). Specially developed sensory trails can be particularly valuable for those with a range of disabilities. Volunteers, people who gather NTFPs and many others talk about seeing change through the seasons and enjoying the changes in vegetation and weather. Windy days, kicking fallen leaves in the autumn and snowy walks in the woods in winter are often enjoyed as much as dappled sunshine through the tree canopy on summer days, as they can provide a variety of experiences.

> I like to see the trees, how they change, the colours of the leaves and perhaps rustling through it. I remember doing that when I was a young child and I love that.
> (Low income group) (Carter et al., 2009)

> Children involved in Forest School go out in all weathers and enjoy sliding in the mud on rainy days and are physically active on cold days to keep warm.
> (O'Brien and Murray, 2007; O'Brien, 2009)

Social development and connections

Shared experiences with others are an important source of benefits from people's contact with woodlands, and can involve meeting new acquaintances as well as socialising with family and friends (O'Brien, 2005; Morris and Doick, 2010; Carter et al., 2011). Results of the UK POF 2011 survey showed that 54 per cent of respondents agreed that woodlands are important to the public because they bring communities together. Evaluations of interventions that involve organised activities, e.g. walking, cycling etc., highlight that it is often the social interaction that happens during the activity that is particularly important, not only in attracting people to get involved in the first instance but also in motivating them to continue their participation in the longer term (O'Brien et al., 2006). For example, the Active England evaluation shows that a key benefit theme was socialising through joining a health walk or an organised cycle ride (O'Brien and Morris, 2009; Morris and O'Brien, 2011). This social dimension enabled people to undertake activities they might not have done alone and to gain support from friends and project staff. Those referred by their doctor to Chopwell Wood to undertake physical activity found support and encouragement from staff particularly useful and developed new relationships with others as they undertook health walks and t'ai chi activities (O'Brien and Snowdon, 2007). When moving to a new area environmental volunteering can be a route to developing new social networks.

> There's the social contact. Over the years I've got to know members of the group really well, they're some of my best friends in the area. It was a good way of getting to meet people when I first moved up to the North East.
> (Female volunteer) (O'Brien et al., 2010)

For disabled users woodlands can be important for socialising and can provide a distraction from problems and concerns (Burns et al., 2008). Surveys at three woodland sites (Bentley Community Wood, Doncaster; Birches Valley, Cannock Chase; Ingrebourne Hill, London) in England highlighted that 69 per cent felt that the sites bring the local community together. Fifty-eight per cent said the sites got people involved in local issues (Morris and Doick, 2010).

Symbolic, cultural and spiritual significance

Meaning and identity

A study of environmental volunteers found that the active, 'hands on', practical conservation activities such as coppicing, footpath repair, vegetation clearance etc. provided volunteers with a strong sense of satisfaction from carrying out meaningful activities and making a contribution, often described as 'putting something back' (O'Brien et al., 2010). Prison offenders undertaking voluntary conservation work in woodlands felt that these activities allowed them to reflect and make positive life changes (Carter and West, 2008). It also helped them to rebuild a sense of self-worth and positive self-identity.

> It's nice feeling part of activity in the open air, society again ... instead of being behind a wall or a fence where you are cut off from the rest of the world.
>
> (Offender volunteer) (Carter and West, 2008)

For some disabled users, being outdoors has a positive impact on their identity (Burns et al., 2008). Woodland users often draw on childhood memories when talking about the values they hold for woodlands and the benefits they gain from them (O'Brien, 2005; O'Brien and Morris, 2009). Climbing trees, family visits and building dens familiarise children and young people with using and enjoying woodlands and this is often a key factor in visits made as an adult (Ward Thompson et al., 2008).

Education and learning

Opportunities for learning and developing skills occur through a range of activities and engagement types. For example, young volunteers talk about gaining skills to help them find employment through particular types of training such as brash cutting.

> I fancy the chainsaw [course] because you can go to local areas and get a job nearby.
>
> (Galloway young male) (O'Brien et al., 2010)

Older volunteers outline more general learning from undertaking activities that are less familiar to them (O'Brien et al., 2010). At Forest School young children undertake their normal learning but in an outdoor environment. This can contribute to formal curriculum learning. Maths learning may involve collecting the right numbers of twigs to place on the campfire, whilst the development of language skills might involve describing their surrounding environment (O'Brien, 2009). Those who gather NTFPs talk about knowledge being passed to them by parents or grandparents, such as how to identify edible species of fungi, for example. In some cases, this knowledge can also be passed on to their children (Emery et al., 2006). Offenders who carry out conservation activities as part of their rehabilitation gain skills that can act as a transition into paid employment on release from prison (Carter and West, 2008).

Economy

Some adult respondents recognise that woodlands can be managed for timber production as part of a multifunctional woodland management system and talked about how this can be important for the local economy (O'Brien, 2006).

> Yes, the forests are where the trees are planted for a reason aren't they. They are regenerated for what they cut down, they plant back and whatever. That is what I understand the forest to be, it's actually working, the forest is actually making money from the trees that they have got grown there. Whereas with woods and copses they are just left to it. There is not a commercial side to it. But I think in the forest there is a commercial side to it. Because you see them felling the trees and then planting the new ones.
> (Female, 20–35) (O'Brien, 2004)

In rural areas, woodlands can also be seen as an important element of local tourism (Edwards et al., 2008). Trees in towns (in parks or on streets) are seen by some as indicating wealthier, more attractive residential areas (O'Brien, 2004). In qualitative research, adults that gather NTFPs stated that these practices made them keen observers of nature, and could contribute to their livelihoods (Emery et al., 2006). For low income respondents the low cost of visiting woodlands is critical, particularly for parents on a tight budget (O'Brien, 2005; 2006). Woodlands are seen as places where you do not have to conspicuously consume and they are seen as cheaper compared to other recreation and health facilities, such as leisure centres and theme parks (O'Brien, 2005; Weldon and Bailey, 2007).

Barriers to accessing woodlands

While those who visit and engage with woodlands can gain a wide range of benefits, it is clear that certain groups within society face a number of barriers that prevent them from visiting. A meta-analysis of existing research by SERG and the Forestry Commission found that different groups experienced a variety of barriers (Morris et al., 2011). A typology of these barriers was produced focusing on two key categories:

- *Physical and structural barriers* – this category covers the physical, environmental and services-related issues that limit woodland accessibility for some

people. The research evidence can be sorted into three subcategories: 1) 'General/over-arching' barriers (e.g. weather), 2) 'On-site' barriers (e.g. access points, signage, and facilities), and 3) 'Off-site' barriers (e.g. lack of information and transport).
- *Socio-cultural, economic and personal barriers* – this category covers wider societal and cultural, as well as personal, values and perceptual aspects. It also covers economic factors which limit visiting.

The analysis of survey data highlighted that amongst people who did not often visit woodlands, mobility is a significant issue for women, older people (55+ years), those in lower socio-economic groups, disabled people and white people. Distance to woodlands is an issue for black and minority ethnic (BME) people. Lack of a car emerges as a significant barrier for women, older people (65+ years), lower socio-economic groups, the disabled, and white people. Amongst those who do visit woodlands, poor weather and lack of facilities prevent low income groups, women and white people from visiting more often. Younger and older people, disabled people, women and low income groups are associated with a cluster of variables relating to mobility such as lack of a car, woods being too far away, and personal mobility issues.

Qualitative research highlights that urban residents (aged between 35 and 59 years) cite barriers such as fear of unknown spaces, of antisocial behaviour and of getting lost. Lack of information and not knowing where to go or what to expect at different sites is an issue for many. For women, concerns about personal safety when visiting alone and concerns about child safety are often significant, particularly in more deprived urban areas. Poorly maintained sites with signs of antisocial behaviour often heighten these concerns. One study found that respondents from low income households faced multiple barriers to accessing woodlands, with many relating to attitudes and general outlook. Many expressed low motivation, or stated that woodland visits were not a priority given more pressing issues. Some BME groups stated that visiting woods is simply not part of their cultural background (Morris and O'Brien, 2011).

Interventions can be used specifically to engage groups that face particular barriers. For example, the Active England woodland projects targeted BME groups to encourage them to become more physically active. The approach taken was to set up organised activities such as health walks and cycle rides on a regular basis for those in the Asian community. Another approach was to facilitate access for a group of Pakistani women, organising transport to take them to a local woodland, with a ranger taking them round the site so that they could experience what it was like and what was on offer. The women spoke about their intentions to return with their families now that they knew where the site was and what to expect from a visit. These approaches, referred to as 'facilitated access', require organisation and staff time and can be resource intensive. However, they can be particularly effective at encouraging use by specific groups that face multiple barriers to access.

Conceptual framework: woodlands and well-being

The key areas explored in this chapter provide the background for the development of a dynamic conceptual framework to detail the various factors that enable, mediate or restrict the realisation of well-being benefits from woodlands (Figure 10.2). The framework can be applied to research case studies, such as woodland sites, or particular interventions and projects, in order to explore and describe how various factors can combine in the 'co-production' of goods and benefits. For example, the factor 'Trees Woods Forests' would include criteria such as the type of woodland (coniferous, broadleaf, mixed, urban, rural), and available access infrastructure and facilities (footpaths to and within the site, car parks, visitor centres, cafés and toilets). Also included would be particular features such as veteran trees, pollarded trees etc. 'Governance' includes criteria such as ownership of the site, who is involved in decision making about the site, partnerships that might operate at a site, as well as any specific interventions to enable access and the realisation of well-being benefits. Specific governance processes may facilitate, enable or enhance the experience through site management approaches and the provision of services such as programmes and interventions that target specific social groups to encourage access and well-being benefits (Edwards and Weldon, 2006). 'Activity/engagement' includes types of engagement with the woodland, including direct (visits,

FIGURE 10.2 A dynamic, non-linear conceptual framework detailing the various factors that can enable or restrict the realisation of well-being benefits gained from woodlands

volunteering) and indirect (woodland views) forms of engagement. Activities can include walking, cycling, picnicking, volunteering etc. The characteristics of 'Individuals / groups' (i.e. age, gender, life stage, group type such as mountain bikers, 'Friends of' groups etc.) refer to the different motivations and norms for visiting. Furthermore, this refers to the fact that certain groups may face particular barriers to accessing woodlands.

Different configurations of the components of the framework can lead to various well-being outcomes for different groups. We can use this model to explore how the various factors interact across different sites to identify whether there are particular combinations that are successful for specific groups. This can inform woodland management and the design of interventions for public bodies, non-governmental organisations, and private woodland owners who are interested in enabling and encouraging access to woodlands.

Conclusions

This chapter has drawn on research undertaken by SERG to identify the common types of well-being people can gain from engagement with woodlands. Well-being is a broad and complex concept and this research highlights how woodlands and forest can contribute to people's overall well-being in a variety of different and surprisingly wide-ranging ways. We undertook this synthesis to explore commonalities in the well-being gained by different sections of society and the research shows that there are common experiences that different social groups experience. However, the context of use and engagement is important so that sometimes people are motivated to carry out different activities based on the benefits to well-being that can be gained, such as walking to relax, cycling to raise adrenaline and picnicking to socialise. Different types or intensities of well-being benefit may arise from undertaking different activities in various contexts and these experiences may vary over people's life course. Those who visit woodlands every month or more tend to describe greater well-being benefits than those who visit infrequently. Barriers to access can be complex and targeted interventions and programmes as well as outreach and 'facilitated access' can be successful in encouraging participation by those who do not visit or who are not familiar with woodlands. Site infrastructure and facilities can encourage use but will often be more successful with those who already visit woodlands rather than those that face particular barriers. Quantitative surveys provide useful information on broad trends that occur at specific sites, within particular catchments or at a national level, while qualitative research, particularly participating in an activity with people followed by group discussion, provides valuable insights into people's experiences and the meanings they associate with woodlands, particular activities and levels of engagement. The results outlined here correspond with some of the previous research that has been undertaken of the well-being benefits people gain from woodlands (Macnaghten et al., 1998; Henwood and Pidgeon, 2001; Bishop et al. 2002).

Reflections: the wider context

The UK NEA (2011), the Natural Environment White Paper (HM Government, 2011) and the *Biodiversity 2020* strategy (Defra, 2011b) all argue that nature has been undervalued. The substantial body of research reported in this chapter provides compelling evidence of people's everyday experiences and contact with trees, woods and forests and how this natural environment is valued by different sections of society. The environment constitutes one element of a national framework of societal well-being measures currently being developed by the Office for National Statistics. Our research illustrates how one specific natural environment type (woodlands) contributes in multiple ways to societal well-being and shows how it can contribute to the various components of well-being, such as health and education. The research also shows how the woodland environment can deliver against broad societal development goals and policy agendas, such as improving health, community development and employment.

As well as supporting these wider policy agendas, the research reported here also provides a useful resource to those responsible for woodland policy and management, and particularly those working to achieve the equal distribution of access to and benefits from woodlands in the UK. The evidence shows that certain social groups have specific needs and may require carefully targeted support in order to be able to access and enjoy the benefits that woodlands offer. Interventions that are delivered in a way that is cognisant of, and sensitive to the specific needs of different groups can achieve significant gains in terms of increases in visitor numbers and the duration of woodland visits by members of excluded and under-represented groups.

Acknowledgements

Thanks are due to all the members of the Social and Economic Research Group at Forest Research that worked on the studies outlined in this paper.

References

Bishop, K., Kitchen, L., Marsden, T. and Milbourne, P. (2002) 'Forestry, community and land in the South Wales valleys', in L. O'Brien and J. Claridge (eds.) *Trees are company: social science research into woodlands and the natural environment.* Edinburgh: Forestry Commission.

Burns, N., Patterson, K. and Watson, N. (2008). *Exploring disabled people's perceptions and use of forest recreation goods, facilities and services in Scotland, England and Wales.* Glasgow, Strathclyde Centre for Disability Research, Glasgow University for the Forestry Commission. http://www.forestry.gov.uk/fr/INFD-7PSL75 (accessed 21/5/2013).

Carter, C. and West, D. (2008) *Policy into practice: employment for ex-offenders an innovative approach.* Edinburgh: Forestry Commission.

Carter, C., Lawrence, A., Lovell, R. and O'Brien, L. (2009) *The Forestry Commission public forest estate: social value, use and expectations.* Forestry Commission, Final report. http://www.forestry.gov.uk/pdf/PFE_social_study_final_report.pdf/$FILE/PFE_social_study_final_report.pdf (accessed 4/6/2010).

Carter, C., O'Brien, L. and Morris, J. (2011) *Enabling positive change: evaluation of the Neroche Landscape Partnership Scheme*. Edinburgh: Report to the Forestry Commission.

Defra. (2008) *Sustainable development indicators in your pocket 2008: an update of the UK Government strategy indicators*. London: Defra.

Defra. (2011a) *Forestry*. http://ww2.defra.gov.uk/rural/forestry/ (accessed 1/2/2011).

Defra. (2011b) *Biodiversity 2020: a strategy for England's wildlife and ecosystem services*. London: Defra.

Defra (2012) Independent Panel on Forestry, http://www.defra.gov.uk/forestrypanel/files/Independent-Panel-on-Forestry-Final-Report1.pdf

Dolan, P., Peasgood, T., Dixon, A., Knight, M., Phillips, D., Tsuchiya, A. and White, M. (2006) *Research on the relationship between well-being and sustainable development*. Report to Defra, London.

Edwards, D. and Weldon, S. (2006) *Race equality and the Forestry Commission*. Farnham: Forest Research.

Edwards, D., Morris, J., O'Brien, L., Sarajevs, V. and Valatin, G. (2008) *The economic and social contribution of Forestry for People in Scotland*. Research Note FCRN102, Edinburgh: Forestry Commission, p8.

Emery, M., Martin, S. and Dyke, A. (2006) *Wild harvests from Scottish woodlands: social, cultural and economic value of contemporary non-timber forest products*. Edinburgh: Forestry Commission. http://www.forestry.gov.uk/pdf/fcrp008.pdf/$FILE/fcrp008.pdf (accessed 5/6/2010).

Forestry Commission. (2011) *Public opinion of forestry 2011, UK and England*. Edinburgh: Forestry Commission.

Forestry Commission. (2012) *About the Forestry Commission*. http://www.forestry.gov.uk/aboutus (accessed 21/5/2013).

Glynn, M. (2007) *An evaluation of the Forest Schools Woodland Improvement Grant in the East of England*. Report to Forestry Commission England, http://www.forestry.gov.uk/pdf/fce-wig-evaluation-report.pdf/$file/fce-wig-evaluation-report.pdf

Henwood, K. and Pidgeon, N. (2001) Talk about woods and trees: threat of urbanization, stability and biodiversity. *Journal of Environmental Psychology*, 21: 125–147.

H M Government. (2011). *The natural choice: securing the value of nature*. London: HM Government.

Interface NRM Ltd. (2004) *West Midlands woodland and health pilot evaluation*. http://www.forestry.gov.uk/fr/INFD-6HCF4N (accessed 21/5/2013).

Kaplan, S. (1995) The restorative benefits of nature: toward an integrative framework. *Journal of Environmental Psychology*, 15: 169–182.

Layard, R. (2005) *Happiness: lessons from a new science*. London: Penguin.

Macnaghten, P., Grove-White, R., Weldon, S. and Waterton, C. (1998) *Woodland sensibilities: recreational uses of woods and forests in contemporary Britain*. Lancaster: Lancaster University.

Millennium Ecosystem Assessment. (2005) *Guide to MEA reports*. http://www.maweb.org/en/index.aspx (accessed 15/2/2011).

Molteno, S., Morris, J. and O'Brien, L. (2012) *Public access to woodlands and forests: A rapid evidence review*. Farnham: Forest Research.

Morris, J. and Doick, K. (2010) *Monitoring and evaluating qualify of life for CSR07. Final annual report 2009/10*. http://www.forestry.gov.uk/pdf/CSR07_final_annual_report_2009-10.pdf/$FILE/CSR07_final_annual_report_2009-10.pdf (accessed 3/1/2011).

Morris, J. and O'Brien, L. (2011). Encouraging healthy activity amongst under-represented groups: An evaluation of the Active England woodland projects. *Urban Forestry and Urban Greening*.

Morris, J., O'Brien, L., Ambrose-Oji, B., Lawrence, A., Carter, C., and Peace, A. (2011). Access for all? Barriers to accessing woodlands and forests in Britain. *Local Environment*, 16(4): 375–396.

Natural England. (2011) *Walking for health.* http://www.wfh.naturalengland.org.uk/ (accessed 10/1/2011).

Newton, J. (2007) *Wellbeing research: synthesis report.* http://www.defra.gov.uk/sustainable/government/documents/Wellbeingresearchsynthesisreport.pdf (accessed 2/2/11).

O'Brien, E. (2004) *A ort of magical place: People's experiences of woodlands in Northwest and Southeast England*. Farnham: Forest Research.

O'Brien, E. (2005) Publics and woodlands: well-being, local identity, social learning, conflict and management. *Forestry,* 78: 321–336.

O'Brien, E. (2006) Social housing and greenspace: a case study in inner London. *Forestry*, 79: 535–549.

O'Brien, L. (2009). Learning outdoors: the Forest School approach. *Education 3-13*, 37(1): 45–60.

O'Brien, E. and Murray, R. (2007) Forest School and its impacts on young children: case studies in Britain. *Urban Forestry and Urban Greening*, 6: 249–265.

O'Brien, E. and Snowdon, H. (2007) Health and well-being in woodlands: a case study of the Chopwell Wood Health Project. *Arboricultural Journal*, 30: 45–60.

O'Brien, L. and Morris, J. (2009) *Active England: the woodland projects*. Edinburgh: Report to the Forestry Commission, p76.

O'Brien, L. and Morris, J. (in press) Well-being for all? The social distribution of benefits gained from woodlands and forests in Britain. *Local Environment*.

O'Brien, E., Greenland, M. and Snowdon, H. (2006) Using woodlands and woodland grants to improve public health. *Scottish Forestry*, 60, 2: 18–24.

O'Brien, L., Townsend, M. and Ebden, M. (2010) 'Doing something positive': volunteer's experiences of the well-being benefits derived from practical conservation activities in nature. *Voluntas: International Journal of Voluntary and Non profit Organisations*, 21: 525–545.

O'Brien, L., Morris, J. and Stewart, A. (2012) *The contribution of peri-urban woodlands to health and well-being.* Farnham: Forest Research.

Office for National Statistics. (2010) *Measuring national well-being.* http://www.ons.gov.uk/well-being (accessed 10/12/2010).

Physical Activity and Health Alliance. (2011) *Path to health.* http://www.paha.org.uk/Resource/paths-to-health (accessed 20/2/2011).

Scottish Government. (2006) *The Scottish Forestry Strategy*. Edinburgh: Scottish Government.

SDRN. (no date). *Wellbeing concepts and challenges: SDRN briefing three*. London: SDRN.

Steuer, N. and Marks, N. (no date) *Local well-being: can we measure it.* Report for the Local Well-being Project, London.

UK National Ecosystem Assessment. (2011) *The UK national ecosystem assessment: synthesis of the key findings.* Cambridge, UNEP-WCMC.

Ward Thompson, C., Aspinall, P. and Montarzino, A. (2008) The childhood factor: adults visits to green places and the significant of childhood experiences. *Environment and Behaviour*, 40: 111–143.

Weldon, S. and Bailey, C. (2007) New pathways for health and well-being in Scotland: research to understand and overcome barriers to accessing woodlands. Edinburgh: Forestry Commission Scotland.

Welsh Assembly Government. (2009) *Woodlands for Wales*. Cardiff: WAG.

11

CHILDREN AS EXPLORERS

Revealing children's views on well-being in intensifying urban environments

Christina Ergler and Robin Kearns

Introduction

Children are experts on their experiences, their lives and what concerns their well-being. Nonetheless, many researchers tend to neglect integrating children directly in the research process. Despite many fine social studies of childhood that work with children, research on/with children is still very adult-centred. This chapter assesses the opportunities and challenges faced in inviting children to participate centrally in a research project. We show that by trusting in children's own expertise and giving up some control in the research encounter, children become involved in the project in different ways, become de facto researchers themselves. This, in turn, fosters children's well-being in two ways: the enjoyment of collaborating; and potentially enhanced insights available for policy through gaining a deeper understanding of children's worlds.

Many urban areas are increasingly challenging to live in – especially for children. The impact of ongoing residential and commercial intensification of urban environments on the well-being of children has been profound. Increasingly, cities are characterised by high traffic volumes and low air quality as well as declining independent mobility and increasing time pressures for parents and their offspring (Freeman and Tranter, 2011). While the interest in urban children's well-being has grown in the past years focusing on their physical, social and mental well-being, research that integrates their views and practices in an intensifying urban environment has been rather piecemeal and generally limited to traditional suburban environments. Not only does children's participation in urban life continue to be subject to adult control, censure and regulation, but this is also the case in terms of their active participation in research. Finding ways of engaging children, rather than doing research *on* them, will not only help to identify an urban design which supports healthy, active lifestyles for children, but will also benefit the well-being of society at large. Yet, the majority of studies have historically and unintentionally objectified children through the choice of research design and methodologies. This seems to avoid integrating children directly into the research process, so as to shed light on their views on well-being, despite an increasing acknowledgement of children's expertise on issues concerning their lives (Christensen and Prout, 2002).

This chapter sets out to illuminate challenges and opportunities in researching children's well-being in vertical and suburban environments by drawing on an interdisciplinary research project undertaken in Auckland, New Zealand. A particular focus is the process whereby children were recruited to be researchers so as to reveal how their neighbourhood experiences contribute to their overall well-being. The chapter critically evaluates the merits of collaborating with children and 'moving beyond passive participation' (Ergler, 2011) to achieve an improved understanding of children's well-being in urban environments and for 'being well' as an outcome of collaboration.

In the remainder of the chapter we first provide a more detailed discussion of children's well-being in contemporary urban environments. The chapter then explores some of the theoretical developments that have contributed to seeing children as capable of researching topics relevant for their daily encounters and the methods applied in this research design. We then lay out the place-specific context in which the study is situated. The second half of the chapter reflects on the improved understanding of children's worlds this study yielded as well as children's understanding of being well that is achieved by the adult–children and children–children collaborations at the heart of this project.

Children's well-being in intensifying urban environments

Sound neighbourhood environments can serve as arenas for the healthy physical, mental and social development of children, contributing not only to 'being well', but also to 'feeling well' in a location (Rissotto and Guiliani, 2006). Time spent outdoors, for example, correlates positively with increased activity fostering children's physical well-being and exemplifying *being well* (healthy, among others things) in an environment. Children negotiate risk and capabilities through their local environment (Mackett et al., 2007; Malone, 2007). Looking at outdoor play through the lens of 'geographies of well-being' (Kearns and Andrews, 2010) allows us to turn away from the negative connotation of health implications of places (e.g. risks of injury) to emphasise positive relationships such as gaining and improving physical competence. Such relationships can positively affect children's self-confidence and self-esteem and may reduce stress and anxiety about 'their being in the world' (Malone, 2007; Wells, 2000). Further, playing outdoors provides a basis for children to enhance understanding of the local environment and themselves. An environmental understanding encourages creativity as children can adjust their surroundings for their play needs (Day and Wagner, 2010). As children generally have a very affective experience of their local environment, being familiar with locations may contribute to *'feeling well'* while being 'out and about' in a neighbourhood.

'Feeling well' can therefore be read in many ways (e.g. good feelings related to community attachment, or related to outdoor play opportunities with friends (Chawla, 2001)). In interacting with peers while playing outdoors, social and cultural skills are learned and transformed, which are increasingly important in a globalising world (Weller and Bruegel, 2009). Malone (2007) summarises these named aspects as 'environmental literacy' or the capability 'to comprehend or read the environment in terms of its key elements'. Well-being here refers to skills learned through interaction with and in an environment, and which can be activated and used in a later life stage to establish a better future, but is not limited to simply meeting substantial needs (Kearns and Andrews, 2010). Nonetheless, there are a diminishing number and size of spaces in which children can independently foster environmental literacy and competence and, in so doing, promote their current and future well-being.

Since economic growth picked up after the Second World War, car dependency, technological improvements and urban sprawl have changed the play environments of children significantly (Chawla, 2001; Dixon and Broom, 2007). Not only the public open spaces in neighbourhoods, but also private play spaces have transformed or shrunk in size (Hörschelmann and Van Blerk, 2012). Reasons for this trend are seen in a changing built environment and in parental concerns over their child's mental and physical well-being (e.g. the concern of 'stranger danger' or traffic safety (Carver et al., 2008)). Appealing indoor activities such as watching TV or playing videogames have also been among the explanations offered as to why children's outdoor play behaviour has changed and their independent mobility has been restricted (Lobstein et al., 2010). Little, however, is known how the recent intensification of urban areas in light of new urbanism and sustainable living ideologies affects children's play and place experiences (Fainstein, 2000; Talen, 1999).

Most studies interested in children's neighbourhood activity patterns are, with a few exceptions (Carroll et al., 2011; Whitzman et al., 2010), limited to suburban or rural environments (e.g. Jones et al., 2010; Mackett et al., 2007). While more sustainable and healthy living for adults may result from vertical living (e.g. based on active transport), consequences for children's well-being in intensifying urban settings remains relatively unknown. The research presented in this chapter is based on twin premises:

- that an in-depth understanding of children's outdoor play experiences and their movements in and beyond their neighbourhood in an intensifying urban environment is essential for creating truly child-friendly cities; and
- that a response to the pressing environmental and health issues of our time lies in new urbanist cities when children's well-being is considered. In this chapter, we propose that in order to be able to reveal such an in-depth understanding in children's well-being, a shift in approach is required.

'Ground truth': acknowledging children's expertise in a research design

Over the past two decades children's geographies has become a vibrant sub-discipline employing a wide range of methods and philosophical paradigms. Early studies were rooted in positivistic spatial science and children were (unintentionally) objectified in the research process (e.g. Blaut and Stea, 1971). Methods were subsequently developed to address these concerns. Children began to be viewed as experts on their own lives and researchers promoted to work 'with' children instead of on their behalf (Christensen, 2000; Holloway and Valentine, 2000). Children became participants and some studies explored the potential of children *as* researchers (e.g. Karsten, 1998; Porter, 2008). Qualitative, child-centred methods (e.g. in-depth interviews, photo-voice) have subsequently been developed, refined and further explored during this period (e.g. Cope, 2008).

Despite many recent attempts to integrate children into the research process, Kellet's (2004) statement that 'participatory research is generally adult-led, adult-designed and conceived from an adult perspective' still prevails. While children have been reconstructed as 'participant' rather than 'respondent', researchers invariably remain in control of the research design and process, which often leaves no time for children's own interests to emerge. To gain insights into what we term the 'ground truth' of children's worlds (Ergler, 2011), this study employed a multi-method approach. In using this term we note that children are not only literally closer to the ground, but they are also closer to understanding their world and how to improve their well-being. The research process, approved by our institutional ethics committee, included 20 Auckland children, who were recruited through school (suburb, 11 children) and summer holiday programmes (inner city, 9 children). The first stage involved asking children to wear a lightweight Global Positioning System (GPS) for four consecutive days (two weekend days and two weekdays) in summer and winter. As the GPS only measures location, distance travelled and speed, children also filled out a travel diary to provide context-specific data. Additionally, to reveal their feelings about a place or activity, children were asked to draw a map of their neighbourhoods highlighting where they like and dislike being active. Next, the first author undertook a semi-structured interview with each child. The GPS maps, which show track logs of each individual representing their mobility patterns, were jointly analysed (along with the elicited drawings and travel diaries) by child participants and the first author. This exercise guided a discussion about outdoor play experiences, children's feelings about them and barriers to accessibility. Through this process children could explain what their drawings meant to them. Although children's agency and capabilities were acknowledged, the research design and data collection was primarily adult-driven.

In contrast, the children themselves drove the second stage of data collection. Children analysed the data collected in stage one at two Saturday morning workshops in December 2010. They explored their GPS logs and drawings through participating in different games. In addition, in both study areas children took the non-local children on a child-guided neighbourhood tour in which they showed the visitors 'good or annoying things to do' in their neighbourhood. The novelty in this approach is that the child did not show the researcher the neighbourhood, but rather she or he showed it to someone of the same age to reveal what is really important for children's well-being in a neighbourhood.

Children were in charge of the guided walk undertaken at these gatherings. That is they decided where to go, how long to stay and what to do at the destination. Further, the 'adult' researchers (the author and five field assistants) only attended the walk for safety and ethical considerations as well as to observe the 10 child researchers who agreed to be part of this second stage. Children were asked to carry a GPS unit, digital camera and voice recorder to capture aspects of the walk, which also gave them the possibility of more fully moving into a researcher's role. They were given the power to decide how and to what extent they used the recorder and camera. The aim was to record the guided walk but, in so doing, hand the power to the children to decide on their use of equipment. This design allowed children to settle on, and highlight, which aspects of their well-being in their neighbourhood are important to them. In the remainder of this account, we argue that in order to be able to move to a deeper engagement with, and better understanding of, children's views on 'being well' in intensifying residential environments, we need to acknowledge the children's position and capabilities in the research process. There are two consequences relating to children's well-being in releasing some control in the research encounter: fostering possible improvements in neighbourhood environments through an improved insight in aspects concerning them; and enhancing well-being because of the sheer enjoyment of collaboration.

Placing study sites: Auckland's central city and the suburb Beach Haven

The Auckland metropolitan area (2012 population approximately 1.5 million people) is one of the fastest growing regions in New Zealand with a population increase of 32 per cent between 1991 and 2006 (the most recent census). Growth projections estimate that 2 million people will live in this area by 2035 (Auckland Regional Council, 2010; Auckland Regional Growth Forum, 1999). The traditional 'kiwi dream' of a free-standing house on a 'quarter-acre' lot is fast disappearing in the face of subdivision and the construction of medium and high-density apartment blocks (Murphy, 2008).

Two areas in the Auckland metropolitan region were selected to investigate how intensifying environments impact on children's well-being through the lens of outdoor play: Auckland Central and the suburb of Beach Haven. Both localities are categorised as highly walkable areas based on the walkability index developed by Leslie et al. (2007) and offer diverse destinations according to the Neighbourhood Destination Accessibility Index (NDAI) (Witten et al., 2011).

Beach Haven is located approximately 5 km north-west of central Auckland and is bounded by wooded hills and an inner harbour coastline. With only two roads in and out of its mostly quiet residential streets, we speculated that children in this suburb may experience less parental surveillance than elsewhere in Auckland. Beach Haven has numerous parks and has long been considered a good place to raise children (Witten et al., 2009). About 25 per cent of residents are under 15 years old and almost 70 per cent of all households consist of families with young children. Although this suburb has been deemed to be relatively deprived (Crampton et al., 2000) with a median household income of NZ$27,000 recorded in the most recent (2006) census, it has strong social networks, often based around schools, sports clubs and ethnic affiliations (McCreanor et al., 2006).

Central Auckland is characterised by a commercial port, motorways reaching directly into the city and high-rise complexes (business and residential). However, apartments have not been built with children in mind and tend to cater in the first instance for students, young professionals and 'empty-nesters' (Carroll et al., 2011). More than 75 per cent of all households have no children and the 2006 median household income was NZ$35,750. Nonetheless, families have begun to move into more affordable central city dwellings prompted by increasing housing prices in the region (Friesen, 2009; Witten and Carroll, 2011). About 3 per cent of central city residents are under 15 years old. 'Playscapes' are limited in the central city due to commercial activity. Two major parks (Myers and Albert Parks) and some smaller open green spaces afford recreational opportunities.

Children as explorers of neighbourhood well-being: a methodological discussion

We turn now to reflect on, and discuss the children's engagement with, the research process. We consider that examples of collaboration between adult and child researcher can improve the understanding of children's neighbourhood experiences and provide, in turn, an improved understanding of children's well-being in an environment of increasing housing intensification.

- First, we discuss how children's views on what underlies feeling well in a neighbourhood sheds a different light on the questions adult researchers have been interested in. Slipping into the role of a researcher we show children as actively shaping and providing a snapshot of their understanding of well-being.
- Secondly, we briefly discuss the merits of including children in the research process more thoroughly than current approaches do. We argue that only they can reveal the 'ground truth' of neighbourhood experiences that contribute to or hinder their well-being.

Releasing power of the research encounter: child researchers' perspectives on well-being

The research process in this study was intentionally left sufficiently flexible such that child participants easily transitioned into the role of 'de facto' researchers. Below we highlight the importance of integrating children into the design process of a research project and trusting in their capabilities.

At the time of welcoming the children at the first meeting, it is highlighted that roles would be reversed to allow children to be the researchers. Therefore, they were asked to reflect on, and record, questions they wanted to have answered from the meeting as they would be 'in the driver's seat' for this stage of data collection (Ergler, 2011). In a second step, one child collected all the questions children felt comfortable sharing on a large sheet of paper. This is subsequently pinned it to a wall for everyone to see to allow reassessment at the end of the process. For example, city children were interested in whether it is 'cool living' in Beach Haven or 'when do you go to school' and Beach Haven children were interested in how city children spend their time (see Table 11.1 for details).

TABLE 11.1 Child-researchers' questions in research project

Questions children shared with co-researchers		Questions children did not share with co-child researchers	
What do you want to know about playing outside in summer and winter from children living…		What do you want to know about playing outside in summer and winter from children living…	
…in Beach Haven?	…in the Central City?	…in Beach Haven?	…in the Central City?
✓ When do you go to school? ✓ What do you do at home? ✓ Is it cool living here?	✓ What kind of games do you play? ✓ What do you do on the weekends? ✓ What do you do all day? ✓ Which time is better? (summer of winter?) ✓ Why? ✓ Where do you live? ✓ Do you have chickens?	✗ What do you do in summer? ✗ What do you do at school? ✗ Are you allowed to play outside in winter? ✗ How do you get to school? ✗ Can you play on the streets? ✗ How many people can play in Beach Haven? ✗ Where can you play? ✗ What do you do in the holidays?	✗ Do you guys get good weather? ✗ How much do you like to game? ✗ Do you get to play a lot in your neighbourhood? ✗ Is it busy in your neighbourhood? ✗ Where do you play? (Inside or at the park?) ✗ Is it bad? ✗ Do you play at the courts? ✗ Do you have lots of friends at your street?

Interestingly, when their notes were reviewed later, children only highlighted very general questions in the forum. Their questions reflected environments and activities that are generally associated with children's well-being: play spaces and locations they frequently spent time in, such as school. In contrast, in their notes children were also interested in how everyone will spend their holidays and if the living circumstances in the central city are similar to the ones in suburban Beach Haven (see Table 11.1). Questions they did not feel comfortable sharing were more detailed and embraced a wider range of topics, which went beyond the focus of this study. This was surprising in two ways. First, children's initial interest was generated by their curiosity to see the other participants' data (Ergler, 2011), but were not limited to these as questions in Table 11.1 show. Second, children also took the role as a researcher seriously, thinking about topics they are interested in and questions they want to have answered. They did not simply repeat questions we had covered during the interviews in stage one. This observation reflects the way children can shed a different light on research. Children ask different questions and observe the world differently from an adult (Mitchell et al., 2007). For children, particular aspects of well-being are important such as the geographies of friendship and school as well as the living circumstances in Beach Haven and the central city. In contrast, we were more interested in their place-based experience of after school hours' activities, and in so doing neglected important aspects of their lives. In child-based neighbourhood research, which is interested in children's well-being, it is therefore valuable to integrate children in the research process as they not only ask different questions, but also they have different concerns. These questions and concerns can be revealed from a genuinely child-based perspective – something inaccessible for an adult researcher due to power and generational issues (Robinson and Kellett, 2004). We consider this issue in more detail later in the chapter.

A further example of children slipping into the role of a researcher is illustrative. Unprompted, two boys were playing with a recorder after we came back from the neighbourhood walk. They freely started their own little project, thus demonstrating that they felt engaged in the research topic beyond the simple relationship between the adult researcher and the child participant, as exemplified in their reflections on the neighbourhood walk.

> Michael: This is Michael (last name) here as a reporter and I would like to ask you a few questions, okay?
> Josh: Okay.
> Michael: What was the favourite bit of the walk?
> Josh: The bush walk!
> Michael: Why was it your favourite bit? What made it so exciting for you?
> Josh: Uhu, oho (giggles) oh the laughing side, because umm (both giggle) because Michael was a chatterbox all the time like this is one of the things.

Michael: I think it wasn't me. I think you were hearing it from McBeth, because he was behind yeah, but anyway (giggle and turn recorder on and off)…This is Michael again as your reporter and I would like to ask you a few more questions. What was your favourite photo?

Josh: My favourite photo? Umm, my favourite photo was down the wharf looking at the view.

The fact that Michael and Josh continued to 'play' researchers after we arrived back at our meeting point shows how much they enjoyed having been being invited into this role and having their questions answered. In this example they not only take their role as a researcher seriously and seem to imitate the questions we had been asking during the previous interviews, but they also adopt a different angle on the process. Photographing involves an aesthetic aspect which transcended our original idea of children 'taking pictures' of places important for them. In order to take a worthy picture you need a 'view'. In retrospect, it may have proved valuable to explain in more detail the documentary aspect of photography to the children in order to better prepare them for this task (Cook and Hess, 2007). However, it would have contradicted our aim of empowering children and giving them the opportunity of deciding on the use of the camera.

For the bush walk, in which we anticipated that nature played an important role in making it a favourite aspect of the local environment (Spencer and Blades, 2006), it was the personal relationship and fun they had that was memorable. Josh revealed that the time in the bush was his favourite aspect of the walk, but not because of the natural environment or the view, which was highlighted in their talk about the photos. Rather, the landscape was the arena in which a fun activity took place, but spoken word and personal interaction created the happy feeling. Diverse neighbourhood environments can be the arena for triggering positive experiences and feeling well in an environment, but also the activities and people with whom children enjoy spending their time contribute to their well-being. The boys clearly demonstrated that activities *and* scenery play a part in their well-being and enjoyment in the participation of this research.

In summary, these two examples show that children moved from being passive participants to active collaborators who asked and answered questions about their well-being and positive neighbourhood experiences. We therefore see the need to collaborate with children to gain an improved understanding of the determinants of their well-being.

'Ground truth': two examples of an improved understanding of children's well-being in urban environments

In the previous section we discussed the benefits of when children become active collaborators in a research project. However, we only touched on the implications that such an approach may have for an improved understanding of children's experiences of well-being in residential environments (see also Ergler, 2011). We now consider the value of engaging children as researchers and of designing research cooperatively. We contend that adult researchers will always be at risk of (mis)interpreting data on children's lives from their adult-centred point of view (Walker et al., 2009). We need the help of children to reveal deeper meaning for, as adults, we are simply too far from the ground truth of children, a metric which is not only related to their height. Children are therefore important researcher collaborators in exploring issues concerning their well-being. Established mixed-method research designs show that improved understandings are gained as different aspects of children lives can be accessed with different methods. For example, Darbyshire et al. (2005) demonstrate the complementary aspects of different methods in children's geographies. By giving children more involvement in the research process, otherwise hidden meanings and insights can be revealed.

In a first example, we discuss the significance of dogs for children's well-being. Studies revealed that dogs generally encourage their owners to be more active, increase their social capital and have a positive impact on mental well-being (Darbyshire et al., 2005; Tipper, 2011). However, none of the children in this study integrated or hinted at the existence of a dog in their maps. Dogs were neither represented as an encouragement to play outside nor were they depicted as a barrier to activity. The only prominent animal drawn by a child was a lion in the zoo which was representative of a place she likes to visit where it is 'fun to watch all the animals'.

Only two of the participants owned a dog. Both lived in apartments in the inner city of Auckland. The two girls told me in their interviews that they walk their dogs frequently and enjoy this most of the time. Lilly highlighted her trips to the local park and how people envy her owning a dog in a central city environment. This makes her stand out of the crowd and gives her a sense of pride. 'I can take him off the lead and people like go "wow there is a dog in the city, there's a big dog in the city". It's kind of cool thinking.' At my second meeting, however, they needed to find a new home for the dog as neighbours complained about his barking. Another participant, Hannah, was only allowed to walk her dog in the fenced car park of her apartment complex. Being the only person walking a dog made her feel awkward at times.

These examples highlight the role dogs play as a mediator for spending time actively outside, but this role was only revealed during the interviews. None of the participants mentioned playing with dogs as a fun activity during the neighbourhood walks. However, the way dogs can be a barrier to activity was revealed through interviews and neighbourhood walks, but to different extents. Three girls talked about fearing dogs in their interviews and all lived in the suburb. This finding may be related to the low ownership rate of dogs in the central city compared to the suburb, but assertions like 'I wished dogs never existed' and 'I hate dogs' as well as listing dogs, for example, along with traffic, 'tagging' and 'yelling people' as aspects of the landscape feared by the children, raised questions about whether this fear actually hinders outdoor play (especially after Maree told me all about her positive outdoor play experiences with friends, but 'where there are dogs I don't know'). The fear of dogs seemed to emerge at this stage of the data collection, but it was hard to place and even harder to determine whether 'dogs' were, on balance, more of an enabler or barrier for outdoor activity and children's well-being in general.

It was nonetheless surprising to note the number of dogs photographed during the local neighbourhood walk in Beach Haven. Two girls took seven pictures of four different dogs, while highlighting their fear of being bitten. Therefore, it was not surprising that these pictures were taken from a secure distance. In some, the dog was a tiny dot on the picture. One event during fieldwork, however, was notable. While the first author was walking with a group of children on a path surrounded by trees, a small dog approached off-leash followed by its owner a short distance behind. The dog was excited to meet people and attempted to sniff everyone. On seeing the dog, Maree immediately cowered behind her friend Isabelle and looked very scared. Her entire body language spoke of fear. The intangible fear of dogs, mentioned by some children during the interviews as a barrier to freedom in the neighbourhood suddenly became real. The knowledge of who owns a dog and which areas should be avoided therefore seems less important than the reality that you can meet a dog at any place. The boundaries where dogs roam and spend time are fluid.

These examples highlight that the meaning and importance of an action may only be revealed in a location-specific context (Cope, 2008; Walker et al., 2009). Sitting in a room and talking about dogs or the fear of dogs is different from experiencing the palpable fear of dogs during an encounter. We conclude, therefore, that it is important for understanding the determinants of well-being among children to conduct research within the contexts of their everyday life and to fully integrate children in the research process. This way the objects or locations they fear or enjoy are more likely to become apparent than through an adult researcher trying to assess choice and constraints at 'arm's length'.

For the second example we introduce McBeth who is an only child and lives with his parents in a one bedroom apartment in the central city. He indicated on his map (see Figure 11.1) that he likes two particular electronics stores. He coloured the rest of the shops on the busy main shopping street in downtown Auckland red, indicating his presumed dislike for them (shown by the 'Dislike' labels). We assumed his preference for these stores were related to buying music discs or that these two shops were simply the least boring ones. We asked him why these were so interesting for him and received the following answers.

McBeth: Because we get, cause we did, mm, we can go shopping and we can see toys and stuff and like you can see a DVD and go through the aisles.
Christina: How do you feel when you go shopping?
McBeth: I feel excited!
Christina: Why do you feel excited?
McBeth: Feels like that, that the one like you can get toys and computer games. […] A place that I don't like? [name of different electronic chain] and mm ….
Christina: Why don't you like [name of different electronic chain]?
McBeth: Cause, I don't really find my games there and toys. And no DVDs at [name of different electronic chain].

This section of our interview suggested that he enjoys shopping and both of his favourite shops have products he is interested in. Children as consumers have increasingly become a target for retailers and marketing strategists (see e.g. Marshall, 2010) and McBeth seems such a consumer. He enjoys wandering through the shops and looking around. However, it appears that he does not get a game, toy or DVD every time he visits the shops, so purchasing does not seem to be the incentive for visiting electronic stores per se. But during the rest of the interview it was not apparent why he enjoys 'playing' in the shops; the deeper meaning of this activity was revealed during the neighbourhood walk in the inner city.

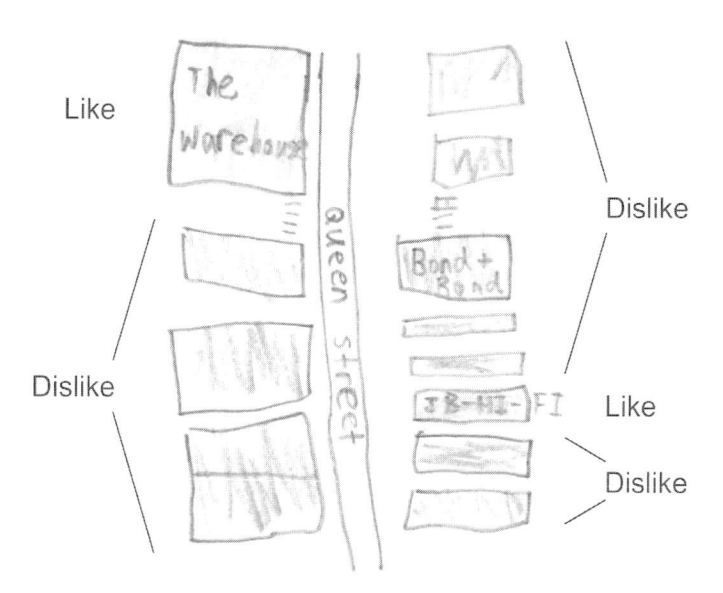

FIGURE 11.1 Extract of McBeth's drawing in summer (central city)

McBeth showed another child, Dexter, the shops he had identified as a good place to play in the central city because they are places where he could play the latest video games without any obligation to purchase anything. It seems that given the constraints of McBeth's daily life (a small family budget, limited child-friendly destinations in the city) he had found a way to make the less-than-child-friendly environment work for him. McBeth had turned some shops into a playground. In the course of the project he showed Dexter various video consoles and they played games without being noticed or told off by staff.

The deeper significance of this unorthodox play area was revealed because children were given a central role in the research project. Instead of showing an adult researcher around and possibly being influenced by a presumption that certain adult expectations should be met (Cook and Hess, 2007), children showed a 'non-local' response associated with their age, deciding on the places to visit and, more importantly, how to spend time in each place.

Conclusion

This chapter has explored the merits and challenges of a research design which attempted to gain a deeper understanding of children's well-being in their neighbourhood. In this endeavour, adults and children became collaborators, moving beyond the classic relationship of adult researcher and child participant with the latter passively agreeing to share their expertise and life experience. We have taken a broad view of well-being, seeing it as a quality arising from interactions with and in lived environments, and which can be a resource towards establishing a better future. In other words, feeling well (and well-placed) today can be a resource to help deal with issues that might arise in that or another place tomorrow. In the case of the children in our study, their place and urban experience – like children in many western cities – will change as residential intensification continues. For many, their worlds will become more vertical and more dominated by concrete. Despite living in 'built-up' cities, children deserved to have their own 'ground truths' acknowledged and given credence in research practice. Through doing so we have the opportunity of including them into the planning and research stages more firmly.

Towards this goal, we have shown that, through a shift in research approach, we may better understand and influence children's well-being.

Firstly, by cooperating with children we, as adult researchers, can gain a deeper understanding of children's complex neighbourhood experiences. This was illustrated by McBeth who utilised shops as a playground, and Josh and Michael's recalling of a fun activity during the neighbourhood walk. By releasing some of the power inherent in the research process, and allowing children to bring their expertise to a project, children act less as participants and more as collaborators. The net result, as we showed, is that child-genuine aspects of neighbourhood experiences can be revealed. These experiences were either not mentioned or obscured among other experiences during previous (more adult-centred) stages of data collection. By collaborating with children, we as adult researchers are in a better position to make policy recommendations which foster children's well-being. Children's agency and opportunities for exploring their neighbourhood may also increase through them having a voice to express the enabling and constraining aspects of the neighbourhood environment that affect their experience of independence. Creating an environment which is safe and comfortable for children to explore independently can also foster a healthy environment for adults (e.g. active transport, safe public places, reduced crime) as children are regarded as among the most vulnerable members of society (Freeman and Tranter, 2011).

Secondly, we as adult researchers are able to influence children's well-being directly during the research process. Enabling children to collaborate on a research project provides them with heightened self-esteem and may put them into a better position to address issues impacting on their lives (Kellet, 2004). More importantly, children can have fun while collaborating and working on a project (Ergler, 2011).

Although we have come a long way from the invisibility of children in geography to giving them voice as adult researchers, we still need to improve our research designs in order to gain a deeper understanding of children's well-being. We propose that there is a need to be more courageous and creative in working with children to reduce the risk that children are simply passive participants in our research processes. Without such a commitment, as adult researchers we risk continuing to reveal only what we think is important for children's well-being.

Acknowledgements

An earlier version of this chapter was published as Ergler. C. (2011) 'Beyond passive participation: Children as collaborators in understanding neighbourhood experience', *Graduate Journal of Asia-Pacific Studies*, 7(2), 78–98. The authors are grateful for permission of the publisher to draw on and extend the original article.

References

Auckland Regional Council (2010) *State of the Auckland Region*, Auckland: Auckland Regional Council.
Auckland Regional Growth Forum (1999) *A vision for managing growth in the Auckland region. Auckland regional growth strategy 2050*, Auckland: Auckland Regional Growth Forum.
Blaut, J. M. and Stea, D. (1971) 'Studies of geographic learning', *Annals of the Association of American Geographers*, 61(2), 387–393.
Carroll, P., Witten, K. and Kearns, R. A. (2011) 'Housing intensification in Auckland, New Zealand: Implications for children and families', *Housing Studies*, 26(3), 353–367.

Carver, A., Timperio, A. and Crawford, D. (2008) 'Playing it safe: The influence of neighbourhood safety on children's physical activity – A review', *Health & Place*, 14(2), 217–227.

Chawla, L. (2001) *Growing up in an urbanizing world*, London: Earthscan.

Christensen, P. H., ed. (2000) *Research with children: Perspectives and practices*, London: Routledge Falmer.

Christensen, P. and Prout, A. (2002) 'Working with ethical symmetry in social research with children', *Childhood*, 9(4), 477–497.

Cook, T. and Hess, E. (2007) 'What the camera sees and from whose perspective – Fun methodologies for engaging children in enlightening adults', *Childhood: A Global Journal of Child Research*, 14(1), 29–45.

Cope, M. (2008) 'Patchwork neighbourhood: Children's urban geographies in Bufallo, New York', *Environment and Planning A*, 40, 2845–2863.

Crampton, P., Salmond, C. and Kirkpatrick, R. (2000) *Degrees of deprivation in New Zealand: An atlas of socio-economic difference*, 2nd edn, Auckland: David Bateman Ltd.

Darbyshire, P., MacDougall, C. and Schiller, W. (2005) 'Multiple methods in qualitative research with children: More insight or just more?', *Qualitative Research*, 5(4), 417–436.

Day, R. and Wagner, F. (2010) 'Parks, streets and "just empty space": The local environmental experiences of children and young people in a Scottish study', *Local Environment*, 15(6), 509–523.

Dixon, J. and Broom, D. H. (2007) *The seven deadly sins of obesity: How the modern world is making us fat*, Sydney: UNSW Press.

Ergler, C. R. (2011) 'Beyond passive participation: Children as collaborators in understanding neighbourhood experience', *Graduate Journal of Asia-Pacific Studies*, 7(2), 78–98.

Fainstein, S. S. (2000) 'New directions in planning theory', *Urban Affairs Review*, 35(4), 451–478.

Freeman, C. and Tranter, P. J. (2011) *Children and their urban environment: Changing worlds*, London: Earthscan.

Friesen, W. (2009) 'The demographic transformation of inner city Auckland', *New Zealand Population Review*, 35, 55–74.

Holloway, S. L. and Valentine, G. (2000) *Children's geographies: Playing, living, learning (Critical geographies)*, New York: Routledge.

Hörschelmann, K. and Van Blerk, L. (2012) *Children, youth and the city (Routledge critical introductions to urbanism and the city)*, Abingdon: Routledge.

Jones, A., van Sluijs, E. M. F., Ness, A. R., Haynes, R. and Riddoch, C. J. (2010) 'Physical activity in children: Does how we define neighbourhood matter?', *Health & Place*, 16(2), 236–241.

Karsten, L. (1998) 'Growing up in Amsterdam: Differentiation and segregation in children's daily lives', *Urban Studies*, 35(3), 565–581.

Kearns, R. and Andrews, G. J. (2010) 'Well-being', in Smith, S., Pain, R., Marston, S. A. and Jones, J. P., eds., *Handbook of social geographies*, 3 ed., London: Sage, 309–328.

Kellet, M. (2004) 'Just teach us the skills please, we'll do the rest: Empowering ten-years-olds as active researchers', *Children & Society*, 18, 329–343.

Leslie, E., Coffee, N., Frank, L., Owen, N., Bauman, A. and Hugo, G. (2007) 'Walkability of local communities: Using geographic information systems to objectively assess relevant environmental attributes', *Health & Place*, 13(1), 111–122.

Lobstein, T., Baur, L. and Jackson-Leach, R. (2010) 'The childhood obesity epidemic', in Waters, E., Swinburn, B., Seidell, J. and Uauy, R., eds., *Preventing childhood obesity: Evidence, policy and practice*, Oxford: Wiley-Blackwell, 3–14.

Mackett, R. L., Brown, B., Gong, Y., Kitazawa, K. and Paskins, J. (2007) 'Children's independent movement in the local environment', *Built Environment*, 33(4), 454–468.

Malone, K. (2007) 'The bubble-wrap generation: Children growing up in walled gardens', *Environmental Education Research*, 13(4), 513–527.

Marshall, D., ed. (2010) *Understanding children as consumers*, London: Sage Publications.

McCreanor, T., Penney, L., Jensen, V., Witten, K., Kearns, R. and Moewaka Barnes, H. (2006) '"This is like my comfort zone": Senses of place and belonging within Oruamo/Beachhaven, New Zealand', *New Zealand Geographer*, 62, 196–207.

Mitchell, H., Kearns, R. A. and Collins, D. (2007) 'Nuances of neighbourhood: Children's perceptions of the space between home and school in Auckland, New Zealand', *Geoforum*, 38(4), 614–627.

Murphy, L. (2008) 'Third-wave gentrification in New Zealand: The case of Auckland', *Urban Studies*, 45(12), 2521–2540.

Porter, G. (2008) 'Increasing children's participation in African transport planning: Reflections on methodological issues in a child centred research project', *Children's Geographies*, 6(2), 151–167.

Rissotto, A. and Guiliani, V. (2006) 'Learning neighbourhood environments: The loss of experience in a modern world', in Spencer, C. P. and Blades, M., eds., *Children and their environments – learning, using and designing spaces*, New York: Cambridge University Press, 75–90.

Robinson, C. and Kellett, M. (2004) 'Power', in Fraser, S., Lewis, V., Ding, S., Kellett, M. and Robinson, C., eds., *Doing research with children and young people*, London: Sage Publications, 81–96.

Spencer, C. P. and Blades, M., eds. (2006) *Children and their environments: Learning, using and designing spaces*, Cambridge: Cambridge University Press.

Talen, E. (1999) 'Sense of community and neighbourhood form: An assessment of the social doctrine of new urbanism', *Urban Studies*, 36(8), 1361–1379.

Tipper, B. (2011) '"A dog who I know quite well": Everyday relationships between children and animals', *Children's Geographies*, 9(2), 145–165.

Walker, M., Whyatt, D., Pooley, C., Davies, G., Coulton, P. and Bamford, W. (2009) 'Talk, technologies and teenagers: Understanding the school journey using a mixed-methods approach', *Children's Geographies*, 7(2), 107–122.

Weller, S. and Bruegel, I. (2009) 'Children's "place" in the development of neighbourhood social capital', *Urban Studies*, 46(3), 629–643.

Wells, N. M. (2000) 'At home with nature: Effects of "greenness" on children's cognitive functioning', *Environment & Behavior*, 32(6), 775–795.

Whitzman, C., Worthington, M. and Mizrachi, D. (2010) 'The journey and the destination matter: Child-friendly cities and children's right to the city', *Built Environment*, 36(4), 474–486.

Witten, K. and Carroll, P. (2011) 'Intensification, housing affordability and families: Learning from the Auckland CBD', in Witten, K., Abrahamse, W. and Stuart, K., eds., *Growth misconduct? Avoiding sprawl and improving urban intensification in New Zealand*, Wellington: New Zealand Centre for Sustainable Cities, University of Otago, 79–89.

Witten, K., Kearns, R. A., McCreanor, T. and Penney, L. (2009) 'Connecting place and the everyday practices of parenting: Insights from Auckland, New Zealand', *Environment and Planning A*, 41, 2893–2910.

Witten, K., Pearce, J. and Day, P. (2011) 'Neighbourhood destination accessibility index: A GIS tool for measuring infrastructure support for neighbourhood physical activity', *Environment and Planning A*, 43, 205–223.

12

LANDSCAPE, WELL-BEING AND ENVIRONMENT

Richard Coles and Zoë Millman

Introduction

In this book, we sought to provide some clarity regarding the role of the landscape in supporting the well-being of individuals and whether it is possible to define or, at least, provide a fuller understanding of the landscape associations that engender high levels of well-being. In this final chapter we review and summarise key aspects of the individual explorations and discussions contained in the earlier chapters. At various points we have attempted to summarise the key elements which impact upon well-being, positively and negatively, or identify the deficiencies of urban landscapes, presenting them as key points which use or paraphrase the terminology used by the authors of the chapters. To understand the full context of these the reader should, of course, refer to the original chapters and their specific source material.

All authors have introduced well-being as a critical issue to society and set their discussion in a range of contexts which consider how the environment is being identified as a health resource. In the main, the context of enquiry relates to urban situations, certainly to urban populations, although the theoretical discussions draw on a wider range of material that includes natural and designed landscapes, residential locations and leisure destinations and which present a substantial source of theory and discussion around specific interventions. The issue at hand, identified in the first chapter, concerns how the experience of landscape, or more widely engagement with the environment, relates to wellness and, in turn, can contribute positively to life experience. Discussion is also centred on the need to understand the impacts of urban living on health and well-being, identifying factors which contribute to positive health and well-being as well as those that are considered negative. Several authors comment further, for example, Lindsay Sowman (Chapter 4): 'The relationship between the environment and human well-being is at the centre of human existence and experience.' He continues, 'It is an infinitely complex relationship, about which we have an equally infinite range of personal and collective social intuitions.'

The idea of personal well-being is regarded differently by each of us, with variables including:

- physical health
- personal outlook
- personal histories and the experiences that form them
- emotions and moods
- the presence and realisation of positive and negative feelings
- interactions with others and how they are perceived.

Each of these variables influences how we perceive our personal well-being, but they also affect how we perceive and respond to our surroundings (Reid and Hunter, Chapter 1). The main thrust of this book is that in addition to the variables above, the experience and perception of the landscape is an equally important variable that both influences and is influenced by our well-being.

In exploring woodlands to improve individual and community well-being, Liz O'Brien and Jake Morris (Chapter 10) remind us that that 'in the sustainable development suite of well-being indicators ... the value and use of green space is one of a number of indicators of well-being', suggesting that the qualities associated with the more natural elements of the environment are as important to the well-being of society as any other indicator. The challenge thus is for those responsible for designing and managing the landscape, and those who hope to improve the well-being of society, to understand these different variables and the processes by which the landscape is experienced and understood. Inviting exposure to landscapes, or facilitating environmental interactions, so that 'latent' positive qualities are accessible, enables users to experience personal well-being in whichever form it may take for them.

Association with the landscape is not passive: the landscape is imbued with meaning and is experienced very specifically by the perceiving individual who gives it meaning in relation to their life experiences, requirements, personal relevance and expectations; all of which define the remit for accessing the landscape and its subsequent interpretation. The personal meaning, interpretation and appropriate rationalisation of the experience broadly defines the individual's 'landscape experience' and leads to an assessment of its relevance to them and ways that it may be used in the future for personal benefit, for example via repeat visits or by modifying a route to work or school so that it can be incorporated into the individual's everyday experience.

We can describe this interaction in various ways and there are a range of terms which do just that. Janice Astbury (Chapter 5) helpfully describes it as a 'social–ecological system', emphasising the complex dynamic at work involving individuals and what becomes 'their' environment as they embed their values in it and incorporate what they view as its functions and offerings into their own identities. In our own work we have described landscape interaction as 'performative' (Millman, 2012), indicating that we are affected by the landscape as we move through it, but also experience the landscape by placing our own values upon it in a loop of exploration and experience to continuously refine its perception and capture the specific qualities that are important and personal to our lives.

Movement through the landscape involves both physical and emotional encounters; sensory experiences including sights and sounds, touching and tasting contained objects, the passage of the foot and movement of the body; and emotional experiences such as the recollection of memories, the creation of feelings and musing on the things we encounter. These things can and frequently do move us into a positive state which can be understood if we employ appropriate means of capturing feelings. It is significant that the approaches used and discussed by the authors more often concern qualitative techniques to collect information, techniques which allow users to express the quality of their experiences and represent the emotional consequences in their own words. Qualitative techniques can include the collection of verbal 'narratives' in which individuals talk about their experiences and feelings, as with the work of Penelope Carroll et al. (Chapter 8) , as they move through the landscape or, as with Erica Ander et al.'s work (Chapter 9), as they handle objects. The narratives created using these techniques illustrate the processes of engagement, construction of meaning and movement into positive states of reflection. Sometimes these methods also help identify negative associations.

In our own landscape work we identified the importance of taking a user-centred approach at an early stage and have been impressed by the elegance of the language used by individuals when invited to express their responses and represent their feelings. Generally individuals indicate that they have derived great personal satisfaction from landscape experiences, having moved from the everyday to a special place of self-reflection. We have found that places have the capacity to instigate associations with personal life events, recalled upon experiencing certain aspects of the environment. For example the sight of a boat or the feel of cobbled paving underfoot has instigated the recollection of other times, places and people in what could be described as a 'Proustian moment'.[1] The nature of these associations makes them completely personal, but the same aspect of the landscape may instigate different recollections in other users.

Explaining landscape interaction

Sara Warber et al. introduce a range of theoretical models which attempt to explain well-being and the environment (Chapter 2). These are drawn from different disciplinary perspectives, many of which have a long legacy. Foremost among these is 'Attention Restoration Theory', which involves restoration from the mental fatigue induced by the everyday stress of navigating the complexity of the urban environment, largely developed by the much respected environmental psychologists, Rachel and Stephen Kaplan. It is argued that exposure to natural environments restores our mental state and observations of green space users do seem to correspond well to the theoretical model. Another is 'psychophysiologic theory' which has a more clinical basis and, again, as Warber et al. discuss, links the experience of nature to human physiology where exposure to, or being in, a non-threatening natural environment creates a relaxation involving the body's fight or flight response; it is suggested that exposure to nature is a mediator for reducing physiological stress. These theories refer to well-being in terms of their mental and physical health benefits, and the idea of feeling well, relaxed and restored.

Within the geography field an equally enticing theory is that of 'sense of place' which suggests that experience of the place itself is psychologically important. Place-related research emphasises the emotional attachment that people have with a specific location, rather than the clinical dimensions, but it does not preclude any of the underpinning psychological responses.

Warber et al. also present the 'biopsychosocial' model which seems to more clearly express the importance of psychological benefits and social support, including barriers to accessing the benefits. In briefly reviewing these theories they seem to indicate that none are mutually exclusive. However, a 'bio-psychological-social-place' model of landscape interaction has much to recommend it in considering the dynamics and nature of landscape interaction. Certainly from users' responses to the landscape we can identify the individual 'bio-psychological-social-place' elements, for example in Warber et al.'s examination of park users. They also introduce what they call a 'spiritual dimension' which they evidence with terms from users' responses such as 'calm', 'peaceful', 'at ease', 'tranquil', 'serene' and 'quiet', but acknowledging that this term might be disputed.

Sowman (Chapter 4) explores the landscape in some detail, presenting a wide range of literature to define current thinking and research. He considers 'the role of landscape and perceptions of place in human well-being' under the broad heading 'towards a landscape of well-being'. Sowman emphasises that there is

> an enduring recognition and understanding of the impacts of various environmental parameters such as clean air and water, nutritious food, appropriate shelter and the like, on physical health and well-being... Even the earliest designed landscapes reflect a sophisticated sensitivity to the healthful, restorative and spiritually nourishing aspects of gardens and human-scale landscape spaces. [But] what is less well understood, however, are the myriad operative and causal factors...

Sowman also presents key theoretical threads emphasising the concept of 'place', human experience and the connections that people feel with the world around them. In exploring the relationship between place and identity he observes that there is little discussion on its relationship with well-being as a specific concept and poses the question, 'what contribution might "sense of place" make to human well-being?' This is, of course, an issue which this volume attempts to address and where we suggest that we should not 'over-define' landscape in terms of well-being but recognise the factors that promote positive engagement and remove the factors that deny such in the confidence that we are releasing the potential of the landscape.

Landscape typologies that underpin well-being

Within these theoretical dimensions there is much scope to consider the landscape qualities that underpin human health, both mental and physical, and which accrue positive associations beyond the basic, perhaps in an effort to identify landscape typologies that are derived from or grounded by their capacity to induce well-being. How might such typologies be developed and what would be their constituent qualities?

Several chapters address this question from different perspectives. Janice Astbury (Chapter 5) emphasises the human–environment interface, which she terms 'interactive landscape', emphasising the individual's control of the environment. Astbury also cites the work of Kaplan and Kaplan – 'people's involvement in environmental stewardship and the results of their efforts have the potential to contribute significantly to human well-being', but she firstly considers the negativity that can be associated with urban living:

- Many urban landscapes convey the message that the city is beyond the control of ordinary citizens.
- They limit direct contact with nature and the ecosystem services that sustain life.
- As such our urban landscapes are often disempowering, sometimes inducing despair.
- These landscapes represent a missed opportunity to empower the large numbers of people residing within them.

She follows this by considering an 'emerging typology of inviting landscapes' which are aimed at promoting interaction with (urban) nature to enhance 'social–ecological resilience', that is, the landscape's ability to mitigate negative experiences and mental fatigue. Landscapes are perceived as inviting when they can be perceived as safe to use, engender feelings of ownership and community, and include nature. So the presence of certain characteristics is important for underpinning positive engagement:

- Safety – users should feel safe and components which engender these feelings should be present.
- Permission to enter – landscapes should be open to all, easily accessible, and their sanctioned uses should be obvious.

- Interest – landscapes should include diverse features with opportunities for fun and exploration.
- Connection – users should feel relaxed enough to make connections, both physically (through movement and the senses) and mentally (through musing), so a local rather than corporate or institutional atmosphere is important.
- Community – landscapes should facilitate community and be community-claimed, so social, inviting and play spaces are important.
- Nature – landscapes should allow users to interact with the natural world (e.g. flora and fauna) and observe natural processes (e.g. weather and seasonal change).

From the various theoretical propositions and explorations of such parameters we can begin to consider landscape or environmental qualities in terms of a 'green space/well-being continuum'. This is rooted in greater understanding of the positivity that can be induced by landscape and which engenders and underpins well-being. Chapter 5 thus helps us consider some of the prerequisites for positive interaction and a means for assessing the qualities of environments that underpin positive engagement. This could form a basis for an audit of existing green space provision and the extent to which engagement is facilitated or prevented and where the physiological responses referred to take place. Astbury's emerging typology helps considerably here, but we should be cautious about defining landscapes of well-being simply from a checklist of landscape characteristics. This could lead to an overly prescriptive approach with limited room for personal interpretation, associations and creation of personal places.

Irene Yerro Vela (Chapter 6) considers the contribution of greenery as a factor of well-being and presents case studies of apartment complexes to illustrate the typology of the spaces created as part of professional architectural practice. She emphasises that:

- Green space provision moves beyond the pragmatic (e.g. aesthetic 'softening' and economical concerns) to a more user-centred approach, where residents are able to make their own contributions to their surroundings, for example through sustainable living.
- The social contribution from green spaces should offer possibilities of use, comfort and well-being rather than impose social behaviours.
- Where (green) semi-private outdoor spaces are framed in an urban context, issues like access to nature, the space for children to play, car-free areas and open spaces for informal meetings constitute a palette of elements to achieve a better quality of life for residents.
- Greenery can be an economic investment that attracts buyers and tenants, and therefore value to architecture.
- Although good quality is often costly, research has revealed that the best green places do not necessarily require large investment.

- Quality (green) outdoor spaces can be achieved with interdisciplinary teams working together.
- There exists a need for a new architecture focusing on sustainable construction and environmental practices.

Yerro Vela discusses the standards available to her architect colleagues, citing the 'green factor systems' that are landscape requirements designed to increase the quality and quantity of planted areas in some cities. She also refers to a range of other international standards which build upon the tradition of green space provision and quality urban environments which we are now equating with the ability to support and engender well-being. We should also consider current European practice concerning ecosystem services which explicitly consider health and well-being in terms of their 'cultural services'.

In our own work we refer to well-being, but are content to consider the interactions that individuals experience and how they recall that experience. What we observe is positivity and delight, a strong sense of ownership and self-reflection, sensory engagements and personal connections, the affirmation of self-identity and layers of meaning which suggest a reconfiguration of the landscapes in question from the everyday to special places of personal significance. These are all engendered by the qualities of the landscape encountered, but also by the absence of negative associations. We have undertaken studies in natural areas such as woodlands, parks and open spaces in addition to urban centres and found consistency regarding a 'landscape/well-being continuum' and the expression of personal delight that is associated with their use. For example, there are clear common aspects of ownership, access and permission to enter the different places, to use them on your own terms and at your own pace. Safety is a crucial element which is often referred to, as is the fear of getting lost; issues relating to accessibility and safety must first be overcome before landscape interactions can begin and these include clear indicators of permission to engage with the sensory qualities of the environment (Coles & Bussey, 2000; Coles & Caserio, 2001).

The levels of positivity that we have seen, evidenced by narratives, can be very high indeed, with participants describing 'being on a high', or 'a little bit of therapy'. These responses are very personal and would have been difficult to predict beyond general terms, since they are absolutely related to the experience of the individual (Millman, 2012). They do relate to discussions concerning 'place', but can equally be described as encounters with 'self'. In the 'landscape/well-being continuum' we must include 'self' and the mechanisms by which the landscape or object are encountered and made sense of.

Performativity – encountering and experiencing the landscape

To move the discussion forward it is appropriate to consider Fiona Bannon's work to understand more clearly how we interact with the landscape/environment

(Chapter 3). Bannon explains in the title of her chapter that she is considering an 'an everyday aesthetic for walking' and

> what it is that intimately supports us in our ongoing emplaced experiences... The fabric of these ordinary, often overlooked, activities is effectively an interlacing of memory, evaluation, reflection and knowledge generation... a shaping of resonant experience where each individual is a connoisseur of his or her perception and thoughts.

She draws on her experience of 'somatic practice' and choreography, expanding on what we referred to earlier as the 'performativity of the landscape' and which she refers to as the '"in-dialogue" with the places' and the 'haptic as part of our ability to forge connections'. Bannon raises concerns regarding the quality of the environment and opportunities to realise connections, referring to John Dewey who comments on 'a dulling and narrowing of life experience and expectation'. Her discussion highlights the individuality of experience and the paucity of everyday interaction, wishing to raise standards regarding the quality of 'place' and essentially moving towards a consideration of the self-reflection, identity, refreshment and vitality engendered during landscape encounters. Bannon draws from a range of sources from the arts, in particular referring to artists who explore and advocate walking (Richard Long; Janet Cardiff; Simon Whitehead) who, with Bannon, emphasise the importance of '[walking as] valuable ... in ... getting to know and unlock the richness of places'. She refers to a 'kinaesthetic sensibility' that occurs when walking, that is, the dynamics and thought processes of the moving body as it encounters space, which include:

- bodily understanding as a felt experience
- the rhythm of walking and the need to be captured by it
- the interdependencies of our physical interaction, intellectual and emotional selves
- the flows and connections made as we move through space and time
- how we get to know ourselves
- ongoing dialogue between one's self and the rhythm of the spaces/landscape
- being responsive to the sights, smells, and sensory attributes of place
- fostering environmental design practice and policy that affords a positive impact upon the individual by re-energising environments.

In our own walking experiences and interventions we invited participants to experience places and observe the 'rhythm of the walk'. The sensory engagement that occurs has moved participants to reflect on 'self', for example where they have remembered family members and past events, been moved by the quality and dominance of water, the presence of the past through heritage sites, or in other circumstances the rhythms of nature and seasonal change, smells, sounds, the quality of light and tactile experiences. Some participants have adopted strategies to ensure regular landscape interaction through repeatedly visiting, leading us to recognise the importance of such engagements as part of a life strategy. It is in these circumstances that there are clear indications of the landscape underpinning well-being.

Object, touch and well-being

Missing from much of the landscape/well-being debate is reference to the qualities of touch and, by association, the importance of objects. For some clarity on this we can learn from the material presented by Ander et al. (Chapter 9) in discussing museum well-being interventions through their project 'Heritage in Hospitals', in which museum objects were taken into hospital wards for handling by patients. Through an examination of 'the health and well-being benefits of touching objects' they emphasise the intrinsic power of objects, the tactile experience, sensory qualities, embodied meaning, and the ways that this might impact on community cohesion, neighbourhood renewal, civic engagement, local participation, the design of safe spaces and environmental sustainability.

The 'Heritage in Hospitals' project is significant in that it adopts a critical approach to assessing the well-being outcomes of the intervention, applying the approach to a range of clinical and hospital situations, using objects from archaeology, Egyptology, geology, and zoological collections. Through this intervention various positive well-being outcomes were observed and reported by patients, including:

- new perspectives
- positive feelings and moods
- learning
- energy and alertness
- reflection on sense of identity
- the opportunity to try something different or inspiring
- feeling calmed and relieving anxiety
- passing time
- social experience
- tactile experience.

The researchers report that it was difficult to separate the social and cultural aspects of the intervention from the specific handling of the objects, but emphasise that each aspect helped produce dynamic interactions with a well-being outcome greater than the sum of the parts. Given the power of objects and the importance of touch, the current paucity of everyday opportunities to touch and experience the qualities of materials and objects within the urban landscape is disappointing, although there are exceptions in the public art sector. When we consider the properties of objects and touch in natural environments (and how they might reinforce well-being), for instance the pleasure and connection felt at picking up a colourful stone from the ground, the shell collected from the beach, touching the bark of a tree or running a hand through the soft stalks of grass, we are reminded of the impoverishment of the urban environment in this regard and the limited invitation to touch as one negotiates a street, sits down or uses a hand rail. Research into the tactile qualities of the landscape and the importance of touch in relation to well-being is overdue. Just as Astbury has advocated the removal of fences that prevent physical access to the landscape, we should be considering the barriers which prevent a full tactile experience. Perhaps taking cues from natural environments?

Participants' perspectives

Several of the chapters focus on the experiences and responses of individuals through the use of qualitative methods targeting a range of user groups and different environments. We have already referred to the work of Warber et al. (Chapter 2) who examine the responses of park users by encouraging participants to reflect on their experiences. By asking the question 'And thinking about after you leave this park, what words would you use to describe how you feel after you leave here?', the authors were able to collect a variety of individual responses. Using the participants' own words they relate the responses to a range of domains, which could be termed the 'subsets of positive well-being' associated with use of the landscape:

- Physical – associated with the physical body, e.g. being physically relaxed or revitalised.
- Affective and Place Attachment – representing users' emotions and personal feelings about a landscape, or how they are affected by their experience.
- Spiritual – referring to inner calm.
- Cognitive – realising personal satisfaction or achievement.
- Social – connections with others and the wider community.
- Global well-being – referring to broad aspects of improvement in health, e.g. feeling 'better' or 'healthy'.

Benedict Spencer et al. (Chapter 7) present another user group perspective by exploring the concept of playable space as a well-being attribute of the landscape for older people. They comment on the 'lack of playfulness in the public realm' and the absence of outdoor spaces that respond to the needs of older people: '…the opportunity for joyfulness, let alone playfulness, is lacking in much of England's public realm, which still has the potential to be transformed from the barely functional to the playful and delightful'.

They add that this can be achieved through 'host[ing] the regular, voluntary, informal and happy anticipated gatherings of individuals beyond the realms of home and work'. This criticism of the (urban) public realm is echoed throughout this book, and although the terminologies used by the contributing authors differ, they all highlight the lack of vibrancy or opportunity in the landscape which prevents the deep level of engagement required to underpin well-being. Spencer et al. focus on the opportunities for adult play, stressing the importance of social relationships formed through various activities and the provision and quality of the facilities available to achieve this. The examination of landscape interaction from the perspective of 'playfulness', with its connotations with 'joyfulness', is an appealing attribute of a dynamic landscape suggesting strong links with well-being. This theme is under-explored in relation to adults; however, the authors are able to cite similar research being undertaken from the perspective of children's play and list a range of terms which can be adopted to define well-being properties of the landscape:

- freedom of personal choice and control
- feelings of personal power/empowerment
- 'pretending', non-literal 'as if' behaviour
- intrinsic motivation
- positive effects of pleasure and enjoyment
- flexible and adaptive use of objects and rules
- understanding leisure as discretionary free time
- leisure as a state of mind.

To support well-being, landscape associations and experiences need to contain intrinsically rewarding experiences which move individuals to a positive state of mind. Chapter 7 also includes comparisons with 'Quality of life factors' and play, further supporting the idea that the terminology of playfulness is akin to the state of mind associated with well-being.

Much of Spencer et al.'s research with older people is related to leisure, where there is less emphasis on novelty (a feature of children's play) and more emphasis on the continuity and reinforcement of past experiences (remembered events and activities and the recall of joyful moments). Our experience suggests that this is also the case as users walk through a landscape. For example, in our studies where users explored their reactions when visiting regenerated canal landscapes (Millman et al., 2008; Millman, 2012) and designed botanical gardens (Costa, 2013), users recalled other pleasurable moments and relationships in direct response to the qualities of the landscapes, forming 'memory loops', or confluences of past and present. The recorded narratives indicate joyful states of mind and a sense of reward at the recollection of their past experiences, indicating that the ability for users to remember while they are in the landscape is an aspect of positive well-being.

Chapters 8 and 11 further explore participants' perspectives from the point of view of children as landscape users in New Zealand. Penelope Carroll et al. (Chapter 8) consider how children perceive their local neighbourhood in Auckland. Discussion is set in the now familiar context of a deteriorating urban environment with a lack of opportunities for children to play (freely and on their own terms), stay active and experience as they interact with the environment. This lack of opportunity is compounded by the current urban intensification in that region and is all the more troubling when we consider that play activities are crucial for children's development. The authors cite a range of information that identifies the negative factors relating to the erosion of opportunities in city neighbourhoods, commenting that spaces for children are being restricted to swimming pools, libraries and organised playgrounds. Children are more active outdoors than indoors but their use of the outdoor landscape is restricted by a range of factors:

- (over) safety-conscious parenting
- car reliance
- adult-centric urban design
- erosion of independent play opportunities
- increasing traffic volumes fuelling fears over children's safety
- a planning process which confines children to specific municipal places
- that children's views are not represented
- 'toxic' cities which fail to nurture children.

They recognise and call for a 'prioritisation of children's needs in service and infrastructure provision ... [and that] cities must provide for the well-being of children' and the need to take a child-centred view, embracing children in the design process. Recognising these issues, Carroll et al. focused on obtaining the views of children regarding how they perceive and use their local environment, which further informs us regarding well-being and the environment. They use a range of methods including 'go-along' walking interviews and travel diaries to capture the experiences, followed by additional interviews with adults. The difficulties that adults have in 'thinking as children' can preclude a child-centred approach and Carroll et al. recognise this in identifying the researchers as 'outsiders' without the 'insider' knowledge of the neighbourhood or the ability to adopt the perspectives of local children; they emphasise the need to develop an appropriate research methodology which is led by the children. These are interesting methodological issues by which the authors resolve to achieve a child-centric view of their local landscape, which includes an understanding of children's daily activities and comparisons with professional perceptions, tested against adult and child focused perceptions of 'place':

- Children/insider perspectives – children defined their neighbourhood in terms of where their friends live. Some ranged widely, while others were fearful, mentioning strangers, drunk people, feeling scared, increased bullying, scary dogs, and it not being 'cool' to use certain spaces.
- Parents/adult insider perceptions – some cited issues of safety away from the school or home, violence from strangers and teenagers, thugs, drunkenness,

adverse media reports and a perceived fear of drowning. Others contradicted this and saw the neighbourhood as good place to grow up.
- Researcher/outsider perceptions – they identified suitable and apparently appealing green places for play and exploration, which were largely deserted, contrasting with well-patronised local shops. During school hours, schools were the focus of activity but were locked at other times with spiked security fences restricting access.

The differences between the adults' and children's responses to the neighbourhood, as an appropriate landscape which was supportive to the children's independent mobility, indicate the importance of involving children in the research process and the range of variables. According to the authors the neighbourhood contained good opportunities for play and exploration, but for the children they were considered fearful places. The implications for landscapes of well-being are that although natural elements appeared to be present, access to them was denied by virtue of social pressures, including the nature of the local community, parent and peer pressures. Many children were prevented from beginning to explore the landscape as they were conditioned to avoid it as part of a strategy for remaining safe. Barriers to access can be subtle and while they include real physical barriers, other, less obvious factors can have a detrimental effect. For example, danger and underuse can be signified by a lack of clear exits from a space or the presence of litter or dumped cars, while aspects or features which do not accord with our personal perspective or not seeing others like us in a place can prompt the user to feel unwelcome. In such circumstances the subtle, negatively perceived factors immediately negate the latent positive potential of places that otherwise appear desirable (Coles & Bussey, 2000).

Christina Ergler and Robin Kearns (Chapter 11) also take a child-centred approach in their investigation of children's views on well-being in intensifying urban environments in Auckland. Like Carroll et al. they emphasise that 'children are experts on their experiences, their lives and what concerns their well-being' and comment on the impacts of intensification of the urban environment in ways that are negative to the mobility and independence of children; they emphasise the need to find ways of engaging with children to find ways to support healthy active lifestyles to the benefit of personal well-being and wider society. They emphasise the importance of taking a child-centred approach which can 'foster well-being in two ways: the enjoyment of collaborating; and potentially enhanced insights … gaining a deeper understanding of children's worlds'. Well-being factors associated with children's use of their environment include:

- correlating positivity (positive outlook) with physical activity
- exemplifying being well with a specific environment
- negotiating (physical and social) risk

- gaining physical confidence
- promoting self-confidence and self-esteem
- reducing anxiety about their being in the world and defining their place in the world
- feeling well from being outside in their neighbourhood
- community attachment
- environmental literacy
- providing precedents for promotion of well-being in later life.

Ergler and Kearns emphasise the importance of children's engagement with the landscape research process and that it 'sheds a different light on the questions adult researchers have been interested in … they can reveal the "ground truth" of neighbourhood experiences that contribute to or hinder their well-being'. The authors demonstrate the process of 'releasing … the power inherent in the research encounter' and comment upon the activities referring to aspects of play.

It also appears that through the transfer of the research process from adults to themselves, the children are given permission to explore the meaning of their surroundings and tasked with discovering how they perceive their environment and how they can represent it in their own terms, that is, learning the possibilities of engagement with the landscape. The authors give an interesting example where the group discuss and consider the impact of dogs in their experience of place. Ergler and Kearns conclude that

> we as adult researchers are able to influence children's well-being directly … enabling children to collaborate on a [landscape] research project provides them with a heightened self-esteem and may put them in a better position to address issues impacting on their lives.

Child-centred work that involves environmental interaction allows children to negotiate a personal position which they can use to explore and experience its qualities. In this way they can learn to associate the positivity of health, play and joyfulness with the environment to an extent that they can become confident, drawing on these skills and memories in later life to revive the joyful aspects of play, to reflect on self and life.

Well-being and woodlands

Reference has already been made to the importance of natural environments in respect of well-being. Extensive work on the restorative potential of woodland environments and their impact on well-being is discussed by Liz O'Brien and Jake Morris from the Social and Economic Research Group (SERG) at Forest Research (Chapter 10) to define woodlands as a major social and cultural resource which can induce great positivity. Inherent in their work are the qualities of woodland environments and how we access them, are invited to access them and which provide exceptional sensory stimulation. Within the woodland context there is an easy transition to the playfulness/joyfulness of the woodland experience and the delights of sights, sounds and smells encountered, contact with the rhythms of nature, the dominance of the natural world, offering opportunities for self-reflection, exploration and making personal 'life connections'.

Woodlands are the antithesis of busy urban environments and offer a powerful antidote to the stress of urban life (Coles & Bussey, 2000). Woodlands also offer opportunities for touching and collecting objects, feeling the bark of trees, collecting cones and leaves, throwing sticks for the dog, negotiating water, and in the design of seating and benches with tactile surfaces, the use of rough timber as well as including interventions to promote reflection and engagement such as art and sculpture trails (Coles, 1995; Coles and Bussey, 2000). O'Brien and Morris identify that 'people are often not aware of who owns the woodlands they visit', but they have strong views regarding the continued existence of a freely accessible, publically owned resource which gives a strong message regarding the freedom to roam. The idea of freedom underpins the positivity of the experience and is a factor of well-being. Within this context the SERG examine ways to increase access to woodland environments and improve their potential as a social, well-being resource through:

- the provision of new woodlands through planting, including in urban areas
- opening up existing woodlands to public access
- physical improvements to woodlands, e.g. providing infrastructure to encourage access
- addressing the needs of individuals and groups including elements that might be regarded as adult- or child-centred or focus on family engagement
- promoting Forest Schools
- promoting volunteering.

Some health authorities are now noticing the well-being potential of woodlands, creating specific ventures with patient referrals to spend time in woodlands as a way to combine the various benefits of exercise and social engagement with the exploration, joyfulness and sensory power of the woodland experience. O'Brien and Morris identify the components of well-being benefits in terms of specific themes drawn from their experience:

- Physical well-being – improving stamina, toning muscles, losing weight, feeling fitter.
- Mental restoration – release from tension and stress.
- Nature and landscape connections – access to natural and cultural heritage.
- Sensory stimulation – engagement with the senses linked with natural processes.

- Social development and connections – shared experiences and meeting people.
- Symbolic – cultural and spiritual significance, meaning and identity.
- Education and learning – personal skills and new knowledge.

Concluding remarks

This book draws on, and adds to, the growing amount of discussion of the conditions of the urban environment in terms of its deficiencies and limitations in supporting the well-being of individuals and society. The wide range of investigations discussed here attest to the value of the landscape in meeting society's well-being demands and emphasise that there is a process of engagement with the landscape which can establish profound synergies through experience and self-reflection.

There are various definitions and terminologies of well-being, many of which are explored in this book. They concern both mental and physical health and include variants on the maintenance and/or promotion of positive outcomes, or the maintenance and acceptance of life's fluxes, peaks and troughs.

Despite issues with defining what we mean by 'well-being', these chapters establish the positive impacts of landscape in various fields and using both qualitative and quantitative methods, resulting in a range of theories to explain the nature of landscape interaction. These demonstrate that the association between individuals and the environment occurs at a range of levels depending on the situation, but emphasise the existence of a process of 'dialogue' between individuals and landscape involving our physiology, mental and emotional states. This is described in various ways, but we suggest the notion of a 'landscape/well-being continuum' (Figure 12.1). This continuum comprises a range of interconnecting components which make a personal, individualistic 'biophysical-psycho-place-kinaesthetic' complex! This idea is as complicated as the name suggests, but when we examine the range of approaches and outcomes discussed here, the sum is thus well described in this manner. We have also referred to this relationship with the landscape as 'performative' to emphasise the way that landscape is read, interpreted and made sense of through experiencing it. 'Eco-sociology' is another useful term to describe the individual–landscape relationship, especially for natural sites, but each of these terms relate to the personal nature of landscape interactions and the connections and meanings created.

We present a range of parameters drawn from the chapters which can be considered subsets of the 'continuum' and which serve to explain its different dimensions. These have been extracted and summarised in this chapter and include 'negative parameters' – those which prevent the continuum from progressing beyond its most basic form and 'positive factors' – those which allow it to form and move people to a deeper level of engagement. Authors identify the parameters to higher levels of association and identify the language used to describe a positive state of well-being, using terms such as joyfulness,

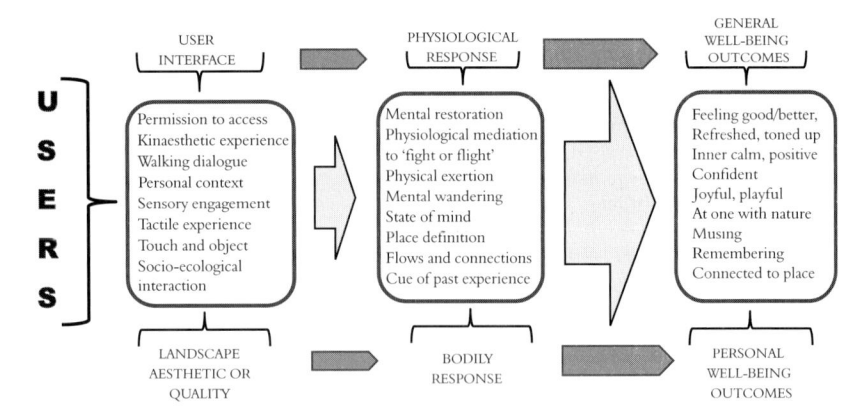

```
┌─────────────┐         ┌──────────────┐         ┌──────────────┐
│    USER     │ ═════▶  │ PHYSIOLOGICAL│ ═════▶  │   GENERAL    │
│  INTERFACE  │         │   RESPONSE   │         │  WELL-BEING  │
└─────────────┘         └──────────────┘         │   OUTCOMES   │
                                                  └──────────────┘
```

U   ┌ Permission to access   Mental restoration   Feeling good/better,
S   │ Kinaesthetic experience   Physiological mediation   Refreshed, toned up
    │ Walking dialogue   to 'fight or flight'   Inner calm, positive
E   │ Personal context   Physical exertion   Confident
R   │ Sensory engagement   Mental wandering   Joyful, playful
S   │ Tactile experience   State of mind   At one with nature
    │ Touch and object   Place definition   Musing
    │ Socio-ecological   Flows and connections   Remembering
    └ interaction   Cue of past experience   Connected to place

```
┌─────────────┐         ┌──────────────┐         ┌──────────────┐
│  LANDSCAPE  │ ═════▶  │    BODILY    │ ═════▶  │   PERSONAL   │
│ AESTHETIC OR│         │   RESPONSE   │         │  WELL-BEING  │
│   QUALITY   │         │              │         │   OUTCOMES   │
└─────────────┘         └──────────────┘         └──────────────┘
```

Notes: The Continuum attempts to illustrate the parameters involved in moving the individual from a passive state to an active state where engagement with the qualities of the environmental encounter move the user into a special 'place' and 'state of mind' associated with high levels of well-being. Using terminologies explored in the chapters, on the left are factors which lead to positive access to the landscape, in the middle section are terms related to the processes of interaction that move the user into a positive state and on the right are listed 'indicators' associated with the achievement of high levels of physical and mental well-being.

FIGURE 12.1 The landscape/well-being continuum

sense of worth, achievement, reflection and remembering. In psychological terms this has been referred to as 'mental restoration' but this term might not be sufficiently robust to describe the process by which users become reflective. Explorations of playfulness in adults help in understanding the movement to a joyful state, which for adults encompasses the pleasure of remembering and in children an assertion of their capability and engagement with the world. These combined experiences define the landscape/well-being continuum, although we emphasise that it is individually constructed. Techniques that investigate the continuum are well informed by qualitative enquiry, especially by the collection of narratives which express the nature of the restorative experience in eloquent and personal terms. Evidence concerning engaging children in landscape and well-being research suggests that measures which encourage people to verbalise their interaction or to engage in specific activities help to develop the continuum.

It is felt that we should not strive to over-define well-being from a landscape perspective, but to apply the principles of the continuum and understand the 'latent potential' of engagement and seek to support individuals and society in realising the well-being benefits of accessing appropriate landscape situations.

Readers are invited to review the terminology and ideas presented in this book, to apply them to their own personal experience and to consider their professional remits related to the design and management of landscape, in the configuration of the environment, in supporting communities, individuals and specific sectors of society, for example older people and children, to develop 'eco-social resilience':

- To consider the levels of sensory engagement that might be generated in real landscapes.
- To take a multidisciplinary approach to the study of well-being and the landscape and to place theory.
- To explore the rhythm associated with landscape, the rhythm of walking, the seasons, contact with nature, and the senses.
- To verbalise their experiences and reflect on their personal engagement with the landscape.
- To consider the typologies of well-being and landscape character presented.
- To place well-being at the heart of the debate concerning the design of places and spaces.
- To re-energise the landscape by releasing the latent energy embodied in the landscape/well-being continuum.

Note

1 '... I carried to my lips a spoonful of the tea in which I had let soften a piece of madeleine. But at the very instant when the mouthful of tea mixed with cake-crumbs touched my palate, I quivered, attentive to the extraordinary thing that was happening in me... Undoubtedly what is fluttering this way deep inside me must be the image, the visual memory which is attached to this taste... And suddenly the memory appeared. That taste was the taste of the little piece of madeleine which on Sunday mornings at Combray ... my Aunt Leonie would give me after dipping it in her infusion of tea or lime-blossom... Immediately the old grey house on the street, where her bedroom was, came ... and with the house the town, from morning to night and in all weathers, ... the Square, ... the paths we took' (Proust [1913] (2003): 47–50).

References

Coles, R.W. (ed.) (1995) *Community forestry in an urban context*, Proceedings of the Front Door Forestry Conference, 21–22 April, Redditch, Birmingham: University of Central England.
Coles, R.W. and Bussey, S.C. (2000) Urban forest landscapes in the UK – progressing the social agenda, *Landscape & Urban Planning*, 52, 181–188.
Coles, R.W. and Caserio, M. (2001) *Social criteria for the evaluation and development of urban green spaces*, report to European Commission, Project URGE-Urban Green Environment, EVK4-CT-2000-00022, available at http://www.urge project.ufz.de/PDF/D7_Social_Report.pdf.
Costa, S. (2013) *Narratives and well-being experience in the landscape*, http://landscapewellbeing@wordpress.com/tag/bcu.
Millman, Z.K. (2012) *Landscape narratives and the construction of meaning in the contemporary urban canal-scape*, unpublished thesis, Birmingham City University.
Millman, Z.K., Coles, R.W. and Millar, G. (2008) *The canal environment soundscape in Birmingham – a pilot study*, Proceedings of the Institute of Acoustics Spring Conference 30(2), 10–11 April. Reading: University of Reading.
Proust, M. ([1913] 2003) *The way by Swann's*. London: Penguin.

INDEX

Access: barriers to access 177, 178, 180, 187, 212; (for) children 142, 143, 193; (to) culture 151; (to) green spaces/landscape 1, 23, 29, 45, 80, 201, 204, 209; (to) nature 87, 106, 205; to spaces 110, 111, 131, 150; (for) older people 119, 120, 122, 123; permission to access 206; (to) woodlands 168, 169, 170, 174, 178, 179, 214
Accessibility: Accessibility Index 189; accessible populations 62; criteria for 45, 123, 177, 187, 206; neighbourhood 189; adult control 184, 187
Actions: general 76, 78, 79, 83, 149; to protect environment 8
Active England (projects) 170, 178
Active/interactive learning 148
Active participation 14, 184, 192
Activities: children's 134, 138, 142, 143, 186, 191, 192; curtailment of 9, 29; harmful 17; museums 150, 169; detrimental 10; physical 110, 113; play 5, 114, 115, 122, 124, 125, 210, 211, 213; political 49; recreational 93, 95, 103, 109, 117, 123; woodland 170, 172, 173, 175, 176, 180
Aesthetic 4, 38–46, 48–50, 54–6, 67, 68, 95, 96, 104, 121, 192, 205, 207; kinaesthetic; 25, 26, 46, 64, 207, *see also* synaesthetic 39
Affective Health Domain 22, 24, 25, 27, 29, 38, 58

AHRC, Arts and Humanities Research Council 157
Amenities 120, 123, 124
Anderson Report (A Common Wealth) 148
Antidote: to sedentary lives 32; to stress 214
Anxiety 32, 154, 160, 173, 185, 208, 213
Apartments 89, 90, 93, 95, 97, 104, 105, 189
Architecture 2, 3, 43, 44, 46, 54, 88, 89, 98, 106, 206
Art: artist collaboration 90, 98, 100, 207; artistic behaviour 117; artists 207; Arts Council England 40, 149; Arts Health and Well-being (report) 40; arts practice 2, 3, 4; museums 147, 151, 154, 156; organisations 147; play in art 113; street art 112; using art 81
Artefacts 151
Associations with the landscape 1, 3, 57, 65, 200
Attention Restoration Theory (ART) 21, 24, 202
Attitudes 58, 63, 149, 178; children's 5; uniting 42
Attributes: of well-being 168; of rhythmanalysis 39; neighbourhood 129; social 136
Auckland (New Zealand) 129, 130–3, 142, 185, 187–9, 193, 194, 210

Index

Authentic: authentic engagement 66; authentic happiness 59
Autonomy (people's) 111, 118–20, 154

Beach Haven (Auckland) 188–91, 194
Behaviours: efficiency 9, 13, 14; environmental 3, 7–10, 12, 14–17; harmful 14; social 87, 89, 106, 123, 178, 205; sustainable 9
Benefits of play 112, 117, 118
Big Society 17, 163
Biking 170, 172, 173
Bio-cultural 54
Biodiversity: general 22, 23, 74, 102, 106, 168, 170, 172; strategy 181
Bio-medical 22
Biophilia/biophilic 54, 75, 80
Biopsychosocial model 22, 24, 30, 203
Biotope Area Factor (BAF) 88
Blood pressure 21
Bodily responses 4, 21, 24, 38–40, 43, 46–50, 57, 194, 201, 203, 207
Bullied, bullying 117, 140, 137, 211

Calming effects 26, 28, 95, 151, 160, 173, 203, 208, 209, 216
Capital: social 78, 193; natural 78; mental 155
Children/childhood: designing for 80, 81, 87, 93–5, 100–6; mobility 129–44, 212; obesity 32, 129, 131; (and) play 110–15, 121, 122; (as) researchers 184–93, 210; well-being 185, 186; (in) woodlands 171–3, 176–8
Choreography 38, 39, 48, 207, see also rhythm: rhythmanalysis
Civic Ecology, see ecology
Coding (analysis) 24, 134, 159
Cognition 42, 48, 58; cognitive health 22, 24, 25, 27–30, 42, 43, 57, 58
Common Ground 119
Community: attachment/building 73, 75, 78–82, 91, 99, 136, 149, 152, 186, 205, 208; identity 60, 61; well-being 152, 167, 169, 201
Complexity: of interaction 42, 47, 120, 168, 202; of spaces (definition) 45, 47, 58, 89
Connections: social 29, 131, 209, 214, 215; with places 32, 46, 50, 57–61, 68, 78–82, 109, 144, 174, 192, 196, 202, 206, 207
Conservation 16, 23, 74, 95, 171, 176, 177

Consumption of goods 9, 10–14, 73
Co-production 179
Countryside 54, 77, 172
Cultural: aesthetics 39; and museums 147, 148, 151; contexts 28; heritage 174; indicators 155; landscapes 73, 76, 78, 79, 82, 88; needs 57, 58, 120; services 168, 206; values 74, 169
Cycling/biking 13, 14, 169, 170, 172, 173, 175, 180

Dementia 151, 152, 158
Department Culture Media and Sport (DCMS) 149
Depression 73, 118, 154; combatting 32
Design: Inclusive Design for Getting Outdoors (IDGO project) 120; (of) research projects 66, 133, 187, 188, 190, see also interviews and methodology; sustainable design 87, 88
Dialogue (in dialogue with places and events) 39, 47, 49, 63, 64, 207, 215, 216
Diaries: photo 64; travel 130, 133, 134, 143, 187, 211
Disabled users 175, 176
Dogs: negative aspects/fears 120, 123, 124, 136, 140, 194; positive aspects 27, 30, 81, 122, 143, 172, 193, 214
Double Dividend 7–10, 12, 14–17
Drawings/draw 187, 188, 195
Drown/drowning 138, 139, 142, 143

Ecology: civic 4, 78; eco-sociology 73, 215; Ecosystem Services 72–5, 78, 81–3, 168, 204
Economy 92, 99, 152, 177
Effortanalysis 47
Environmental: citizenship 3, 8, 12, 14, 15–17; health 53; stewardship 72, 204
ESRC, Economic and Social Research Council 17, 60, 64
Eudaimonia 8, 10–17
Exalted View 8, 14–17
Exercise (physical) 25, 26, 110, 116, 121–3, 171, 173, 214
Exhibitions and museums 147–53
Experience: Experience of Landscape (Appleton) 54, 55; experiential enquiry 4, 46; (of) nature 21, 22, 29, 30, 55, 203; (of) neighbourhood 185, 186, 189, 191, 192, 196; (of) place 57, 58, 61; sensory 40, 41, 42, 49
Exploring (activities) 137, 138, 151, 197

Families 95, 97, 103–5, 138, 178, 189
Feelings 10, 11, 25–9, 32, 45, 49, 58, 111, 118, 119, 159, 168, 173, 186, 201, 202, 210
Forest/forestry: Forestry Commission 168, 170, 172, 173, 177; Forest Schools 170, 171, 214; UK Forest Research 5, 167, 168, 213
Freedom: free 59, 102, 111–20; to roam 214
Friends Programmes 153
Fun: having 80, 109, 115; *see also* play

Gardens, gardening: 23, 53, 143, 203, 210, 104, 105; vegetable 101–3, 105, 106
Genius Loci 50, 57
Global: environmental problems 72, 87; well-being 24, 25, 27–30, 50, 209
Go Along Interviews 133, 134
Gore Bay (New Zealand) 62, 63, 66
GPS (Geographical Positioning System) 133, 143, 187, 188
Green Space Factor System 88
Green spaces: (and) children 136, 143; (and) health 22–4, 29, 30, 32; (and) housing 104, 105; infrastructure 32, 74, 75; social contribution of 87, 88, 106
Gross Domestic Product (GDP) 153, 167
Ground truth 187, 189, 193, 196, 213
Grounded theory 147, 159

Habitat Theory 54
Happiness: definition of 153; (and) well-being 11, 13, 59, 73, 117, 151, 155, 157, 158, 167
Health: Arts Health and Well-being (report) 40; health frameworks 21, 22; holistic concepts 28, 31; models of health 21, 22; spiritual 30; WHO definition of 39, *see also* public health and cognitive health
Heart rate (effects of nature on) 21, 29
Hedonia 8, 10–12, 14–17
Heritage in Hospitals Project 5, 148, 157, 158, 160, 163, 208
Home/at home 58, 80, 83, 109, 135–7
Housing projects 87–90
Human scale 45, 53, 77, 203

Identity: place 21, 57, 58, 60, 61, 203; self 130, 176; spatial 91, 99
Imageability 45
Independent mobility (of children) 129–31, 133–5, 141–4

Infrastructure, green 74, 75, 80
Insider/outsider perspectives 133, 135, 136, 143, 144
Interviews: CATI (computer assisted telephone interviewing) 130, 133, 134, 142; Go Along Interviews 133, 134
IPF (Independent Panel on Forestry) 168

Joyfulness 25, 28, 109, 118, 209, 210, 213–5, *see also* laughter

Kids in the City Project 129, 130, 133, 141
Kinaesthetic 43, 46, 48, 64, 207, 215, 216

Landscape: connections and interactions 56, 174, 202, 203, 206, 210, 216; landscape architecture 3, 55–7; typologies 204
Laughter 114; and play 117, 118
Learning (lifelong) 148
Leisure: leisure time; 111–6; (and) woods 170, 177, 210
Life satisfaction 5, 111, 153, 154, 168
Love (for places) 26, 28, 29, 106, 175

Mapping 63–5
Marmot Review 111
Maslow's Hierarchy of Needs 59, 111
Meadow 102–4, 106
Measuring well-being 153, 155–7; Relative Stands Theory 59; Needs Satisfaction Model 111; Psychological General Well-being Scale 154; Positive Affect Negative Affect Scale (PANAS) 157, 161; Visual Analogue Scale (VAS) 157, 161
Media reports 131, 142, 144, 212
Memory (general) 38, 44, 47, 57, 58, 67, 151, 161, 202, 207, 213; banks 151; loops 210; maps 47
Mental: capital 155; fatigue 21, 202, 204; health 119, 150–2; restoration 173, 214, 216; stimulation 2, 28
Methodologies/methodological approaches: 22, 56, 62–4, 112, 130, 133, 134, 147, 148, 156, 159, 169, 187, 193, 209, 211, 215, *see also* interviews
Millennium Ecosystem Assessment 168
Mobility: decline in 5; increased 44; (and the) city 46–9; (and) older

people 120; children's 129–31, 133–5, 141–3, 186
Models of well-being 3, 4, 31, 46, 202, *see also* measuring well-being and well-being
Museums: Museum, Libraries and Archives Council (MLAC) 148, 150; sector 147–53; (and) well-being impacts 155–7

National Ecosystem Assessment 168
National Health Service (NHS) 149, 161
Natural cycles 74
Natural England 168, 171
Natural environment: experience of nature 55, 77–9; (and) health 20–21, 31, 32, 54, 75, 76, 78, 168; Natural Environment White Paper (UK) 181; (and) restoration 21, 203; nature mystics 29; watching 172
Narratives 65, 77, 82, 202, 206, 210, 216
Needs Satisfaction Model (for quality of life) 111
Neighbourhood: (and) children 129–44, 185–97, 211; participation 104; neighbourhoods 1, 5, 98, 100, 109, 110; Neighbourhood Destination Accessibility Index (NDAI) 189
New Economics Foundation (NEF) 153
New Zealand 63, 129–32, 142, 185, 188, 210

Obesity 20, 32, 44, 73, 129, 131
Object handling and museums 157–9, 161
Office of National Statistics (ONS) 7
Older people: 5, 109–11, 119, 178; (and) play 115, 121–4, 209, 210; older women 115, 117
Our Healthier Nation (report) 39
Outdoor play 129, 131, 132, 136, 185–8, 194
Outsider 130, 133, 135, 136, 143, 144, 211, 212
Owner assessment (of landscape) 96, 104
Ownership: and dogs 194; patterns 89, 170, 204, 206; public realm 119, 168, 170, 179

PANAS (Positive Affect Negative Affect Scale) 157, 161
Park Prescriptions 32
Participant researchers 130, 133–6
Peace of mind 28
Perception: general 45, 59, 130; insider/outsider 135, 136; of safety 80, 134; neighbourhood 133, 134, 138; residents 129, parents 137, 142–4
Performative/performativity 202, 215
Photography, photographs 133, 134, 139, 158, 161, 162, 174, 192
Physical: activity 30, 32, 44, 114, 119, 122, 129–35, 141–4, 175, 212; Physical Activity and Health Alliance 171
Physiology 21, 203, 215; Heart rate (effects of nature on) 21, 29
Places: place theory and associations 44–50, 56–61, 80–2; third age places 109, 110, 125; place attachment 24–9
Planners (urban, City) 44, 47, 77, 79, 89, 107, 143, 167
Play: children's 122, 135, 136, 140, 143, 211; opportunity for play 110, 129, 135, 212; play by adults 110–3, 121, 124; Play For a Change (review) 112, 117; playscapes 189
Population density 62, 131
Preference theory 54
Pro-environmental behaviour 7–10, 12, 14–16
Psychology, positive 29
Psychometric scales 163
Psychophysiologic theory 21, 24, 29, 203
Public health 1, 2, 44, 150, 163, *see also* health
Public realm: general 45, 109, 110, 119, 124; (and) play 117, 119

Quality of life 5, 20, 22, 54, 61, 111, 118, 129, 144, 155, 210; CASP-19 measure 111; the Needs-Satisfaction Model 111
Quality criteria for walkable spaces 45

Recreation: recreational activities 74, 93, 95, 112, 114, 116, 131, 143, 189; (and) woods 170, 171, 178
Red Hat Society 115
Relative Stands Theory 59
Relaxation: general 1, 24, 28, 29, 32, 33; response 21, 203
Renaissance in the Regions (museums report) 149
Restoration: of the environment 78; mental 173, 214, 216; restorative affects 21–4, 27, 29, 30, 68, 202, *see also* Attention Restoration Theory (ART)
Rhythm: of nature 207, 214; Rhythmanalysis 39, 46; rhythmic motion 39, 41, 44–50, 207; 214, 217
Risk: perception of 142, 143; taking risk 67, 122, 185, 212

Rootedness of place 58, 61, 64
Rules, restrictions 76, 96, 103, 112, 120, 134, 210

Safety 26, 80, 206, 120–4, 206; and children 19, 129, 131, 134, 142, 178; traffic 186, 211
Seating provision 120–2, 214
Sense of place 21, 23, 24, 29, 46, 49, 50, 57, 61, 62, 64, 66, 67, 77, 168, 203, 204
Sensory: experiences 40, 49, 174, 202; sights 202, 207, 214; smells 207, 214
Social and Economic Research Group (SERG) 5, 168, 169, 177, 213
Sociology 21; eco-sociology 215
Somatic practice 38, 49, 207
Spiritual 14, 22, 24–32, 49, 53, 54, 58, 61, 68, 176, 203, 209, 215
Stress reduction 21, 29, 32, 55, 61, 75, 173, 185, 203, 214, *see also* PANAS
Sustainability/sustainable development 20, 32, 88, 106, 129, 168, 169, 186, 201, 206
Symbolic meaning 56, 168, 176, 215
Synaesthetic 39

Tenants views 95, 96, 102, 103, 205
Third age/third places 109, 110, 125
Timber products 172, 177, 214
Tranquil/tranquillity 26, 29, 30, 33, 203
Transparency (of spaces) 45
Trees (engagement and contact with) 168–70, 172, 174–7, 179
Topophilia (concept of) 29
Touching of objects 152, 161, 208, 209, 214, 216
Tourism (and museums) 152, 177

United Nations Convention on the Rights of the Child 129, 144
Urban: design 32, 44, 45, 79, 109, 119, 129, 130, 184, 211; 'Five D Relationships' 45; planning 33, 129, 130, 141, 144; sprawl 129, 186

Values: cultural and social 5, 9, 11, 74, 75, 149, 169, 178; natural 54, 78; personal 11, 14, 178; (and) place 58
Verbal: methods 49, 63; narratives 202; verbalise 216, 217
Vertical living 186

Video games 196
Violence: fear of 137, 138, 211; freedom from 59, 75
Visitor: experience 148, 188; to Gore Bay 63
Visual: interest 44; Visual Analogue Scale (VAS) 157, 161
Voices of participants 65
Volunteering (conservation) 16, 114, 153, 169, 171–3, 175, 180, 214

Walking: (and) children 131, 135, 137, 142, 143, 194; (the) dog 193; interviews 130, 133, 211; in the city 39, 43; Laban Movement Analysis 46; Walkability Index 188, 189; to school 135, 143; walk (general) 26, 38; Walking to Health (report) 171; walking practice 44–50, 207, 217; (in) woodlands 3, 4, 169, 170, 172–5, *see also* kinaesthetic and rhythm: rhythmanalysis
Wardens, park 123
Water/waterways: general 53, 54, 59, 74, 81, 139, 140, 143, 203, 207, 214; fear of 81, 139, 140, 154
Well-being: definition 167, 168; emotional 28, 55, 151; eudaimonic 11–17; global 24, 27–30, hedonic 11–13; indicators 168, 201; interconnected model 31; (and) museums' work 147, 152, 154, 208; personal 7, 8, 10–16, 168, 201, 216; The Needs-Satisfaction Model of Quality of Life 111; place and landscape 60, 61, 67, 68; Psychological General Well-being Scale 154, *see also* measuring well-being
Wellness 4, 7, 13, 16, 30, 40, 64, 154, 161, 200
Wilderness experience 28, 30, 77
Wildlife, observing 26, 121
Woodland policy 181
World Health Organization (WHO) 39

Young people: activities 143; well-being 150, 154; woodland visits 176

Zurich: university 100; municipal government 104; housing studies 87–9, 97–9, 106